Regent's Study Gu[...]
General Editor: Paul S[...]

C000108594

Outside-In

Theological Reflections on Life

© 2006
Published by Regent's Park College, Oxford OX1 2LB, UK
in association with Smyth & Helwys Publishing, 6316 Peake Road,
Macon, GA 31210, USA

All rights reserved.
Printed in the United States of America.

The paper used in this publication meets the minimum
requirements of American National Standard for Information
Sciences—Permanence of Paper for Printed Library Materials.
ANSI Z39.48–1984 (alk. paper)

Outside-in: Theological Reflections on Life

Library of Congress Cataloging-in-Publication Data

Weaver, John (John David)
Outside-in : theological reflection on life / John Weaver.
p. cm. — (Regent's study guides ; 13)
ISBN 1-57312-472-9 (alk. paper)
1. Church work.
2. Theology, Practical—Textbooks.
3. Christian life—Textbooks.
I. Title.

BV4401.W37 2006
253—dc22

2006024700

Cover art: *There is too much pain in the world* by Simon Walker
© Simon Walker and Regent's Park College, Oxford

Regent's Study Guides

Outside-In

Theological Reflections on Life

by
John Weaver

Regent's Park College, Oxford
with
Smyth & Helwys Publishing, Inc.
Macon, Georgia

Dedication

*For students and congregations with whom
I have learned about being church*

Contents

4. Integration: Examples of Practice

5. Action: Mobilizing the Church

6. New Experiences: Growth in Community

Preface

The central theme of this book is theological reflection, that is, asking questions about the ways in which God is at work in the world and in human lives. Throughout the text I have sought to provide a variety of ways in which these questions might be asked, addressed and answered. As a help for individuals and groups, each chapter includes three exercises designed to aid the process of reflection.

Why? What is my reason for writing?

I believe that it is time for the church to stop playing games. I believe that Dave Tomlinson[1] is right when he describes the church as a cosy club that proclaims middle-class conservative values and passes them off as Christianity. Many Christians are never challenged to see faith and worship encompassing the whole of life; there is a tendency for the church to be the particular club that Christians attend in their spare time. For them it may represent an oasis from the tough and, sometimes, brutal world in which they spend the rest of their life.

This is an unsatisfactory state of affairs for all concerned, and is far removed from the Christianity of the New Testament. My desire is to provide ways in which people inside and outside the church may think about the Bible and faith in the light of the issues that affect their daily living.

What? What do I expect as a result?

Through the use of an action-reflection model, in small group discussion, I believe that people will become excited about the relevance of the Bible for their lives. I believe that the Bible stories will be seen to relate to our own stories, that people will make the connections for themselves. As experiences are shared and conclusions are suggested, there will be an ownership of what has been learned, which will make it more likely to be remembered and applied. The heart of this process is that each person's experience is valued and each is able to express something of what he or she has learned. When these thoughts are placed alongside an understanding of scripture, church tradition and sociological analyses it will be possible for group members to express a response.

Who? Who is this book for?
Initially it is for those who will be the enablers of this process within the life of the church. Using a variety of examples from different areas of ministry—preaching, Bible study, pastoral issues, work, and politics—I hope to be able to excite ministers and church leaders about a different way of being church. I have seen this approach used in a number of situations in Central America and I have tried out these ideas within a variety of different groups in this country: with students, with lay preachers, with an elderly church Bible study group, with an evening congregation, and with lay and clergy groups. In each situation I have been thrilled and indeed surprised by the response. I share something of these experiences through this book with the hope that they might be an encouragement to others. This approach really does work and makes a difference to the ways in which people think about their faith.

I am indebted to students, both past and present, at Regent's Park College, Oxford, and the South Wales Baptist College, Cardiff, and to a large number of church groups, with whom I have learned, as we have shared our experiences of life and sought to understand the Bible together. I am grateful to Paul Fiddes and Fiona Floate for their careful reading and helpful comments on the manuscript during its development. Lastly, I wish to express my grateful thanks to my wife, Sheila, who has not only put up with my time spent 'locked' in the study, but has also been my careful 'sense-checker' and challenging critic.

John Weaver
Cardiff,
December, 2005

Note

[1] Dave Tomlinson, *Post Evangelical* (London: Triangle/SPCK, 1995).

1
Outside-In: Being Church in a Complex World

Time for reflection

On 31st July, 2005 the BBC news website carried the headline: 'Student dies in racist axe attack'.[1] A-Level student Anthony Walker, 18, died in hospital after a gang of up to four white men attacked him in Huyton, Merseyside, on Friday 29th July, 2005. He had been taunted at a bus stop with his white girlfriend and a male cousin. They fled but were set upon in a park.

Merseyside Police said that the couple were subjected to a 'torrent of racial abuse' as they waited for a bus outside the Huyton Park pub. Anthony and his companions did not retaliate against the abuse and left to find another bus stop. But they were followed and as they walked through McGoldrick Park they were attacked by a gang of three or four men. Anthony's girlfriend and cousin saw a man carrying an axe bludgeon him, and ran to get help. When they returned minutes later they found him slumped on the ground with massive head injuries. The axe was embedded in his skull.

Anthony Walker was taken to Whiston Hospital and later transferred to Walton neurological centre where he died in the early hours of Saturday 30th July, 2005. Merseyside Police Assistant Chief Constable Bernard Lawson said, 'What we are dealing with here is an unprovoked and vicious attack on a young black man which we believe to be racially motivated. This was a despicable act and we are absolutely determined to find the people responsible.' He added, 'We believe the offenders are local and we believe it is the responsibility of the local community to give these people up. There are a lot of decent people in the local area who are absolutely shocked at what has happened.'[2]

Anthony was a churchgoer who was also a keen basketball player. The BBC's Richard Wells said local people had told him that those who knew him said he 'wouldn't hurt a fly'. Assistant Chief Constable Lawson commented: 'Anthony was a young Christian studying for his A-levels and wanting to be a lawyer. Those dreams for him and his family are now dashed.'

When we read of an incident like this our minds flood with images, memories and emotions. We remember similar incidents such as the murder of Stephen Lawrence in Eltham, London in 1993 or the London bombs of July 2005, the attack on the World Trade Centre in New York, 11th September, 2001, or the numerous incidents involving Nationalists and Unionists in Northern Ireland from 1969 to 1998.

We recognize our feelings of anger, horror, fear, anxiety, despair and shame. It is important that we recognize who we are as participators and observers of the world in which we live out our Christian discipleship and ministry.

Numerous issues are raised by such a case study. Some that come readily to mind are:

• Ethnic and religious tensions.
• Mixed marriages and relationships between people of different ethnic or religious groups.
• Racial intolerance and racism.
• Living in a multicultural society or global village.
• Allowing the actions of a minority to set the pattern.

Christian thought, reflection and action is not an optional choice for the disciples of Christ. As both Jesus and the apostle James put it, faith without action is dead (Matthew 25:31-46; James 2:14-26). We will continue to reflect upon the murder of Anthony Walker at the beginning of each chapter, throughout the book.

The issues are complex, and so a framework for our thinking or a model for reflection and action will be useful. Moving to Cardiff and beginning a new course in practical theology, I wanted to explore models for theological reflection which would be an integral part of the whole course. My first contact with the class, all ordinands (Anglican, Baptist and Methodist), was two and a half weeks after '9/11', the bombing of the Twin Towers of the World Trade Centre in New York on 11th September, 2001. I began the session with a series of slides that replayed the events of that day from the initial impact of the aeroplanes, through the collapse of the towers in clouds of dust and smoke, to the aftermath of twisted steel being picked over by rescue workers. We then began to discuss our feelings, observations, knowledge, and reflections. The following emerged through our discussions.

What were our first thoughts about the experience?

• Shock, disbelief, bewilderment, numbness, fear. *The question is: what?*
• Horror, pain, need to do something, grief. *The question is: why?*
• Anger, vengeance, hatred. *The question is: who?*
• Revenge, retaliation, retribution, punishment. *The questions are: when? How?*

At this initial stage there seems no room for the Christ-like qualities of forgiveness, love, justice, reconciliation. *The question is: which way?*

We then began to explore how we might attempt appropriate reflection:

• How do we deal with the raw emotions we all feel?
• What do we expect of our political leaders?
• What do we expect of church leaders?

This led on to a discussion about appropriate action:

• A time for being there; being with people; absorbing their pain, anger and fear; a time to listen and say very little.
• A time to step back; to demonstrate the courage of wise leadership; to let justice overrule emotion.
• A time to suggest an alternative way; to stand for justice and truth. (Remember the first casualty of war is truth.)

Finally we considered some reflection on the longer view:

• Why did the terrorists strike?
• What does the West learn from these events?
• Is justice wider than bringing terrorists to trial?

- How can justice be best served?
- What can a technologically advanced army do against a small group of determined people armed with knives and their own life?

As a group we developed the following outline for reflection:

Description
- What happened on 11th September?
- What has happened since?
- What is happening now?
- What does the church say?
- What does the church do?

Reflection
- What did you feel?
- How have your feelings changed in time?
- What do you feel now?
- What do you learn from this?

Critical discussion
- What should be done?
- What do these events tell you about international politics and the nature of our world?
- Are the political decisions right?

Theological reflection
- Where is God in all this?
- How have these events affected your faith?
- What are the theological issues?
- What does God expect of God's people?
- What prophetic voice do we bring?

Pastoral care
- How do we support and care?
- What counsel is needed and for whom?
- What prayers can we pray?
- What professional assistance is required?

Practical theology
• Who is involved?
• What assistance can the church offer?
• What ministries are employed?
• What training is required for those who counsel in such circumstances?

From this discussion and similar theological explorations with students I have developed my own version of a pastoral cycle as a model for theological reflection, which is printed as figure 1. Several versions of the cycle of action and reflection were offered by Laurie Green in his book *Let's Do Theology* in 1990, and these have since been very widely used.[3] A rather different and interesting approach has been suggested by Elaine Graham, Heather Walton and Frances Ward in their recent book, *Theological Reflection*;[4] but I am proposing a modification of Green's scheme which, while having significant differences, is indebted to his insights. The succeeding chapters of this book will follow this version of the pastoral cycle, as indicated by the diagram.

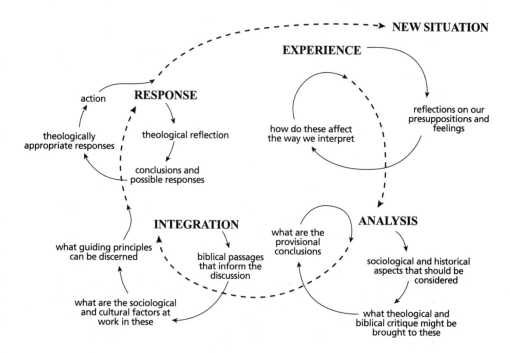

figure 1.1

Recognizing the need

Many Christians have a surprising ability to live in two worlds: the private world of faith and the public world of work and daily life. The sort of reflection indicated by this introductory brainstorming session with a group of students may rarely occur within the programme of a local church. Yet to follow Christ in our daily lives involves asking God questions of each and every part of our lives. Bringing the private and public worlds together is the main task facing the church as it seeks to engage with the whole of life in the mission of Christ.

Consider the following three experiences:

• When I was lecturing in Geology, my secretary had a notice that she would put up on her door on Fridays. It said, 'Today is POET'S day' and was accompanied by the translation, 'Push Off Early Tomorrow's Saturday!'
• As an itinerant preacher I have become a connoisseur of deacons' prayers prior to services. One prayer that I often hear goes something like this: 'Lord, take from our minds all the concerns of our work and life last week and all the problems of the coming week, as we come into your presence to worship you.'
• Returning to school at the beginning of a new week, my wife was faced in one staff room by a colleague who sat huddled over a mug of coffee saying, in a weak, mournful voice, 'Mondays don't suit me.'

These comments underline the division that seems to exist between the world of work, everyday life, and our worship of the Living God. Worship has too easily become a comforting escape from the complexity and challenge of contemporary secular life, with the result that God's people tend to evade their responsibility to be salt and light. There is a flight from reason, where worship becomes a welcome respite from a tough and demanding world. We also deny God the opportunity to encounter us in the concerns of our life in the world: to challenge, direct, forgive, and bring peace.

Our ministry as God's people in the world is hindered and diminished when we are sucked into a 'churchy' mode of life, dominated by church structures and organizations and when Christian teaching and preaching fail to help us to make connections between faith and life. In the face of a complex changing world, church and our Christian faith run the danger of becoming a safe haven or comfort zone. We are happy to pray for Anthony Walker's family, but are ill-prepared or indifferent about issues of racism, unemployment, boredom, alcohol abuse and other ills of society.

Church programmes do not always address the needs of congregations living out their lives in a 'post-Christian' society. While congregations are often challenged, prayed with and affirmed in their Christian lives, the massive cultural boundaries which Christians cross each time they move either into or out of the gathered community of faith are largely ignored. Once we honestly face this cultural divide, it becomes painfully obvious that as churches we are often lacking in the help we give to our congregations, as they wrestle with the ever increasing complexities of living as disciples of Jesus.

Members of church congregations gather together on Sunday with the stories of the world that they have been 'reading' — at work or at home, on television, radio, newspaper and magazine, and hear stories from the Bible, whose relevance to their lives are rarely demonstrated. Pastoral ministry should be engaged in helping believers understand and interpret the biblical text in ways which resonate with their daily experience, helping believers bring their successes and failures, ambiguities and insights into the life, worship, care and support of the gathered community. Communities of faith struggling with their Christ-like discipleship will look for leaders, who in appropriate language and creative styles are able to encourage them in the task of relating their life and belief. In the quest for a mobilized church, there is a clear need for the training and 'equipping of the saints' (Ephesians 4:11-12) in living out the Gospel in every aspect of life. This is particularly necessary if we are to address the issues that arise in the workplace environment, in communities, relationships and in the increasing time spent in leisure activity.

How do we go about mission at the beginning of the twenty-first century and how are the people of God being prepared for ministry? We are all engaged in full-time ministry and mission for Christ; this is the essence of our discipleship. While worship may be seen as central to our Christian existence, mission is the life-blood of our faith. In this we never stop learning from the Holy Spirit, from our reflection upon scripture in the light of our experiences in the world, and from the experience of others. We recognize that each church member, and indeed non-member too, has a contribution to make; we all have our different experiences of life. We can develop some general principles for working out our faith in life, work or ministry under three headings: reflection, integration, and formation.

- *Reflection.* The emphasis is not on telling people 'how to do' but rather get them to draw on their own experience and ask questions about life and the place of God in the world. Reflection begins with experience. It moves on to explore the Bible—its application and interpretation. It moves further to consider actions and events in the world outside the church. It then asks: what is God saying in all of this?

- *Integration.* It is my belief that we should seek, wherever possible, to enable congregations to integrate their faith and biblical beliefs with the practical experience of daily living. To do this, we will encourage our congregations to relate their biblical insights back into the practical, pastoral, and social issues of their lives outside the church, and bring their experience of the world as questions to their Bible study and the worship life of the church. The success of this clearly depends on our ability to break down the compartmentalism that may exist in the mind of each person. This may therefore require a paradigm shift in the approach to Christian discipleship, both for the teacher, preacher or minister, and for congregation members, as we seek to see our faith worked out through our life in the world.

- *Formation.* The result of reflection and integration will hopefully help people towards a Christ-like discipleship. To put this another way, it is not so much teaching people 'how to', but helping them 'to be.' We each want to be open to the shaping of the Holy Spirit so as to be the person that God can use in the ministry of his church.

For the clergy this would be, for example, not how to take a funeral, but learning to face our own death. Not how to counsel the bereaved, but understanding our own feelings of loss.

For Junior Church leaders this would be, for example, not how to run an effective Sunday School/Junior Church, but to understand what children feel and how they think, learn and perceive the world.

For worship leaders this would be, for example, not how to lead worship, but what worship is, and how to help the congregation to encounter the living God.

For every member of the congregation it will mean taking their abilities and the experiences seriously; and from these helping us to work together in exploring our theology of life and discipleship as the people of God.

Putting it all into practice is no easy task, and there is no one right answer. There will be a constantly changing agenda as we address changing needs in a changing world. But I believe that these principles of reflection, integration and formation are integral to our growth as disciples of Christ.

Breaking the mould
Imagine two people meeting at the weekend.

Kathryn: What sort of a week have you had at work?

Alan: It's been a long hard week. It feels as if the whole of my life is computerized. Letters have been replaced by e-mails, orders are dealt with 'on-line,' and decisions are largely made through 'tele-conferencing.' The whole works has been wired so that every department is plugged into the main computer. Stocks are automatically monitored, orders with our suppliers automatically placed, invoices automatically sent and paid. The design office has tapped into the Internet and has immediate access to programmes, information, models, designs, and know-how from every part of the globe. It's a real headache for me, especially as I grew up in a world without computers—I find it almost impossible to keep up with the explosion in information technology. I also keep looking over my shoulder at the younger managers, who take it all in their stride—is my job safe? I'm too old to find another job now, being over forty!

Another effect of all this is that we no longer need a lot of our staff, especially in the despatch department and the finance office. I don't know how I'm going to tell some of the men and women that they are surplus to the firm's requirements — some of them have been with us for over thirty years.

Where does my faith fit into all this mess? Still, enough about me, what has your week been like?

Kathryn: I'm sorry to hear about your problems, but I feel that mine have been even worse. I have two situations that are causing me a great deal of lost sleep. I have one of my female members of staff complaining of sexual harassment — one of her colleagues is forever giving her boxes of chocolates and inviting her out; and won't take 'No' for an answer. I'm trying to mediate — explaining to her that he really is quite harmless and having been single all his life has little experience of how to relate to the opposite sex; while I try to tell him that his advances are not being responded to and that he is causing the 'lady of his affection' a great deal of hurt. He's so naive, I don't think he has a clue about what I'm telling him.

But worse still is the other situation. One of the Year 10 girls is apparently being bullied by other girls in her class. They send text messages that taunt or criticize her about her weight, clothes, and lack of friends. I've had her parents into school twice this week to complain and to express their fears that she is getting very depressed. The girl herself will say little or nothing about it, but is increasingly off school. I have listened very carefully and tried to counsel both them and their daughter. We have a bullying policy, but it is very difficult to enforce, when there is no concrete evidence. How can I try to bring a Christian perspective to all of this?

Alan: Doesn't sound as if either of us has had much chance to witness to our faith in Jesus this week.

Kathryn: (looking at her watch) Well, it's about time for the service to start — at least we can praise the Lord in worship and get away from all our problems for a couple of hours.

Does this sound familiar? It is an all too common conversation. Christians often have a tendency to be schizophrenic, thinking God-thoughts on Sunday, but leaving God out of the equation of work and everyday living. One of the legacies of the Enlightenment has been the withdrawal of Christian faith from the public world of technology and scientific fact into the private world of beliefs and values. Today we see this worked out through individualism and a privatizing of religion, but also, and perhaps more damaging, in the separation of world and church, flesh and spirit, daily living and Christian worship, which is a feature of some evangelicalism.

In today's complex world, religious faith, taken as a whole, serves as a welcome oasis for many people. John Hull has rightly suggested that it may be valued 'precisely because there one can escape from the problems and demands which crowd in upon us from the newspapers and the television.'[5] He is right to note that, for many people home and church are havens from the confusion of a postmodern world. While Monday to Friday are spent among the pressures and questions of a technological world with its pluralistic values and beliefs, Saturday is spent in the safe haven of home, and Sunday in the safe haven of the church. For countless others in modern society, Saturday and Sunday are indistinguishable, forming a part of their working week. The truth is that many people would rather that the church avoided too much teaching, especially where that teaching engages with their daily lives, because such ministry would confront the false values of careerism and consumerism on their own ground. Such avoidance may produce a comfortable Christianity for many in the congregation, a 'peace of mind' for adults, but many idealistic young people find themselves growing up with confusion. When those young people voice their feelings, they become like the little boy in Hans Christian Anderson's tale and proclaim that 'the Emperor is stark naked!' and the result is that they leave the church behind as an irrelevance.

Yet the world presents them and us with other problems. We cannot live without meaning and purpose. Christian discipleship is a full-time occupation, seven days a week. The Christian faith needs to relate to every part of our lives, for there is no part of our lives with which God is not involved. The Good News is that God is able to transform every part of our existence. The first sign in the Gospel according to John is of Jesus who transforms water into wine. He can transform our watery existence into the richness of the life redeemed by through his blood.[6]

Sadly however, with an emphasis on performance in worship, methods for increasing congregations, courses to convince non-church people of the faith, or simply concern over the comfort of the fabric and plant of the church buildings, the Church appears to have no interest in what happens in the life and work of the congregation away from church activities. The shocking truth may be summed up as "Church isn't":

• isn't real, radical, or relevant;
• isn't scratching where people are itching;
• isn't ready for the 21st century;
• isn't even, in large part, meeting the needs of the people who attend its services of worship.

I am, of course, making generalizations, and there are, thank God, many exceptions. Nevertheless, it will prove worthwhile, if we are brave, to ask people who faithfully attend our churches Sunday by Sunday, why they come and what they think. We might get a few surprises! We might begin by trying to answer the question honestly ourselves. Often church services are designed for a small group of insiders, who like to do things in a particular way that they find comfortable and supportive. If this is the case, we have moved a long way from commitment to being the kind of community of the Gospel which is seen in the early chapters of the Acts of the Apostles, and from its members' concern to live as Christ in and for the world.

We need to keep asking: What on earth is the church for? We can identify a number of areas, which we should address of concern:

• Through our involvement with church are we being strengthened in our discipleship?
• Are we being helped to be effective Christian disciples within our social context?
• Are we being encouraged to engage our faith with life and work issues?
• Are the activities that we engage in at church helping us to be effective in the mission of Christ where we live?

- Is there a place within the church's programme to explore the social and local community context and to look for the power and presence of God?
- Is our church community a place where those who don't know Jesus will feel welcomed? Do we *present* Jesus—for example, are we a demonstration of Christ-like love? (1 Corinthians 13:4-8; Romans 12:9-21)[7]

If we all live in the world, why is the church an alien environment to those whom we live with for the rest of the week? The answer may be that we have created a church culture that is divorced from our daily lives, let alone from the life of those outside the church. I was speaking at a meeting where the minister originated in the North-east of England, and spoke like someone from Newcastle, that is, until he was asked to pray, when his voice intoned a churchly accent with no colour or interest! It is one thing to follow our call to be counter-cultural, it is quite another for that counter culture to be rooted in the language and sounds of generations long dead.

There needs to be a reality and integrity in all we do and say. True Christian discipleship will be honest, open, and vulnerable. It does not pretend that the violence and injustice in the world, the suffering of the innocent, the pain and bitterness of broken relationships, the doubts and unanswerable questions of life and faith, the stress of work, and the finality of death, do not exist. We proclaim a Jesus, who in the words of the writer of the Epistle to the Hebrews, was tempted in every way that we are, yet did not give in to temptation (4:14-15). Jesus knows what it is like to be me, and to be you. This writer tells us that we can approach God through Christ (4:16). Jesus Christ is the agent of creation, he is the revelation of God's glory, he is the perfect revelation—he is truly God and truly human. This God knows me in the humanity of Christ—he knows my life and understands what it means to be me. This is Good News for ministers and congregations alike. The creator of the universe is not some distant uninterested power, but in Jesus understands what makes me tick, what makes me laugh, what makes me cry, and accepts me for who I am.

But too often the church looks to be life-denying rather than life-affirming. We have emphasized a sacred-secular divide, which our Christian forebears would not have recognized. We are led to believe, as Mark Greene writes,[8] that some parts of our life are not really important to God — 'little' things like work, school, sport, TV, politics, sex — but that anything to do with church, such as prayers, worship services and church-based meetings, is. Many people have never heard a sermon on the theology of work; the God-given joy of sexual relationships within marriage; our political responsibility; or how to challenge the many opinions produced by the media. Mark Greene quotes one committed church member: 'I teach in Sunday school 45 minutes a week and they haul me up to the front and the whole church prays for me. I teach in school 40 hours a week and no one ever prays for me.'[9] I am sure that this is why so many people in response to the question, 'What work do you do for God?' answer with their jobs in the church.

We want to be able to live out our faith and find Gospel answers, real good news, for our lives in a hurting and questioning world. Mission is the essence of life for all Christians and we never stop learning. When I sat my driving test (for the third time) I was relieved to hear those comforting words, 'Mr. Weaver I am pleased to be able to tell you that you have passed,' but then challenged by the examiner's next sentence, 'Now you can begin to learn to drive!' The same must be true of the mission and ministry of the church. We continue to learn from the Holy Spirit, from our reflection upon scripture in the light of our experiences in the world, and from the experience of others.

Our challenge is to be the people of God in and for the world. Sadly, in many places, especially in the western world, congregations have abdicated their involvement in ministry in favour of the clergy, and the mission of Christ has become focused on the church as an end in itself. We are encouraged by the early church's understanding of baptism as being into full-time service in the power of the Spirit (Romans 6:1-14). We are challenged to understand worship as the whole of life (Romans 12:1-2; Ephesians 2:8-10) and recognize that Jesus did not call his disciples to be merely attenders at the weekly morning church service. Latin American theologian, Gustavo Gutierrez, points us to the key passage — Mark 8:27-35 — where the confession of faith and the practical business of following imply each other. He says, 'the challenge is to be able to preserve the circular relationship between orthodoxy and orthopraxis and the nourishment of each by the other.'[10]

What we believe should affect, and be seen, in what we do. Luke recalls that the first disciples left everything behind and followed Jesus (Luke 5:1-11). In this story Simon Peter, Andrew, James and John had found out that Jesus was not only an amazing teacher, but also, in the light of the great catch of fish, knew more about fishing than they did. As long as Simon's boat is a 'floating pulpit' the owner has no objection to Jesus being in command, but as soon as it reverts to being a fishing boat (or workshop, or classroom, or kitchen, or conveyer belt, or hospital, or family home) then surely the fisherman (mechanic, teacher, housewife, operator, nurse, mother) is in charge—for that is his job. We listen to Jesus' words, we ask for his help, we long for his healing and power; but for Jesus to interfere in our job, our home, our leisure, our lifestyle seems different—it's not religion is it? But Jesus the carpenter turned preacher, tells Simon the fisherman, how to fish! There's just a tiny hint of a thought about 'teaching grandmothers to suck eggs'—yet the result shows that Jesus actually knows more about Simon's job than Simon does.

From this story we draw the truth that God is concerned to be our guide and help in all of life. It is therefore foolish to separate worship on Sundays from daily work and living. Yet it is too often the case that in work and in daily life people are called upon to be innovative, productive, creative and participative, while in church to be passive, conforming and controlled. In life there is frequently conflict, but in church conflict is denied, avoided or suppressed. In work we have reviews and appraisals, our performance and the outcomes of our work are evaluated, while in church it is a matter of doing our best (hopefully) and leaving the rest in God's hands. In church preachers and teachers may be tempted to avoid the issues of work and the harsher realities of daily life, where there may be controversy and where they may themselves feel vulnerable, and, instead, concentrate on the character of God and the Bible, where they are more comfortable, even experts.

The result is that many in the congregation are largely left unsupported in their everyday lives. When church ministers do take an interest in their people's work it is often to engage teachers in the Sunday School, builders on the fabric committee, and bankers to oversee the church's finances. I believe that such thinking is inadequate and unsupportive and fails to recognize either the depth of experience that congregations have, or the resource for mission that the people represent, or the pastoral needs of those involved in demanding daily occupations. Francis Dewar rightly observes that a calling is far wider than ordained ministry.[11] The importance of this point comes to the fore when people who feel that God is calling them, immediately and instinctively think that this must mean the ordained ministry of the church. This problem may arise because our experience in the world outside of church programmes is undervalued, and there are few encouragements to allow our faith to permeate and guide our daily living. As a result, when God's call is heard there may be confusion. We need to rediscover the sense of vocation—God's call to exercise our ministry in our daily employment, paid or unpaid (see chapter 4). I believe that the direction of our thinking should be 'from the outside to the inside', from mission out in the world to reflection upon it within the church: in short, *'outside-in', not 'inside-out'*.

When the only Christian work that is of value is ministry within the church, we fail to use our God-given gifts through the whole of our life. God invites us to discover our true selves through offering our lives into his hands. But Francis Dewar maintains that this is followed by a second invitation, which is to give ourselves wholeheartedly to what we do. We respond to God's promptings, changing direction, taking those risky steps of faith, which are followed by God's confirmation, and in the future by further steps.

To help us in our reflection about God and his activity in the world we must take the concerns of life, work, and our cultural context seriously. People are constantly crossing back and forth across the cultural boundaries between 'church' and 'world', and we all need help in making the connections. Biblical texts must encounter our social context and produce a new way of living for the followers of Jesus. Our witness, ministry and part in the mission of Christ involves every aspect of our lives.

I believe that there will need to be new styles of teaching and church programmes that enable church members to explore their life experiences and relate them to their understanding of the Christian faith, and vice versa. Ian Fraser notes that 'in much of the world church, the membership is no longer leaving theology to 'theologians' but hammering it out at white heat in the fire of experience, tempering it as weaponry for the fights of life.'[12] While classical theology is made up of research and well-argued conclusions, the theology of the community of faith is a theology of the road, as is illustrated by the book of Exodus. Here we find the God who reveals himself, who is holy, who liberates, who builds a relationship with his people, and who accompanies them in their wanderings. These are the theological reflections of the community based on their experience of God.

We see much the same in the account of the appearance of Jesus to the two disciples on the Emmaus Road (Luke 24:13-35). Here we find Jesus asking the question: 'What are you discussing together as you walk along? Tell me about it: what's your story?' We learn from Jesus' way of dealing with people, his interest in them, his understanding of their way of life. First of all Jesus gets alongside and listens. He then asks them to tell their own story, which they do including all their dashed hopes. Then Jesus begins to explore their story in the light of the scriptures and the promises concerning the Messiah. Finally, at their invitation, he sits down to meal with them, where they recognize him and respond by returning to Jerusalem to share what they have learnt with the rest of the disciples.

Exercise 1.1

a. Where does your faith and Bible study interact with your family life or work, your leisure activities, or local, national and world events?

b. Name some specific events or life experiences that have caused you to question your faith or what the Bible has to say.

A model for change

Here are two key questions:

- Is the church communicating the Gospel to those who do not venture within its doors?
- How do we make connections?

Belief in God in British society remains constant at about 72%, but belief that Jesus is God's son is much lower. Opinion polls tell us that 52% believe in heaven; 43% in life after death; and 32% in hell. In 2001 7.8% of the UK's population attended church, and of these only 16% read the Bible regularly, while 32% of church attenders had not read the Bible in the previous year.

Who is Jesus? A good man, an example of how to live, someone to follow, a crucified man, a church man, probably an historical character, a mad man, or merely a common expletive? The story is told of a woman who went into her local jewellers to buy a cross and chain for her grand-daughter's confirmation. The young woman behind the counter asked her: 'Do you want one with a little man on it or do you want a plain one?'

In the UK we live in a society where fewer and fewer people attend church or come into contact with the Gospel story. Where does any under-standing of the Cross and Resurrection of Jesus Christ find a starting point? Martin Robinson[13] describes this present time as an age of unbe-lief, where rationalism is faced with new doubts and where there are new questions about belief and unbelief. He recognizes a gradual divorce between Christian faith and a western culture where many people want to see a removal of religious belief, since it is perceived as having evil effects on humankind. Some would see events in Iraq, Afghanistan, the activities of Al-Qaeda, and the proposed UK law (2005) to ban incitement to religious hatred, as proof of religion's harmful nature. Yet, at the same time there has been a growth of interest in spirituality as expressed through the flowering of a variety of religious groups coming under the umbrella terms of New Age and Neo-paganism.

We are also faced by a world in which there is a loss of meaning, and, in consequence, a loss of hope. Lesslie Newbigin suggested that we are reduced to nothing but the development of self until 'we are wheeled off to the crematorium.'[14] In the field of cosmology Steven Weinberg, Professor of Theoretical Physics at the University of Austin, Texas, and a Nobel Prize winner with Abdus Salam on the symmetry of forces in the early universe, declares in his book *The First Three Minutes* that the more the universe seems comprehensible, the more it also seems pointless.[15] Weinberg believes that doing science gives human beings some sense of grace in the midst of the tragedy of being trapped in a hostile world. From his perspective it would appear that there is a paradox of despair: doing science gives point to living, but the discoveries thus made present exis-tence as pointless.

To such a world as ours we have a Gospel of hope. A fragmented society places the quest for community at the top of its agenda. Having lost the church community, we have numerous self-help groups and counselling agencies. The breakdown of families and of relationships within families adds to the isolation and loneliness that many people feel. Patterns of family life, of parenting, and building committed and stable relationships are no longer being presented to many children and young people. The ministry of reconciliation, and the Christian message of value, love and purpose, demonstrated in the cross of Christ, are vital in our society.

However, Gospel engagement with our contemporary context is not an easy, nor a risk-free, task, and we will encounter questions, and indeed answers, that we may find surprising and unsettling. In confronting the issues which we face each day at work, or within our families and community, we will value opportunities to discuss and reflect upon those concerns, drawing on the experience of others, upon scripture and church tradition.

In encouraging congregations to find new ways of exploring the mission of Christ in the world and, indeed, of being church, we might take an initial look at how the pastoral cycle (figure 1.1) might be used with church congregations. A group might begin by telling their own stories, expressing their hopes and fears and their most pressing needs. The group may then focus on a particular issue of importance in their church or community. At this early stage it will be important for each member of the group to own their thoughts and feelings about the issue in question. With any emotive issue or one where there would likely to be strong opinions, such as AIDS, issues of human sexuality or relationships, it is important that people own their own views. A useful model to help people to own their personal experiences and feelings has been developed by Jonathan Adams, based on the work of Joanna Rogers-Macy.[16] It uses the following pattern, using AIDS as an example:

• In pairs one as speaker, and the other as listener. The speaker talks for one minute with each of the following starters:

a. *I first heard about AIDS . . .*
b. *At that time I thought . . .*

c. *What I now feel about AIDS is . . .*
d. *From now on I will . . .*

• The pairs reverse their roles: the speaker becomes the listener and the listener the speaker.
• Presentation of well researched information about AIDS followed by discussion as a group, who have owned their own knowledge, thoughts, feelings and intention

Other approaches might include: brainstorming the subject, posing questions, using photographs or images, in fact anything to keep the cutting edge of the group's discussion sharp and to enable members of the group to own their personal experiences and ideas. In this way we move on to reflect on our stories and experiences, but to do this we will need to have some form of guideline to prevent us from following too many blind alleys. The following two models, developed in clinical pastoral education,[17] may be of help the group to maintain the focus of their discussion.

First there is a model open to a variety of uses, including the exploration of a pastoral encounter through a verbatim talkback (a word-for-word recollection of a pastoral conversation):

    i. A verbatim report of an incident is given by one member of the group.
    ii. The issue for discussion or help is identified.
    iii. The listeners discuss what they:

        a. heard
        b. felt
        c. imaged/imagined
        d. concluded.

    iv. The report presenter says what he or she feels about the observations that have been made.
    v. Theological observations and insights are given.
    vi. Conclusions may be drawn and action proposed.

Second, a similar model involves:

    i. Role play of a pastoral encounter.
    ii. Processing of the role play by the group:

      a. observations
      b. human themes—feelings and issues
      c. theological themes
      d. making a pastoral care plan.
   iii. debriefing and evaluation.

In the following chapters we will explore the ways in which such models allow us to define the issues and move on to analysis and further reflection as we integrate the experiences, and our reflections upon them, with scripture and church tradition. In each situation we will give time to an objective analysis of the story or experience, as this may be a highly emotive issue that will need verification. For example stories coming out of a situation of conflict such as Northern Ireland, Israel/Palestine or Kosovo and her neighbours, or perceptions of relationship breakdown by the parties concerned, may be almost entirely subjective.

For the mission of the church in its local community it is not enough to rely on the impressions of the congregation. For example, when a church in Northamptonshire, where I was the minister, was considering employing a family worker in conjunction with Spurgeon's Childcare,[18] a full consultation with the Social Services, other caring agencies, the schools, doctors and police was carried out to verify the need for such a worker within the community. Only when the need was confirmed did we proceed with the appointment.

Our analysis of any situation or experience can be helped through observations and research in the human sciences. From psychological studies we will ask questions such as: how do people in situations such as these normally behave? What categories or issues should we be addressing? From the social sciences we will ask the question: what patterns have been observed in other groups and communities? We will also want to ask questions about the political issues and the decisions that are involved in that arena.

We will reflect on such analyses in the light of our Christian faith, and we will ask where God is to be found in the situation or experience under consideration. Other questions will include: How does our story fit with the Bible story? How does it accord with the story of the church down through the ages? As we look at how God has acted and been experienced in the past we may find pointers for how God may be experienced today. At this point we may find ourselves challenged by a saying ascribed to Mark Twain, that 'it's not the parts of the Bible that we don't understand that worry us, but the parts that we do'. We may find that the Bible contradicts or challenges our experience and we will have to find ways of bridging the gap between the world of the early church and our own world. We will need to prayerfully reflect upon our experience and analysis and ask what God might be telling us through them. I have suggested elsewhere that I believe that when the church does this it can be described as 'the children of the Father; meeting together in the presence of the Spirit; and seeking together the mind of Christ.'[19]

To guard against detached or uninformed statements, we bring the understanding of our Christian tradition into connection with our contemporary experience, and in this way ensure that our understanding concurs with that of the church universal. Stephen Pattison[20] helpfully encourages people to imagine that they are involved in a three-way critical conversation between:

• their own ideas, beliefs, feelings, perceptions and assumptions;
• the beliefs, assumptions and perceptions provided by the Christian tradition (including the Bible), and
• the contemporary situation that is being examined.

The final stage in the process is our response to the reflection and analysis that we have undertaken. We are called to be a servant people, to be Christ in and for the world, our faith is to be an active faith, and it is upon our activity that Jesus declared we are judged (Matthew 25:31-45). Liberation theologians express discipleship as orthopraxis, 'right action', rather than orthodoxy, 'right belief'; or as expressed in the Epistle of James: faith is enlivened by works (James 2:14-26). We are called to deny self, to take up the life of cross-shaped, self-sacrificing love, and to follow in the way that Jesus leads us (Mark 8:34).

All sorts of possibilities for response will have arisen during the reflection and integration stages, but by the end of the process a clearer picture will be emerging. Laurie Green[21] helpfully expresses the purpose of the theological enterprise as:

- *Contemplative*—finding the knowledge of God for which the soul longs.
- *Instructive*—learning about God's nature and action in the world.
- *Transformative*—working with God's saving intention in the transformation of ourselves and of society.

It is important that in framing our response we ask a number of questions:

- Who is it for, and what is our intention?
- Are we enabling others through this response?
- Are we addressing symptoms or causes?
- Who will be involved in the response?
- What do we hope to achieve? (There should be evaluation and accountability.)
- Will our response present the Gospel of Christ?

Working out our aims, setting goals, and developing a strategy with practical steps for implementation is vital. This will lead us into new experiences, some of success and some of failure, some of excitement and some of disappointment, and out of our reflection upon these will come new responses. In all this we recognize that the pastoral cycle that we have been exploring is not a simple circle, but a circle of circles of integration and reflection at every stage, as shown in figure 1.1.

An ongoing process

When I was lecturing in Geology, I spoke to a senior colleague about the research that I was doing, and about the ways in which my ideas were changing. He said to me, 'If you can look back on research that you did five years ago and still be happy about it, then either you are brilliant or you've stagnated.' Then, after a moment's thought, he looked at me and added, 'and few are brilliant,' with the implication that 'John, you're not one of them.' I would want to say similarly that if we can look back on our Christian lives five years ago and see no changes that have now taken place, no experiences from which we have learned, then either we are perfect or we have stagnated, and I would want to add that only One is perfect. Our prayer is that of Richard of Chichester:

O most merciful Redeemer, Friend and Brother,
may I know Thee more clearly,
love Thee more dearly,
and follow Thee more nearly,
day by day.

The process of theological reflection that we are developing is not a closed circle, which suggests that 'we have made it,' but rather, as shown in figure 2, is a spiral in which our understanding through reflection of one situation leads us on to new experiences and new understandings. This is one way of seeing the journey of our discipleship.

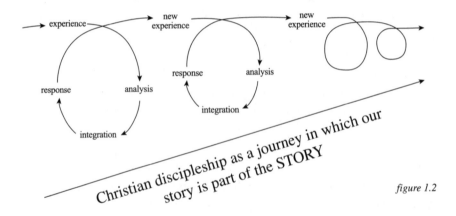

Christian discipleship as a journey in which our story is part of the STORY

figure 1.2

The main difficulty of this approach is that, for those of us who began our education before the 1970s, it is probably in marked contrast to the way in which we were taught in school. This means that whether we are in the role of 'teacher' or 'student' we will probably experience feelings of insecurity. For the 'teacher' there is the insecurity of not being in control: those being taught will not only take an active part, they will also, to a greater or lesser extent, set the agenda and bring their own insights. For the 'student' there is the insecurity of being expected to offer contributions to the learning process, rather than being able to sit back and act as a sponge, receiving information. The 'teacher' will need to have new skills, especially the ability to enable and facilitate discussion and contributions; to begin with a blank sheet of paper rather than a sheaf of notes; a readiness to learn from the 'students' and to have the 'teacher's' own ideas and presuppositions challenged. This might be seen as a dangerous adventure, but it is exceedingly rewarding. It does however require a greater amount of preparation, as the 'teacher' will have to be familiar with a broad range of information and background material. The 'student' will need to have a willingness to be an active participant in the process, rather than a passive receptor of information. It will mean being willing to share his or her own experiences and understanding and to have these challenged by others in the group.

There is an openness here that becomes demanding as 'students' are forced to work out what they believe and think, instead of sitting back with a 'take it or leave it' attitude. In this way there is no division between 'teacher' and 'student', leader and congregation, but rather there is a group of people who are learning together with one who enables this to happen. This is not, of course, to deny the need for the imparting of information by the leader, nor the acquiring of knowledge by the learner.

This approach to learning is particularly important in the context of the church community, where we are attempting to understand the relevance of our beliefs for our life in God's world. Whether we are talking to children or to adults, to Christians or to interested enquirers, or to the uninterested outsider, we need to start where the people are, with their experiences, their understanding and their lives. A key issue in this is the sense of working and learning with each other. We are not doing things *for* or *to* people but we are learning *with* others. It is important to recognize the principle of the incarnation, of God with us, revealing God's own self in everyday experiences of life. The first church was based on community living, on shared experiences and their reflection upon those experiences. It is notable that the writers of the biblical material never set out to prove the existence of God, but rather reflect upon their experience of God's presence in their life and the lives of the people.

For effective growth in discipleship and community the church needs to create spaces and times for the constant interaction of people as they discuss their lives outside and inside the Christian congregation. Such interaction will provide the tools for those conversations that are part of their work, family life and leisure, their meetings in the street, in clubs, pubs, and in each other's homes.

We work *with* our friends, colleagues and family, we work *for* clients, customers or employers, and we can do things *to* inanimate objects or to enemies. Immanuel is God with us, and the servant church of Christ is with people in their lives, seeking to bring about transformation, justice and peace. We recognize the value that Jesus placed on individuals and the respect that he had for human dignity and we seek to follow this pattern. People will often refuse assistance because it is seen as charity, which takes away their self-esteem. Working with people will avoid the danger of the church being classified as 'do-gooders,' with a paternalistic or condescending attitude. The local people are the experts, they know their own situation and needs. The church should always seek to get alongside people to listen, enable and empower, rather than to manipulate or impose ideas upon them. We need to understand the situations which people experience before we can find appropriate ways of sharing the good news of Jesus Christ with them. Bob Holman's examination of the Easterhouse estate in Glasgow demonstrates such an approach.[22]

Holman rightly criticizes the politicians and journalists who visit such urban priority areas, concerned to speak about the problems of the poor, or about the habits of a growing 'underclass' in our society. He is able to make such observations because he has chosen to live in Easterhouse and has sought to work with the people, empowering them to find hope in living. His book centres upon the stories of Carol, Bill, Erica, Anita, Denise, Penny and Cynthia. The first important point to note, therefore, is that the poor have names, they are not a statistic in a Government survey. Secondly, and far more importantly, they write their own stories; they have chosen what to say, and they tell it in their own words. In this way they have been given the power that is so often taken away from them by well-meaning (and not so well-meaning) social workers, churches and other charitable people, who seek to do things for them. The stories are of harsh, chaotic, desperate and despairing lives, and if we are able to empathize with the writers, we discover that their lives are full of pain and a sense of hopelessness. Yet, when we step outside the worldview of our own backgrounds and experience, we recognize that these are not the stories of victims, but of survivors; not weak people, but strong people; in talking about their lives they are given dignity and control.

For reflection to develop its full potential there is a need for the leader and group to value each other and work together. The dynamics of the group will be enhanced by openness, honesty, vulnerability, and a desire to see change. As Paolo Freire and others have emphasized,[23] a group needs to be helped to recognize that they already have access to resources, knowledge, skills and incentive. The leader's role is to endeavour to stimulate and strengthen discussion, provide information and suggest sources of help, and to enable thinking and analysing to take place within the group. Leaders must recognize that they are also learners and that they do not have all the answers. The leader must be prepared to receive new insights from the rest of the group.

The attitude of the leader is vital and the most important initial questions for any teacher to ask are: Do I value the experience of others? Am I continuing to learn? Have I closed my learning circle, or do I have a spiral of reflection and response in my understanding? What we, as leaders and teachers believe about people and their ability to enter into creative thinking and discussion, to contribute knowledge and insight, and to come to good decisions, will greatly influence the working of the group. This because what I think about others, and what I believe about myself and my ability to stimulate this process, will influence my approach to the group and will communicate itself in subtle and intangible ways.

During the last few years I have been learning conversational Welsh. Learning to speak Welsh is important for communicating within a Welsh speaking culture, even if the majority understand English. Being in a Welsh class for at least 5 hours every week has placed me on the other side of the teacher/learner divide. I have become aware of those tutors who are able to help the learning process and those who are less helpful. Those who give space for the learner to experiment, to get it wrong, and to have a go at pronouncing difficult words are valued by the class. The best of all are those who give constant encouragement, who say *Da iawn* (very good) or *Ardderchog* (excellent) in response to your attempt, and then repeat your sentence incorporating what you should have said, rather than saying 'Wrong!' and then just telling you the correct version.

When a group is working well the teacher learns and the learner teaches. In exploring principles for discipling within a congregational setting leaders will want to develop their own ability to listen, to learn, to grow out of their and the group's insights and experiences.

Exercise 1.2
a. Where does your church enable you to discuss the issues that you identified in exercise 1.1?

b. What groups or meetings might your church organize that would help the congregation to explore the relationship of faith to life and work?

A transformed church
In the last half century there has been a growing rediscovery of the church as a community; a biblical concept of co-operation and working together. The more general use of phrases such as the 'body of Christ', 'body ministry', 'fellowship' and 'the priesthood of all believers', has underlined 'lay' involvement in the mission and ministry of the church. With this has come the recognition of the need for training. Such training is an integral part of being a disciple, and should best take place in the context of the local church, drawing on the experience of those who would be trained. In our growth as disciples of Christ we cannot be merely onlookers. We search for understanding that will open up new horizons, awaken our imagination, look for answers and clarification of our questioning spirits. We have to encourage people to overcome a rationalism that does not allow for surprises in history or in our current life. We have to dream, to be able to question the present and look for a new future. Tradition and the insights of previous generations are important, but like our own dreams, must be submitted to the critical reflection of the community of faith. This is the only way to overcome the 'we've always done it this way' syndrome, and yet guard against the assumption, 'it must be better because it is new.'

Our knowledge of God comes through our relationship with God, and our ability to hear and respond to God's word comes from a renewal of our mind through the Spirit. This is not something that is restricted to a clerical élite. Ministers and leaders must be in touch with reality and with people. They will be accountable to their community, and the community of faith will be their critic and guide. Theology is learnt and is challenged through the activity of the people of God, which is something that is seen throughout the life of the early church as demonstrated in Acts of the Apostles and in the Epistles. All of us must be ready to have our presuppositions and treasured traditions turned on their head. A key passage for the mission of the church is found in Acts 10, where God shows Peter that religious sensitivities and traditions can be overturned when the priority is to share the Gospel.

When it comes to understanding the life of society, it is the ordinary people who provide the expertise. Before theologians can begin to comment on an industrial dispute, or proposed redundancies, for example, they will need to understand the value systems that underlie the political, social and economic lives of workers, managers and politicians. Faith must always be seen as a lived faith, not as a series of propositions written down in a book. The role of church leaders is to help their people to put the lived faith into a proper context—that of the community of faith throughout the world and throughout history. We will need to learn from church tradition and from the world church. For example, there are the developments of the action-reflection model within the base ecclesial communities of Latin America, where reflection upon life and upon the Bible leads to action to improve the life of society. But we cannot directly transfer these to our own context. We will need to learn to be sensitive to the Spirit and learn to reflect theologically within our own culture and upon our own experience.

Christian leaders must always value the experience of every person within their community and enable them to discover God in what they already experience and know about life. Leaders will encourage their congregations to recognize their competence and responsibility for such reflection, and the resultant response. We need to enable people to break free of their dependence on 'educated theologians,' or the latest celebrated Christian writer or speaker, and discover the places where God reveals God's own self to them in their everyday lives.

The integration of the Gospel story and church tradition with the present situation and experience of people is a vital part of the process, if it is to remain distinctively Christian. Our present situation is everything that makes up our physical, emotional, intellectual and spiritual life at personal, interpersonal and social levels in the reality of our world. Our reflection will recognize the present and the past that has created it, and will look to future possibilities and choices. Such reflection requires openness to discovery and uses reason, memory and imagination in the process. The dialogue develops within the community of faith, as in love, humility and faith we listen to each other's stories, and, through accountability and critique, we build each other up in our Christian faith.

The story is important for the development of community, as we see it in the Jewish celebration of the Passover, and as we discover it in the Christian celebration of the Eucharist. But then we recognize that each individual Christian's story is a part of the larger story, as it reflects the activity of God in human lives. Out of the church's story comes the vision of the Kingdom of God, what God wants to do and is able to do in lives that are open to his purposes. Given the reality of our sin, especially in terms of self-centredness, this vision of the Kingdom is always 'not yet', and this is a limiting factor in all our praxis.

In his book on the nature of religious education, Thomas Groome encourages us to see the goal of our meeting together:

> In the community encounter between our own stories and the Story, between our own visions and the Vision, we can come to 'know God' in an experiential/reflective manner. It will be a praxis way of knowing that arises from our own praxis, from the praxis of our community of pilgrims in time, and from the praxis of God in history.[24]

We might explore Groome's suggestion through considering the vital place of story in the Lord's Supper, the celebration of the new covenant in Christ through the sharing of bread and wine.

Story number one. Moses, under instruction from God has asked Pharaoh to let the Israelites leave Egypt. His refusal has resulted in God's sending a number of plagues, the last of which is the death of the firstborn of every living creature. The Israelites are to hold an evening meal; a lamb is to be killed and eaten, its blood daubed on the door-posts of their houses; it is eaten with unleavened bread, herbs and wine. When God's angel of death moves through the land he passes over the houses of the

Israelites, which are marked with the blood of the lamb, but strike down the first born of the Egyptians. Pharaoh lets the people go, though later he changes his mind and chases after them. But God leads the people to safety through the Reed Sea and makes a covenant with them at Mount Sinai. They go on remembering all of this at an annual celebration of being the people of God (Deuteronomy 16:1-4).

It was this meal that Jesus celebrated with his disciples on that fateful Passover eve.

Story number two. Twelve hundred years have passed. Jesus knows that his life is coming to an end and he wants to celebrate one last festival meal of the people of God, with his close friends. It is Passover time, and they celebrate the Passover meal. Jesus has made all the arrangements and there is an upper room in a house prepared for the event. During the meal Jesus does the strangest of things: he takes off his outer clothing and begins to wash the disciples' feet and calls them to follow his example. At the supper he calls them to celebrate a new covenant of love. 'Love one another', he says. 'As I have loved you, so love one another.' Follow my example, serve and love; sacrifice and give. He then speaks of the bread and the wine as his body and blood. (Mark 14:22-26; John 13:1-15, 15:12-13)

Jesus gives new meaning to the Passover—it is a new covenant of forgiveness and love, for friends and enemies, which is in Christ and his death. We are to become people of this new covenant through becoming one with Jesus in his death and resurrection.

Story number three. Twenty years have passed and the church of Jesus has spread through much of Asia Minor. As a result of the evangelistic ministry of Paul it has reached Corinth. In obedience to Jesus' command at his last meal, the church everywhere celebrates the supper, often as a part of their fellowship together, and as part of a love feast. It marks their love for each other. Sadly, in Corinth, there were plenty of divisions and not much fellowship. The better off do not like sharing their food with the less well off, and so the people are eating in separate groups. Different leaders are exalted by different groups; some express their superiority through the spiritual gifts they possess; and some declare their strength through the risks their faith allows them to take. Paul, rightly, attacks them for this: 'it's not the Lord's Supper that you are celebrating, when you take the bread and wine during your meal. It can't be the Lord's Supper because you are divided—there's no love being shown here'. There is little evidence of the new commandment of love that Christ demonstrated and called for at the Last Supper (1 Corinthians 11:23-29).

This meal is a celebration of being the people of God, the body of Christ, a loving fellowship. We are now part of this story.

Story number four. Our own fellowship has its story to tell, its expression of being a Christian community. Within this fellowship each disciple shares with others his or her own needs and concerns, together with the whole church's concerns for the community within which they live. The story here is held open for you, the reader, to fill in.

As we reflect on these four stories, we can perceive some of the transformations of meaning that happen between them. There are new elements and insights each time the story is told, and each re-retelling also makes us hear the earlier ones in new ways. However, the development of our literary culture seems to have removed the personal element—the communication of the story from one person to another. Placing the story in a book removes it from the drama of the liturgy within the community. It also leads to individualism and debate, where everyone has their own private interpretation. The Gospel is no longer focused in a person but in a book. In some ways the institutional church has lost the emphasis on a living faith, and we need to rediscover the journeying, pilgrim church, who tell, listen to, and live the ongoing story. The Passover or Lord's Supper help us to recover such story-telling, for the Supper is the place where the story is retold, re-enacted, and where the people enter into the story.

Discipleship does not depend on literacy. Terry Dunnell challenges us by asking how Christians learned about the Gospel before the invention of the printing press.[25] There is a need for the church to recover the art of story telling. The church should be a community that lives by the story. Jesus was a great story-teller. Dunnell helpfully draws our attention to the fact that

> Story is the language of experience, and telling a story to a group or face
> to face with friends is totally different from reading a book. Just listen to

the story-tellers in Native American or Aboriginal tribes! It is fun, engaging and spontaneous. It is emotional and evokes tears and laughter and above all, it creates community. Stories will bind people together and the deeper the meaning of the story the deeper the relationship.[26]

Individual daily reading of the Bible is something new. Before its wide availability, the Bible was generally read in community. Before the printing press the focus of the church was around the altar: the story was told in symbols, images and in words. We look to create a form of church in which the congregation are able to become teachers of the faith through personal testimony, and leaders and developers of liturgy through their own living experience of God. It is out of their shared witness and worship that the congregation becomes the ones who make the Lord's Supper relevant to the life of the world.

Such a vision of the church requires different leaders. They will encourage people to tell their stories and reflect upon them, asking questions such as: What does this teach us about God? How does this help us to understand how God works in the world and through human lives? What might this suggest about God's desire for us, our community, our world?

We will need to recognize the contribution that every church member and non-church member can bring from their experience of life, work, community, relationship, and understanding of the Bible. It is possible for a theologically trained minister to be the one who needs instruction from the community of faith, for in the theology of life and of industry and commerce it is the 'lay' people who are the experts. Congregations are at the cutting edge of the church's witness and service and have knowledge of the issues relevant to their communities and workplaces. We must move away from the view that the mission and ministry of the church is the task of its leadership toward an understanding that Christ's concern for the world is the challenge for every disciple. We seek to develop a community of faith that functions as a redemptive community in and for the world. This is the place where Christians learn their discipleship, and learn to relate their faith to their life and work. Doing theology is the ability to engage in a living dialogue between contemporary issues in faith and the witness of scripture and church tradition. (This we will develop more fully in Chapter 4.) In addition we will have to move away from western thought-forms which have the tendency to see truth as an intellectual construction or proposition rather than a person. We will need to recover the relational nature of the Gospel that we see exemplified in the ministry of Jesus.

We might ask how the Bible can continue to be the primary means by which God communicates with people, when their chief source of information is the TV set or the computer. Terry Dunnell is concerned about non-book people in our society, especially among the young. He rightly identifies that there are important questions for the church to address as it seeks to communicate the Gospel.[27] Such questions will include: How do people in this very visual age gather the information they need in order to make decisions? What methods will be most appropriate for evangelizing and discipling non-book people? How do we bring non-book leadership into the church? What might the Gospel feel and look like from the perspective of a non-book person?

We also ask these questions in relation to children, for people with learning difficulties, and for people in old age, when mental faculties begin to wane. In these circumstances pictures, images, stories, emotions and relationships will be more helpful. It is both challenging and disconcerting that when one minister asked his leaders, most of whom were professional women and men, what part of the Sunday service they received most from, they were unanimous in identifying the children's address.

We need leaders who are able to move beyond an approach that merely imparts information. Preaching, as a spiritual gift, has a power and immediacy that brings the congregation face to face with God and God's word, but teaching and Bible studies should also be more than academic exercises. Leaders will want develop creative ways of helping people to build trusting relationships, where they can tell their story and listen to the stories that others have to tell. We learn from the questions and doubts of others, and from our own failures and successes, as well as theirs.

We must therefore recognize the importance of the operation of house groups and fellowship groups as both learning environments and growth in Christian discipleship. Jane Vella, through forty years experience in community education throughout the world, says that until the gap between teacher and learner is closed, the dialogue limps and the learning is impaired. Her basic assumption is that adults have enough life experience to be in dialogue with any teacher, about any subject, and will learn new knowledge or attitudes or skills best in relation to that life experience.[28]

Vella's principles for guiding adult educators are concerned with the learners, the process of learning and the situation in which that learning takes place. The learners need to be able to build relationships through a non-judgemental, affirming group, in which they feel safe. Learners will need to trust the competence of the teacher or group leader, the feasibility of the objectives, and be able to voice their own expectations. The leader will need to demonstrate respect for the learners, seeing them as subjects rather than objects, who are able to make decisions about learning.[29]

Vella and other writers about adult education[30] also maintain that the process of learning will need to have an immediacy, as adults will not have time to waste, and will want to recognize the immediate usefulness of the course. Vella observes that failure to demonstrate this is the most common reason for people dropping out of programmes. Learning and growth take place not only with the mind, but with emotions and muscles, and it is important that the learning process includes reflection and doing as well as the taking in of facts. A Chinese proverb says: 'I hear and I forget; I see and I remember; I do and I understand.'

It is often said that people remember 20% of what they hear, 40% of what they hear and see, and 80% of what they discover for themselves. It is also useful to find ways of reinforcing the points that are being discovered, through repetition, and sequential learning which moves from the simple to the more complex.

Within any group learning situation there has to be a clear recognition of roles, but having recognized that the teacher is a resource of information and an enabler, we also realise that the teacher or leader is a fellow learner. It is important that learning is seen as a group activity. This togetherness is both an important process and principle, especially for those of us who are training future leaders for the church. Finally it is important that all the learners are engaged in the learning task and that there is accountability both for teacher and learner. The whole group experience and learning process should be accountable to the participants.

We can summarize the model of learning that I have been advocating as: empowering the participants, taking the form of a dialogue, actively engaging everyone, leading to follow up and evaluation, and always being focused on the growth and development of people. We will want to add to this that the church, as a place of learning like this, is a prayerful community with a missionary concern for the promotion of the Kingdom of God and God's justice. As such, churches will reflect on their location in society, seek to give practical expression to this vision and seek to bring it about. A commitment to community is vital in all this, as growth for the individual comes through actively participating in dialogue with others, the situation, the Bible and basic theology. The continuous interplay of reflection and action is the model that allows this to happen, for it is a process that starts from where we are; it challenges us to grow as persons; and it strives to create an environment of love and acceptance that alone makes growth possible.

Here a committed community becomes the one vital element—a community, where in our vulnerability, honesty and lack of understanding, we can develop as disciples. The centrality of the Lord's Supper for our fellowship and worship becomes clear, as we continue to reflect upon our growth in Christ. In exploring the nature of small communities, James O'Halloran rightly recognizes the importance of the Supper in the expression of community when he says that Christian disciples must: 'first look at their own lives and try to make sense of them in the light of the scriptures, just as the early Christians looked first of all at their own life experiences and then sought to interpret and make sense of them in the light of the whole Christ-event.'[31]

Exercise 1.3

a. What points have been raised through this introductory chapter that you would like to explore further on your own or in conversation with others?

b. In the following chapters, where we will examine experience, ways of understanding and exploring our experiences, and the integration of our experience with our faith and interpretation of the Bible, what issues will you want to address?

Notes

[1] http://news.bb.co.uk/1/hi/England/merseyside/4730559.stm; accessed 03.08.05.

[2] Within two weeks of the crime two local men were arrested and charged with Anthony Walker's murder.

[3] Laurie Green, *Let's Do Theology: a pastoral cycle resource book* (London: Mowbray, 1990/ Continuum 2004).

[4] Elaine Graham, Heather Walton & Frances Ward, *Theological Reflection: Methods* (London: SCM, 2005).

[5] John M Hull, *What Prevents Adults from Learning?* (Philadelphia: Trinity Press International, 1991), p. 7.

[6] See chapter 3 pp. 98-99 for an exposition of John 2:1-11.

[7] I am indebted to a number of authors referenced in this chapter and in chapter 5 note 20 for the thoughts expressed here.

[8] Mark Greene, 'Imagine', *Idea* (Magazine of the Evangelical Alliance), March/April 2003.

[9] Mark Greene, 'Imagine', p. 21.

[10] Gustavo Gutierrez, *The Truth Shall Set You Free* (New York: Orbis, 1990), p.104.

[11] Francis Dewar, *Called or Collared? An Alternative Approach to Vocation* (London: SPCK, 2000).

[12] Ian Fraser, *Reinventing Theology as the People's Work* (Glasgow: Wild Goose, 1988), p. 11.

[13] Martin Robinson, *The Faith of the Unbeliever* (Crowborough: Monarch,1994).

[14] Lesslie Newbigin, address given at the Gospel as Public Truth Conference, Swanwick, Derbyshire, 1992.

[15] Steven Weinberg, *The First Three Minutes* (London: Bantam Press,1979), quoted by Angela Tilby in *Science and the Soul* (London: SPCK, 1992), pp. 20-1 and 262.

[16] Jonathan Adams, *An Approach to Group Discussion about AIDS* (Wallsen:, A&W Training Network, 1993), and Joanna Rogers-Macy, *Despair and Personal Power in a Nuclear Age* (New York: Orbis, 1982).

[17] Joe Gross, 'A Model for Theological reflection in Clinical Pastoral Education', *Journal of Pastoral Care*, 48 (1994), pp. 131-4.

[18] Spurgeon's Childcare is a Christian organization that works in partnership with local churches in the UK and overseas in providing support for children and their families. For further information, see website: www.spurgeonschildcare.org.

[19] John Weaver, 'The Church Meeting' in Derek Tidball (Editor), *Baptist Basics* (Didcot: Baptist Union Publications, 1993).

[20] Stephen Pattison, 'Some Straw for the Bricks: A Basic Introduction to Theological Reflection', in James Woodward & Stephen Pattison (eds), *The Blackwell Reader in Pastoral and Practical Theology* (Oxford: Blackwell, 2000), p. 139.

[21] Green, *Let's Do Theology*, pp. 105-8.

[22] Bob Holman, *Faith in the Poor* (Oxford: Lion, 1998).

[23] For helpful explorations of group reflection and adult learning see: Paulo Freire, *Pedagogy of the Oppressed* (New York: Seabury Press, 1970) and *Education for Critical Consciousness* (New York: Seabury Press, 1973); Thomas H Groome, *Christian Religious Education: Sharing our Story and Vision* (San Francisco: Harper & Row, 1980); Jane Vella, *Learning to Listen, Learning to Teach: The Power of Dialogue in Educating Adults* (San Francisco: Jossey-Bass, 1994); Frances Ward, *Lifelong Learning. Theological Education and Supervision* (London: SCM, 2005); Catherine Widdicombe, *Group Meetings that Work. A practical guide for working with different kinds of groups* (Slough: St Pauls, 1994).

[24] Groome, *Christian Religious Education*, p. 193.

[25] Terry Dunnell, 'Christian Education and the Non-Book Culture' *Viewpoints* (National Christian Education Council), 1 (1996).

[26] Dunnell, 'Christian Education', p. 6.

[27] Dunnell, 'Christian Education', pp. 4-6.

[28] Vella, *Learning to Listen, Learning to Teach*, p. 3.

[29] Vella, *Learning to Listen, Learning to Teach*, p. 12. Learning-by-doing is important and Vella, p. 12, has four useful questions which fit with the pastoral cycle: What do you see happening here?—description; Why do you think it is happening?—analysis; When it happens in your situation, what problems does it cause?—application; and What can we do about it?—implementation.

[30] See the works of John Daines, Carolyn Daines & Brian Graham, *Adult Learning Adult Teaching* (Nottingham: University of Nottingham Continuing Education Press, 1993, 1996).

[31] James O'Halloran, *Signs of Hope: Developing Small Christian Communities* (New York: Orbis, 1991), pp. 115ff.

2
Experience: The Context Defined

The family of murder victim Anthony Walker, 18, who was killed with an axe in a racist attack on 29 July 2005, described him as a 'very kind, loving, caring, young man, who gave so much of his life to help other people.' His older sister Dominique, 20, said her brother loved playing football and was an Arsenal fan, but his main sport was basketball and he had trials for the Liverpool and England basketball teams.[1]

His mother, Gee Walker, made an emotional appeal for help in tracing her son's killers at an 800-strong vigil for the murdered 18-year-old in Liverpool on Tuesday 2 August 2005. Mrs Walker said she felt overwhelmed by the 'sea of faces' looking at her and the support from strangers. She stated that she was receiving letters from people in America, Canada, and Ireland—people she did not know who wrote letters of condolence. Her apology for wearing sunglasses because of her swollen eyes drew a round of applause from the congregation. She said, 'I have to tell you about Anthony, he was everybody's son', and she added, 'I am sure he is looking down at you all bouncing his basketball.' 'I am sorry for the people that have done it, and if you know anyone then come forward, they don't deserve to walk the streets,' she urged.

Anthony's older sister, Dominique, fought back tears as she issued a public appeal for help in catching her brother's killers. 'This is no joke, he is flesh and blood, my little brother, he was only 18.' 'It is not over, you just don't know, you just don't know what you have done.' She also said she forgave his attackers. Speaking of the gang who used an axe to kill Anthony, she several times used the phrase 'we have to forgive.' Quoting from the bible, she said: 'Seventy times seven we have to forgive, that's what Jesus said. So we have to, we have to forgive.'[2]

It is at this point that some Christians find they part company with the family. Forgiveness is a major sticking point in pastoral ministry, because, depending on the seriousness of the offence, people generally find it difficult, if not impossible, to forgive. The words of Jesus, read or preached, often produce a negative or angry reaction: 'For if you forgive others, when they sin against you, your heavenly Father will also forgive you. But if you do not forgive others their sins, your Father will not forgive your sins.' (Matthew 6:14-15.)

But when I have spoken with some of my congregation who have reacted against such a text, I have discovered that they have misunderstood the meaning of forgiveness and the reconciliation that lies as its goal. We need to correct the belief that forgiveness means just assuring the wrong-doer that 'everything is all right' and that what has been done 'doesn't matter.' This is a 'happy ending' scenario that leaves the wronged person feeling cheated. As Anthony Walker's sister said: 'This is no joke, he is flesh and blood, my little brother, he was only 18.' To offer forgiveness is a statement that something is wrong, badly wrong. The forgiver is saying, 'what you said to me, thought about me, or did to me, is wrong'. The act of repentance is similar. The one who repents is saying, 'I recognize that what I did, said, or thought, is wrong'.

When we consider the reaction of Dominique Walker or of Gordon Wilson, the father of Marie Wilson, a victim of the Enniskillen Remembrance Parade bombing by the Provisional IRA in 1987, we find ourselves wondering just how we would have reacted. Gordon Wilson was a man of Christian faith (he attended Enniskillen Methodist Church), and came to national and international prominence with an emotional television interview he gave to the BBC, when he expressed forgiveness to his daughter's killers and pleaded with loyalists not to take revenge for her death.

It is very difficult for us to understand the reactions of others in many traumatic situations, not only those of forgiving a wrong. I still remember the funeral of Mark Baghurst, aged 3 months, held at Belper Baptist Church, Derbyshire, where my wife and I were members. Mark had been born with a heart defect, but after extensive hospital treatment he died. His parents were at peace and almost joyful through the whole time, including the funeral. As our children were toddlers at the time, we wondered how they were able to react as they did. Sheila and I expressed our feelings to an older and wiser Christian in the fellowship, who said: 'God does not give you grace for imagined ills, but is there for the realities you face in life.'

At the first stage of the pastoral cycle (see figure 1.1) we need to explore our experience, both as individuals and as members of society. We need to face up to our feelings about our own life and about the communities in which we live. We need to understand why we react the way that we do to the feelings and emotions of others, as they are caught, like the families of Anthony Walker and Mark Baghurst, in the tragedy of violence and suffering. And to do this, we need to understand the whole context in which we are placed, both in our personal lives and in our world.

Identifying our experiences

Our life experiences are extremely important in the whole learning process. We recognize that our early nurture contributes greatly to the way in which we perceive the world around us. As babies and small children we learn through the senses, especially through touch and taste. Our parents or the adults with whom we live and grow are important influences on our behaviour and our emotions. However, it is in our teenage years, from about 12 to 18 that our perception of the world, in which we live, develops.[3] Out of this period of our lives come questions of our own identity—Who am I? What is the meaning of life? Why does the universe exist?

If I may be excused for taking myself as an example, my own formative years were the 1960s, marked by a growing liberalism, tolerance and togetherness. It was the time of 'The Beatles' and of 'Flower Power,' and 'free love.' It was also a period of uncertainty, of 'live for today', when the threat of nuclear war hung over the world. In the church this was the time of ecumenism, Vatican II, and the 'Death of God' debate.

It is also important to think about where we grew up, our family background, and what our parents' occupations were. We recognize that there are local cultural differences, even within a small area. For example, my wife and I both grew up in South Wales in the 1960s, but Sheila grew up as the daughter of a coal miner in a small valley town, while I grew up as the son of a school teacher in the capital city, Cardiff. These different backgrounds led to differing views over many areas of life. church-going was the norm for almost everyone in my school; 34 out of the 36 in my class, when I was 13 years old, went to church at least once per month, and the other two attended the Jewish synagogue! I grew up in a Christian home and my spiritual development was one of gradual nurture. We attended a Baptist church as a family, where both my parents were actively involved. It was a typical Welsh Nonconformist church, where the meaning of the Bible was questioned, and its relationship with contemporary life explored.

I can see the ways in which these experiences coloured and still shape my thinking. Yet alongside these foundational experiences there have been the new experiences along life's journey. These would include: studying Geology at University and beginning to examine the questions that science raises for Christian belief, something that I have continued to explore;[4] the realization at the age of 25 that Christian discipleship is 24/7; God's call to train and serve as a Christian minister; leading a church that was experiencing charismatic renewal in the 1980s; and returning to university teaching of practical theology in the 1990s, whence I have continued to explore theological reflection and adult Christian education. These experiences illustrate for me that the learning cycle or pastoral cycle becomes a spiral rather than a circle (see figure 1.2), and we can all readily find the same pattern in our experience.

With any new group, whether beginning a practical or pastoral theology course or coming together for Bible study, I often work through an exercise outlining the world and church events of the previous 60 years, which helps us all to consider the events and cultural context that may have influenced our thinking. I start by asking each group member to tell me their age. If we agree that 12 to 18 are the formative years in moving from child to adult, then a person's age will define the period of recent history within which he or she was growing up. So if someone is 35 years old in 2006, their formative years will have been the 'Thatcher years' of market forces, individualism and a growing materialism. In the church this would have been the period of renewal movements, church growth programmes, and Willow Creek. Whereas if someone were 55 years old in 2006, their formative years will have been similar to mine, the 1960s, as outlined above. In addition we would consider family background and circumstances, and questions about church experience and our journeys of faith. Those, for example, who grew up in a Christian home, worshipping in a fairly liturgical church, and gradually accepting the Christian faith for themselves some 20 years ago will have a very different perception from someone who has come from outside the church, had a 'Damascus Road experience' a couple of years ago, and has been worshipping in an independent charismatic church. Drawing a map of our personal journey of faith is helpful in understanding this aspect of our experience.

All of these are generalizations, but may serve to illustrate the way in which our experience will affect the way we perceive and learn. When running through this exercise in the Baptist Polytechnic University in Managua, Nicaragua, in 1995, I pointed out that someone who was 25 years old would have grown up with the Sandinista revolutionary government and the Contra War, whereas someone who was 45 years old would have grown up under the Samosa dictatorship. These were two very different experiences. A similar exercise with students in the United States recognized the significance of the presidency of J.F. Kennedy, Woodstock, the Civil Rights Movement, the Vietnam War, and the later era of Presidents Regan and Bush Senior, in shaping opinion and outlook on life.

We recognize that new experiences will connect with old ones. We have filters that affect how we perceive reality, and influence greatly what we learn and do not learn. We have seen that important influences include our growing up, our culture, our education, our work experience, our pilgrimage of faith, our church experience, and our relationships. We will be conscious that all of these are likely to have an influence on our learning together. But paramount for the functioning of any group will be an emphasis on the worth of each person and a recognition of the value of their experience of faith and life.

Helping others to explore their experiences

Congregations are aware that frustrations arise when too few people are doing all the work. It is vitally important that people are helped to recognize their own gifts, and to realize that in the business of daily living out their faith they have expertise gained through their experience. The role of those involved as leaders in the congregation is to enable people to reflect together upon their experiences and recognize the various places where God has been involved. But how do we help this to happen?

We all need to be able to express how we feel and what we know or understand in a comfortable setting. This is best achieved in small groups where mutual trust develops and each person feels confident and secure in expressing his or her thoughts. Here all are encouraged to tell of their own experience in their own words. Anne Hope and Sally Timmel are right when they reflect out of a Third World context that 'participation of people in shaping their own lives and to write their own history means they need to speak their own words—not the words of someone else.'[5]

They are right when they note that sharing information should not be confused with participation. Participation means dialogue which is based on people being able to share their perceptions and offer their opinions and ideas, and having opportunity to make decisions or recommendations. No one has all the answers; no one is ignorant; everyone has experience; and we look for a mutual learning process. To do this we will need skill and sensitivity, especially as many (especially older) people will have grown up with a top-down direction of learning or imparting information through education, management, health service, and government. The result will be that many adults will be suspicious of this kind of discussion group and will, as a result, be slow to get involved. Frequently, this is due to a fear of embarrassment or the insecurity of being in an unfamiliar learning environment. It is therefore important that we shape groups where the members have the assurance of being accepted for who they are, where concerns and experiences are shared in ways that help members to get to know each other and grow in trust, and that each member is clear about the purpose for meeting together.

Along with other writers on adult learning,[6] I recognize that adults have a wide experience and will have learnt a great deal from life. They tend to learn quickly about things that are relevant to their lives and their powers of observation and reasoning grow with age. However, we also need to be sensitive to the vulnerability that adults may have within a new learning environment, and recognize that they have a sense of personal dignity, which should be preserved.

One way to get a group working together, and thinking about how the members can learn together, is to ask everyone to focus on something they have learned outside formal education, but which is important for their daily life. These should be things that they *remember* learning. Examples might include tying shoe laces, flying a kite, baking a cake, riding a bicycle, applying make-up, or driving a car. In each case a person might be asked: Why did you learn it? Who helped you learn it? What was the relationship between you and the person who helped you? What was the situation in which you learned it? In what way did you learn it? Can you remember anything that made your learning easier or more difficult? The results are shared and will give clear insights into how we learn.

Exercise 2.1

a. Think about yourself:
- How old are you?
- What was happening in the world during your teenage years?
- What is your social and cultural background?
- What is your church experience?

b. Can you identify ways in which your experience and background have shaped the person you are today?

Recognizing who we are

Listening to each other's stories of our life journey helps us to recognize common turning points and features. When looking at our faith, our human formation and transformation, we should take seriously the fact that our adult identity and faith has been shaped by our earliest years and relationships. Stages of faith and human development describe general features of human growth—they are every person's stories. Jean Piaget and Lawrence Kohlberg studied ways of how we know, describing stages of thinking and moral reasoning.[7] Piaget's developmental theory is based on biological functioning which stresses that cognitive development is the result of the person's adaptation to their environment through accommodation and assimilation. Piaget considers that certain processes underlie all learning whether in simple organisms or in human beings.

What Piaget does not consider in his analysis of knowing is the area of emotion and affection—he rather looks at rational objectivity. However, for James Fowler, faith involves both rationality and passionality. Fowler speaks of the 'logic of connection' and the 'reasoning in faith.' Fowler then stresses the importance of imagination in knowing, and the power of symbols. He also associates moral reasoning with faith in his recognition of seven stages of faith.[8] These stages are pertinent not only to the development of faith but to adult learning, so it is worth looking at some of them in a little detail.

At his stage 3, *Conforming Faith* (12-19 years), Fowler suggests that adolescents need 'mirrors'—to reflect their changes in appearance and new looks. So the views of others become important for the image of self. They worry about being accepted socially and sexually. For these people God is seen as having inexhaustible depths and is capable of knowing the mysterious depths of self and others. Faith is synthesized rather than analysed. Faith concepts are grasped but the person will go along with the faith crowd. Transition to the next stage comes through noticing contradictions in the lives of valued leaders, or through a break, such as leaving home. But Fowler recognizes that some adults never in fact pass beyond this stage at all.

Stage 4, *Choosing Faith* (18-40 years), includes taking seriously the burden of responsibility for commitments, lifestyle, beliefs and attitudes. At this stage tensions develop between self-fulfilment and self-actualization as a primary concern on the one hand, and service to other people and being for them on the other hand. Many adults do not reach this stage and for others it does not arrive until their 40s. Beliefs are analysed, compared and contrasted. Reactions can be pluralistic or fundamentalist.

Stage 5, *Balanced Faith* (mid-life), is a time of re-working and reclaiming of the past—an opening to the voices of the 'deeper self.' There is in faith a willingness to live with paradoxes and inconsistencies. The views of other faith traditions are appreciated as enriching rather than threatening.

Finally stage 6, *Selfless Faith* (maturity), is—according to Fowler—a rare stage which he identifies with Martin Luther King's non-violence, Ghandi's selflessness, or Mother Teresa's self-sacrifice on behalf of others. These persons embody costly openness to the power of the future; they create liberation and shock waves. We might suggest that they are Christ-like and challenge us in our calling as his disciples.

The identification of such stages in the behaviour and the perceptions of how children and adults learn and grow in understanding are generalizations based on observation. They are neither laws nor even principles, but they do inform our understanding about the ways in which people think. They are, as it were, outlines for people's stories, patterns within which stories tend to be told. In our faith communities we share our interpretations and experiences of the world and of living.

Stories help us to understand ourselves, they convey truth, they help us to make sense of the world in which we live, and they help us to express and come to terms with our emotions. In a world dominated by technology, computers and global economics, all of which have the tendency to crush us and deny our personhood, stories help us to define ourselves. Story is the language of experience, and telling a story to a group or face to face with friends is totally different from reading a book. Telling stories is fun, engaging and spontaneous, full of emotion and passion, and as a result creates community.

Imagination is an important element as it allows us to enter into the experience of others. The stories that other people tell help us to understand them and their behaviour. In telling stories we use our deepest feelings and commitments. Our own stories change and develop with our experiences. Self identity becomes an important aspect of our story, of 'who I am', of 'what it means to be me', of who I am in relation to God, and to my family and other people.

Stories also help us to understand the world; they give reason for action. For example there are the stories that politicians tell, such as the stories that Tony Blair and George W. Bush told about Osama bin Laden and al Qaeda as part of their justification for the invasion of Iraq in 2003. Then there are the stories that are told in the Middle East, in Palestine and Israel, which tend to be stories from the past which are told to justify the present. These include Bible stories, the Crusades, Lawrence of Arabia and the settlement of 1918, the Holocaust, the 1948 settlement and war, the 1967 war, and recent atrocities blamed by one side on the other. Stories are used to build up communities or to strengthen identity, for example the stories told in Northern Ireland by the Unionist and Republican communities. We might note that a good society hears and seeks to understand the stories told by the other side. We can observe that justice may be defined by the ways in which stories are heard and judged.

But within these larger stories, adult individuals will go through different experiences during their lives. They will recognize different issues as important at different stages. We have already reflected on this progression in terms of the development of faith. Another perspective is offered by Jack Dominion in his book *Make or Break*,[9] where he presents a model for the different stages that marriage might progress through and the differing tensions that may arise. If we think about relationships with others more widely, we can make the following general observations about styles of life at different periods.

- *18-30 years*. Most of us engage in a search for social identity, find a job or begin a career path, look for a marriage partner, and adapt to new relationships. Whether lasting relationships become established or not, people are concerned about self-worth, housing, money, work, leisure, sexual intimacy, and children. Much of the emphasis of television programmes, adverts, holiday opportunities, and the lifestyles of the stars of entertainment or sport place an emphasis on looks, pleasure, achievement and success. This has the effect of creating problems of self-worth for many young adults.
- *30-40 years*. The development of our skills and experience reach their height with the possibilities of enhanced job prospects and responsibility. There are house moves, community roles, a growing family or adjustment to singleness. The physical appearance of the rich and famous in the media causes problems at this life stage also. Psychologists in UK and USA have recognized increased incidences of depression amongst women, who look at the natural signs of ageing in their own bodies, but are faced with television images of 30 and 40 year old stars still looking 25, as the result of cosmetic surgery and botox injections.
- *40-50 years*. There may be a plateau in work or possibly a career change. Non-work activities grow in importance. Physical ageing becomes more obvious with the increased possibilities of illness. Caring for ageing parents and/or teenagers is likely. During this period there may be a so-called 'mid-life crisis' brought about by a failure to realize expectations in work or in our relationships. Extra marital affairs, alcohol abuse, stress at work, and depression may be the presenting symptoms.
- *50-60 years*. This time often involves a struggle to maintain pace of life, and to address the mental and/or physical demands of our jobs and the constant need to keep up-to-date with advances in the workplace. Jack Dominion suggests that for married couples the departure of children may lead to further breakdown in relationships, although the positive

aspects can be the enjoyment of grandchildren, leisure, and financial security. However, it should be noted that as couples begin their families later, or have second families, many will have children and teenagers at home during this phase of life.

• *60-75 years*. This period will likely include retirement (in the future at 68-70 in the UK, in all probability), decline in health, and change in social life, with the death of friends and relations, and the reality of our own death. If health and finance allow, there is likely to be an increase in leisure activity, including travel. The downside may include: unemployment, thwarted ambition, ill health, depression, or increased impotence with the resulting stress through the loss of being able to share affection in a sexually intimate way.

• *75 years to death*. For many this will be a period of survival—health and finance will reduce, and there will be an increased dependence on others. There may be a reduction in leisure activity, with an accompanied reduction in self-worth. This may result in a retreat to the past to block off the reality of the present.

While we recognize the enormous changes that are now taking place in the area of life expectancy, lifestyles and human relationships, these generalizations or 'story-outlines' may still be helpful for our understanding. All of these psychological, intellectual, growth, and relationship issues are part of what makes me 'me', and you 'you'. They must be recognized as we consider how we relate our faith to our life and work. These aspects of character and experience will affect our attitudes, our openness, and the positions we hold in the world and in the church.

Recognizing who others are
Obviously we cannot experience every aspect of life and development before we can enter into a dialogue with others. We cannot fully understand another's work, cultural context, or environment, if it is not our own. We must seek ways of bridging such chasms that exist, within churches, and between the church and the community it seeks to serve. To understand the community and social context fully we would need to experience it ourselves. We can walk to other parts of our own community and listen to the people. But awareness comes from experience. We need an immer-

sion experience, which means an exposure to faithful people living, for example, with poverty or with affluence, with singleness or with pre-school children, with management pressures or with mental illness.

First at Fordham University, New York, and more recently at the University of Central America, San Salvador, Dean Brackley has involved first year students in a community service course which involves such an immersion experience. At Fordham students were sent to work with church communities in the Bronx, while in San Salvador they experience life within some of the poorer barrios of the city, or in village communities in the campo. Brackley has recorded three early stages of reflection that these students pass through in their encounter with the poor.[10]

After getting over their initial fear, students first of all are thrilled and surprised to find that they are accepted, that these are 'ordinary folks,' just like them, and that they can be of some use to the people. In addition they begin to recognize that these people are experiencing injustice. At the second stage, realism breaks into their romantic picture, as they discover that amongst these people there are bad as well as good, there is anger, bitterness and violence, and there are those who are confidence tricksters. The third stage is one of asking serious questions of the situation and of what realistically might be done to help. The nature and causes of the problems, such as homelessness, drug addiction, and broken families, are considered. 'They begin to tug on the string of their local situation,' says Brackley, 'and run up against the complexity, the structural nature, and the enormity of the evil and injustice around them.' At this point there may be the danger of being overwhelmed by the immensity of the problem, becoming angry, cynical or merely dropping out. But if they—and we—counter that temptation, the result of such an immersion is to become committed to effecting change. Brackley maintains that this is not a happy experience, since the poor will break our hearts. We look, listen, feel, smell, taste and then reflect. We ask questions: what moved us? and why? We ask what warmed our hearts, inspired, challenged, or confused us. Only through such experiences are we challenged to think analytically, reflect theologically, and respond with appropriate action.

A similar point is made by Denham Grierson[11] when considering the beginning of ministry in a new church. Dialogue with people who live in the parish is key to our understanding of that community. There is a need to understand what may be a new culture, even an alien situation. For example, those who have lived all their life in a town will find that a rural community is alien in many ways, and *vice versa*. There is a need to listen to individuals and to the church, to understand their personal and shared experiences. The spiritual journey of the congregation is often the key to understanding the outward expression of its life. For example, when a congregation says, 'We tried that once and it didn't work', they may actually be reflecting on the fact that last time they tried 'that' it was a painful spiritual experience. There is also a need to recognize that the congregation's life is always in process, and no one sequence of events will completely define its life and faith. The congregation expresses its nature through the symbols, stories and artefacts that it preserves.

A new minister is a 'participant-observer', sharing in the activities and sentiments of the people. This involves face-to-face relationships, and direct contact with their shared life. He or she does not come as an expert, but rather as a learner who, in order to learn, participates in the life of the people. There is a need to get alongside people and listen to their stories, together with an empathetic involvement. All of these are important aspects of the development of trust and of community building.

We should also take note of the important questions that sociologists and psychologists present for the church. Their interest in religion arises through links with guilt, desire, sin and the control of behaviour. Belief, practice and experience find correspondence with the primary psychological categories of reason, will and memory. Psychologists are agreed that the elements of personal religion bring together a *knowledge* of particular doctrines with *practices* concerning 'God.' Knowledge includes beliefs or disbeliefs, attitudes and values about truth and falsity, and the credibility of those doctrines. In addition there are those experiences that give authenticity to some direct awareness of God. These might be, for example, conversion, joy, peace, or the presence of the Spirit. They are accompanied by practices such as rituals and sacraments in social contexts and situations that allow and validate belief. What a person believes is demonstrated in how he or she lives (see Matthew 7:15-23 and James 2:14-17), and religious commitment is always in a social context, defined by particular church traditions.

In western society the Reformation church has tended to subdue the body and extol the mind. The main emphasis has been placed on preaching, teaching, Bible study, and prayer. But in the last thirty years there has been a rediscovery of the presence and power of the Holy Spirit, and this happened together with a new discovery of symbols, images, music and movement. However, we are warned by psychologists that music, dance and incense may enhance such experiences as conversion through 'brain excitement', which is in essence a mechanism for emotional control. They also suggest that some religious practices, such as going to church or giving money, may involve elements of appeasing guilt or of belonging to the right group.

Religious commitment is always in a social context, defined by particular church traditions. A solitary Christian figure is almost a contradiction in terms. Many social scientists see religion as a compensation for deprivation. However, sociologists recognize that small congregations tend to be stronger and exhibit greater commitment than larger churches, because the people know each other and, as a result, are more inclined to support and care for each other. Social relationships give social identity and also give social order.

We need to recognize that all of these factors need to be considered when we examine church growth or decline. Success or failure may not necessarily reflect the relevance of the Gospel that is proclaimed, but rather sociological and psychological factors relating to its presentation, and to the social groupings within the local community.

In conclusion the root of the word education is *e-ducere*, literally 'to lead forth' or 'to bring out' something which is potentially present, although not yet visible. Congregational leaders have the roles of enablers, facilitators, interpreters, and so are resource people. This may mean the development of new ways of learning together and of being church. This is part of the overall task of helping the whole congregation to find deeper expressions of their shared existence.

Exercise 2.2
Construct a faith map or life journey highlighting the events that have shaped your faith. You may draw such a 'map' as a graph (with highs, lows, and plateaux) or as a winding road with pictures or images that rep-

resent particular events. You may wish to share this with another member
of the group of which you are a part.

Understanding our social context

At the beginning of the Second World War France and her allies depended
on the 'impregnable' Maginot Line, a line of forts facing Germany. It
failed because the German army simply skirted around it or flew over it.
In criticism it was said that 'the trouble with the Allies is that they are
always ready to fight the last war!' The same complaint is often levelled,
rightly, at ministers and churches—we tend to be better at answering the
questions and operating within the culture of the last generation.

Martin Robinson[12] describes this present time as an age of unbelief,
where there are new questions about belief and where even rationalism is
faced with new doubts. He recognizes a gradual divorce between
Christian faith and a western culture where many people see religion as
having evil effects in the world. However, while he picks up a significant
trend, the picture is a mixed one; at the same time there has been a growth
of interest in spirituality. In our so-called postmodern, post-rational, post-
Christian society, spirituality is being demonstrated in all sorts of ways.
The church must also learn from such as instances as the expressions of
public grief following the death of Diana Princess of Wales, the reactions
to September 11th, and the increasingly common practice of placing flowers at the side of the road where a road death has occurred. In the 2001
census 71.7% of the population of England and Wales, 37.3 million,
described themselves as Christian. Our concern is not to preserve the
church but to share the Gospel with the people within our communities,
and opportunities abound for which the church must be equipped.

Two key areas of change are necessary:
- Church communities need to become much more open, interactive, personal and expressive—easier places to come to, easier communities to
  belong to. I am not advocating a change of message or a watering down
  of the Gospel of life and hope. But I am suggesting a change of
  approach and an engagement with the questions and concerns of the
  society in which we are to be Christ incarnate.
- We need to return to Jesus' instruction to 'make disciples', enabling
  Christians to become life-long learners and practitioners in communities

that are focused on equipping their members to go where people actually are. This requires a radical shift in much of current pastoral practice and in the readiness of individual Christians to commit themselves to life-long learning.

It is these areas that must be addressed as a priority. We can speak about youth work and preaching, about pastoral care, evangelism, and the social needs of the community, but first of all we will need to *understand* our context. For understanding our context will affect the ways in which we approach all these other areas.

The twentieth century proved what the philosopher Nietzsche predicted: as societies move away from God, they do not get happier, they get unhappier. They don't get more loving, they get more selfish. In the past 40 years individualistic values have been driving our society. These are enormously powerful, but they are not delivering the satisfaction people crave. A society that is not meeting its people's needs is ready to hear good news that might.

The statistics do not make for happy reading. The UK has some highest figures in Europe for teenage pregnancy, youth crime, divorces, and drug and alcohol abuse. We have the lowest level of unemployment, but this is offset by the fact that we work the most hours, and commute further than others in Europe. The result is that quality of life and relationships is reduced. There is an increasing trend of people living alone, and a dramatic rise of interest in 'cyber sex' involving live web cams and chat lines, which is spoken of as sexual fulfilment without the drawback of relationship. In 2005 nearly 20% of the UK population were taking anti-depressants. There is a loss of trust in politics and in almost everything else, as we become more individualistic and self-centred.

In the light of its 2002 census, the youth culture magazine *The Face* wrote, 'If identity crisis is a form of madness, then Young Britain 2002 is a schizoid manic-depressive with bombsite self-esteem. Our status as the most boozed-up, drug-skewed, pregnancy-prone wasters in Europe is pretty much unchallenged.'[13]

We inhabit a universe made up of billions of galaxies, like our own Milky Way, each one containing billions of stars like our own sun. We understand more about the complex genetic make-up of our bodies and have made enormous strides in the identification and cure of diseases. We are able to transmit and access information from all around the world in microseconds. Yet we live with risks and fear of the unpredictable and the bad actions of self-centred human beings, individuals and governments, such as the murder of Anthony Walker or the destruction of whole communities by the Mugabe-led government of Zimbabwe. Our hedonistic lifestyle is the 'new opiate of the people' — it stops us reflecting. Hope and identity for many people is in material possessions as portrayed in television adverts. For example, an advert (in 2005) for a new generation of mobile phone begins with an amateur golfer trying to drive a ball up the fairway, his (inferior) mobile phone lying on the ground in front of him. He is making a total mess of hitting the ball, evidenced by large divots of turf. Some other golfers are seen approaching, he looks at the ground in front of him, and with an accuracy thus far lacking, dispatches his phone into the distance with his iron. The voice-over says: 'life is full of enough embarrassing moments, don't let your mobile be one of them.'

Yet amid this materialism, many people are still searching for some kind of spiritual reality, for some centre to their lives, as seen by the flourishing of New Age, Neo-paganism, and a host of 'Mind, Body and Spirit' publications and shops. Here is an opportunity for those who know the reality of Christ's presence and the transformation that Christ brings to life. The missionary God is active in the world. We may, however, be in danger of confining our understanding of Christ to our restricted experience and limited knowledge. We need a vision of Christ with cosmic and eternal dimensions, a Christ who transcends all our best and most extravagant thoughts about him, and all our most wonderful experiences of him. Once we begin to grasp something of this, we will recognize that Jesus Christ is good news for today.

Our society has changed and the church is no longer at the centre. The churches need help to come to terms with this new situation. For centuries the church was at the centre of British society, but in the last 100 years it has gradually become more and more marginal. Our calling as the church today is to engage in mission from the margins, and this means the church will need to change. It needs seriously to face the fact that a culture gap has opened up between the church and the rest of society. We find that the story of the gospel is not well known, or not known at all, outside the church. What goes on behind the doors of the local church is unknown territory for most people in our communities. The language, practices, values, and meetings of the church are alien. Many churches, as a result, find themselves communities cut off from society, as separate as a pigeon racing club among non-pigeon-fanciers.

For many churches, while the members have no doubt about the reality of their own experience of Christ, mission seems very difficult, old methods no longer work, and the gap has just grown too big. There have been rapid cultural and social changes. The church is often presented as an institution dwelling in the past and failing to interact with the present or even be inspired by the hope of future possibilities. Statistics inform us that many churches will close within a generation. For example, Welsh Nonconformist churches, whose membership in 1904 accounted for 33% of the population, now find attendance less than 5% with 70% of the congregation over 70 or under 10 years of age. Many are failing to see the signs of the times and neglecting to see the spiritual discernment and vitality needed to address the challenge.

Yet the church is not uniformly in decline and there are growing churches in almost every part of the British Isles. Some churches are heavily involved in community projects and care of the disadvantaged. Such contributions are increasingly recognized by local and national government, for example the Kaleidoscope Project for drug-users, based at John Bunyan Baptist Church, Kingston upon Thames.[14] However, generally the media image of the church is not good. Instead of simply complaining about this, we might suspect that where customer satisfaction is the greatest advert for any project, we are failing. Having recently moved into a new area, we needed the services of an electrician, a plumber, a carpenter, a builder and a decorator. Naturally we asked friends and neighbours to recommend people that they had used and found efficient and trustworthy. We might ask: do members of congregations have sufficient confidence in their church to recommend it to their friends and neighbours?

The church no longer has a strong public voice. It is criticized for its failure to address the needs of the young, of women, and in its attitude to gays and lesbians within church and society. It is attacked for irrelevant preaching and dull services. This deep crisis is reflected in discontent inside and outside the church. Our problems are not only with the world outside the church. The church itself is sick, maybe terminally ill—half way between denial and bargaining with God, to use Elizabeth Kubler-Ross' terminology with regard to the stages of grief.[15]

Every crisis has elements of threat and opportunity, and we need to honestly address the current situation. The church is haemorrhaging with 53,000 leaving every week in Europe and North America. Evidence suggests that less than 5% have ceased to believe; they have left the church rather than ceased to follow Jesus Christ.[16] The unique nature of Sunday has all but disappeared under a tidal wave of shopping, leisure and sport, and it is further submerged under a lack of free time. Clergy are no longer people of influence and status to be consulted, and there is a collapse of plausibility in some of the basic assumptions of Christianity. The church is becoming culturally isolated and there is a lack of common ground between the language of the pulpit and the intended audience. Added to this, the impetus for incarnation has been lost—church programmes rarely encourage members to go out to meet and be with people where they are.

People are seeking a spiritual journey but see the church belonging to a bygone era or having a spirituality that is shallow and repressive. It is difficult for the church in the West to be mission-minded, when it is engaged in survival. A church in mission mode will tend to be open, flexible, reflective, experimental, dynamic and energetic, while in survival mode it retreats into being conservative, exclusive, careful and static. But there is no need to be negative, as there are positive opportunities. The Promised Land lies before us, but the question remains: will we go forward into the challenge of the hostile and unpredictable or return to what is comfortable and known? (Numbers chapters 13 and 14).

We have 'seeker-sensitive' events, but surely now is the time to address the concerns of the church-leavers. The following provides a useful agenda, based on some of the ideas in Alan Jamieson's book, *A Churchless Faith*:

• Provide opportunities for people to explore, question and doubt. Open up a safe place where it is all right to say 'prayer doesn't work'; 'God has left me'; 'I don't know whether I believe x or y or z.'

- Explore a theology that speaks of journeying rather than having arrived. Present a 'Pilgrim's Progress,' where we can speak of failure and struggle, dark places and the absence of God.
- Build a supportive community which provides resources for people who have failed or who find themselves in the dark places. Be a community of nurture and spiritual direction.
- Be able to live with a variety of models of God and how God acts in the world. Be ready to admit that God is bigger than any one theological perspective.
- Develop a model of an honest Christian life, which emphasizes integrity rather than a legalistic treadmill of 'oughts.'
- Make space for the expression of emotions and intuitions, where images, dreams and feelings have a place.[17]

We need to focus on what is really important. We have privatized sin with our emphasis on personal morality, especially in terms of sexual conduct, while our part in the major sins of injustice, oppression and poverty in the world are almost ignored. We make an enormous fuss about Dan Brown's blockbuster novel *The Da Vinci Code*[18] and the film of the book, because it repeats in a fast-paced, fictional story some common myths and heresies of the past, while we make little comment upon the arid commercialism and destructive racism that blights the lives of the young and old of our society. The prophetic voices that spoke out against slavery have been replaced by siren calls such as the one at the turn of the twenty-first century to boycott Disneyworld and Disney products because of their equal opportunity policy over the employment of gays and lesbians.[19]

Our modern church, like the society in which it finds itself, seeks to exclude suffering. This leads to deception and game-playing. Also like society, the church has sought to exercise power and control, which is usually in the hands of white, male, wealthy, intellectual, heterosexuals. The result is that others are excluded and move on. If they stay they are marginalized. But a community which reflects the life of Jesus will be a community of generosity and sharing, of friendship and belonging, of mission and identity, of freedom and risk-taking. As such it cannot but help stand out against the deeply held values of western culture.

How can the church create Christian communities that help release the strength of the people where they are? We might begin by asking our congregations and then responding carefully to their answers. Good leaders will seek to find out what the issues that matter to their people, their community, their society and country are. Many people in our churches are struggling to integrate their faith and their life and work. They need help with the questions that they face each day both for themselves and from their friends and neighbours.

We recognize that 'witnessing' is not some special gift or particular programme which gives assured results. Rather it is simply a matter of telling it as it is. It is not a matter of winning an argument but about having a conversation. This of course means listening to the other's view, questions, passions, fears. The Gospel spread through the house groups and conversations that the members of the early church held with their neighbours and friends, all empowered through the activity of the Holy Spirit and validated in changed lives. We need to give people the confidence to have such conversations. This will be achieved through a greater degree of participation in church services, especially through story-telling and testimony (about last week, not the last century!).

Tom is a farmer, who came to personal faith in Jesus Christ when he was 38 years old. For his fortieth birthday he wanted to hold a special party for all his friends and family, both non-Christian and Christian. It began with Tom's favourite classical music pieces played by a string quartet and piano, followed by lots of good food. But between the music and the food Tom, not a public speaker, gave his own personal testimony, in hesitant speech, of growing up in a Christian family, of finding the truth of the Gospel in his late thirties, and of the difference that Christ had made to his family and farming life. It was a powerful witness and a creative way to celebrate a significant birthday.

One major role for church leaders is to enable the congregation to find natural ways of expressing their faith. To encourage such discipleship there is a need for discussion, storytelling and reflection with others; expression of doubts, lively debate and argument with others; and a prayerful openness and supportive love and care of each other. There is a need for home groups, prayer groups, and sometimes groups that have a single focus. We need to empower the church's greatest resource to live as disciples of Christ.

The church once more finds itself to be engaged in working from the margins. The traditional position saw the church at the centre of society; the modern position saw the church relating to society; the postmodern position sees the church relating to different groups and sub-cultures in different ways. We have moved from church buildings in the centre of towns, often the church spire or tower being the highest point on the sky-line, to church buildings dwarfed and hidden amongst towering office blocks and shopping malls, to churches meeting in cinemas and schools.

Churches in almost every place are coming under increasing criticism for their performance, programmes and policy statements. We need to acknowledge that God may have something very important to say to the church through its strongest critics. In a marginal position, perhaps now is the time for the people of God to ask themselves some difficult questions:

• Where is God at work in the world and in people's daily lives?
• How can we best become involved in God's mission in the world?
• How do we share the Good News of Christ, who makes sense of life and brings peace to troubled hearts, with people who are not part of any church congregation?
• Where can we meet people?
• What are the concerns and questions of our neighbours and friends who do not attend church events?
• What are the bridges, across which the Gospel can travel?
• How can we help people to find the real Jesus, rather than the Jesus of TV caricature, or childhood memory?
• What sort of church will we build?

We live today in a society that is dominated by human achievements, by material well-being and by insatiable demands for pleasure and satis-faction. There are many rivals to Christianity—not so much in the other world religions, but rather in the materialism, scientism, individualism, and New Age pluralism of our world. It is into this society that we have been called to be Christ's missionary people. So many people are search-ing for meaning, satisfaction and achievement—but often in the wrong places. The search is part of the restlessness of life, which Augustine, some 1600 years ago, saw as God-given, declaring that 'we are restless until we find our rest in God.'

Passive participation is another feature of our culture, developing through our ever-growing attention to television. People are failing to engage with the real world, and there is the constant danger of being numbed in our response.[20] Another danger is that the media can shape our views and opinions of the world. Modern art and the media presents despair, fragmentation, hopelessness and violence. It is here that the world needs an expression of hope through despair and of the possibility of reconciliation for broken relationships. Such a hope is portrayed in the cross and resurrection of Jesus. The problem is that the church is also full of passive participants, which is demonstrated in our failure to engage the world. This raises questions about our presentation of the Gospel, our style, language, and format. In chapter 3 we will consider the way in which Jesus addressed people. He did not preach very often, and certainly not to those outside his own close group. He used direct prophetic words, statements of truth, miracles accompanied by explanation, and parables— stories related to the actual life and happenings of the community, on the issues of the day. We need to articulate the Gospel from the Gospel, instead of dwelling exclusively on Paul's theology which was directed at churches who were, in large measure, getting it wrong.

There has also been a change in the realm of education. Children no longer sit behind rows of desks learning by rote or by taking notes. Learning is experience based, varied, deductive, moving from one activity to another. Young people discuss, debate, question, investigate, and use all the equipment of a technological and computerized age.[21] This style of learning, as I suggested in the previous chapter, might usefully be employed in the mission and ministry of the whole church. There are a significant number of issues here that have an impact on the presentation of the Gospel in our current social context. But alongside this we need to examine the spirituality and belief of people.

Our spiritual context

A recent report describes unbelief in a way that may be as prevalent amongst church attenders as amongst those who never darken the doors of a church: 'unbelief is not so much the conscious rejection of faith as it is the continuance of a belief which is increasingly unconnected with a living religious tradition'.[22] The sort of 'unbelief' described here is characterized by a number of features. Faith is felt to be an alien, although comforting, culture: it holds onto the past as being superior to the present (showing a delight in poetic-sounding words even when the meaning is not understood, and in rigid forms of music which are considered as 'classical'), it has little contact with the reality of daily living, and—defined as 'church-going'—is a chosen leisure activity. Such a view of faith is opposed to change and probably has little future. This is a picture of a society in which, in practice, people doubt whether there is anything that is transcendent to material reality. It is a society in which people have a sense of being lost, feeling that they are not valued and their opinions do not count for anything. The world seems to be an empty place and marked by moral and ethical confusion.

Maybe the changes in the activities of society in general on Sundays will force us to reconsider what the people outside of the church most want from living and what is their experience of life. Alan Coren, speaking in a radio debate on 9th December, 1993, observed that shopping is now one of the most popular leisure activities: even 57% of men like shopping. More than 60% of the population would like to be able to shop on a Sunday. The sound of the cash register has taken over from church bells. 'There are now bells at Brent Cross[23] to call people to Sunday shopping' noted Coren wryly. We will, rightly, want to emphasize the need for a day of rest and refreshment, designed by God for all humanity, but if we truly believe that the Gospel is Good News, then we will have to encounter people where they are and not where we would ideally like them to be. Time to listen again to the late John A.T. Robinson, then Bishop of Woolwich, writing in April 1963 in the *Daily Mirror* about his book *Honest to God*:

> What drove me to write my book was that what matters to most people in life seems to have nothing to do with 'God'; and God has no connection with what really concerns them day by day.

At best he seems to come in only at the edges of life. He is out there somewhere as a sort of longstop—at death, or to turn to in tragedy (either to pray to or to blame).

The traditional imagery of God simply succeeds, I believe, in making him remote for millions today.

What I want to do is not to deny God in any sense, but to put him back in the middle of life—where Jesus showed us he belongs.

For the Christian God is not remote. He is involved; he is implicated. If Jesus Christ means anything, he means that God belongs in this world. . . . Let's start from what actually is most real to people in everyday life—and find God there.[24]

Perhaps John Robinson was ahead of his time, or perhaps the church was simply unable to hear. Whatever the reason, I believe that his words still speak to us today. Where is Christ?—in the world; but the church is not. Time for a radical rethink, perhaps? The church is called to be in the world but not of the world. The trouble is that we seem to be of the world (in our materialism, self-centredness and even our intellectualism) but not in the world (through our living out of the gospel in Christ-like concern).

We are the 'gathered church', meeting in worship on Sundays and in our mid-week fellowship groups, in order to be strengthened to be the 'scattered church' during the rest of the week. It is as the church scattered that we are involved in the mission of Christ. The role of the minister and church leaders is to equip the body in the mission of Christ (Ephesians 4:12). We readily use the language of 'the Body of Christ' and 'the Priesthood of all believers' when we worship together, and when we celebrate the Lord's Supper. But at the Supper we share one loaf, the one body of Christ, in order to take the broken pieces of the one loaf into ourselves and to go out into our various spheres of living to be Christ in and for the world. All the believers have shared in Christ's death and resurrection to be the one priest—to be Christ to our neighbours, community and world.

Grace Davie has explored the way in which religion has been practiced in the UK since 1945 and has produced an interesting classification of the expression of belief in our contemporary British society:

the inner city	belief depressed
the suburb	belief articulated
the city centre	civic belief
the countryside	belief assumed[25]

She sees these labels as generalizations that give the overall flavour of belief in different areas and strata of society. Belief still persists in the inner city, but there is a lack of evidence of religion making a difference to life, and because there is a general distrust of all institutions it means that there is no desire to practice this belief. The middle class suburbs find the greatest expression of belief and of disbelief—always ready to talk about religion, but not necessarily ready to commit to practice. In rural areas religion is still seen as part of a way of life, though in many places this is fast disappearing. City centre churches are still used to express national grief, anxiety or thanksgiving and celebration, or for funerals of 'the great and the good': examples are the annual Remembrance Service, the filling of Liverpool Cathedral (the largest in Europe) for the funeral of Anthony Walker, on 25th August, 2005, the remembrance service after the murder of 16 schoolchildren and their teacher at Dunblane in March 1996, and the servide held at Glasgow Cathedral after the first Gulf War on 5th May, 1992.

It would be wrong to conclude that these events hold no spiritual meaning for people. I believe that it is still important to ask, for example, what lessons should have been learned from the death of Diana, Princess of Wales, on Sunday 31st August, 1997. Her death shocked the world. I was in Kentucky, USA, where even the local news broadcasts carried the funeral live and the local newspaper carried a special edition. As Cardinal Basil Hume put it, her death made many people 'pause and reflect, to ask questions about life and death, their meaning and purpose.' Why did millions give flowers, write in books of condolence, and cry in public? What prompted over one million people to come to London to 'be there' for the funeral, and 60% of the population of the UK (over seven years of age) to watch it on TV? What brought traffic on the M1 to a voluntary standstill and closed shops and supermarkets on the busiest day of their week? One young Christian leader described it as the most important spiritual event of the past 25 years.

But, one might ask, what was spiritual about this? We notice that personal grief was expressed in religious ways, for example, with flowers and candles. Corporate mourning was expressed in a time-honoured religious way as across the nation half-muffled church bells were tolled. There was personal cost involved as people made journeys to London or gave tokens of their grief. Religious language was used, such as 'shrines' and 'pilgrimage'. Finally, millions participated in specifically religious services of remembrance. All this raises questions for the Christian church:

- Was a nominal Christianity awakened, and if so to what effect?
- There were public expressions of adulation and grief, but what does it mean for worship and for a worshipping people?
- Diana identified with the ordinary and the marginalized. How do we help people to see that serving God is a step beyond humanitarian concern?
- Are there modern parables to be told through Diana's life?

The people of God are a pilgrim church, a church for others, and a sign and a sacrament for the world. An event like the death of Diana, Princess of Wales provides the church with a challenge to meet human need. This not only applies to this event, but is repeated on a small scale in almost every local tragedy.

The European Values Systems Study in 1990 gives us figures worth reflecting on. In the UK overall there is a 71% belief in God, rising to 95% in Northern Ireland; but there is only a 13% weekly attendance at church (Northern Ireland 49%) while 57% have never been to church at all (Northern Ireland 19%). In England and Wales over 80% of the population will never go to church, except for weddings and funerals — mostly funerals these days. A lot of people are ready to talk about spiritual things (27% in a survey we carried out in Rushden, Northamptonshire, in 1991), but the churches are not always ready for them. To address the questions and issues being raised by such people will be demanding of church members' time.

Hard factual information has been provided by the English Churches Census, a snapshot of church life, taken on October 15th, 1989. This revealed a picture of a church that declined steadily over the period from 1975 to 1989. The total number of adults attending church dropped from 4,093,000 in 1975 to 3,706,900 in 1989. The 1975 churchgoers were divided as: Roman Catholics 38%; Anglicans 32%; Free Church 30%. By 1989 these figures had changed to Roman Catholics 35%; Free Church 34% and Anglicans 31%; and by 2000 the projected distribution was: Free Church 38%; Roman Catholics 32%; Anglicans 30%. Within the Free Church the fastest growing churches are the Independents (including the House Churches), the Pentecostals and the Black-led churches. At the same time there is a marked decline in the Methodist and URC churches. The figures reflect the growth of the more charismatic evangelical churches, both among the established denominations as well as the new churches. But overall, current figures show that decline in church attendance has continued in England, falling from the 13% in 1990, quoted above, to 7.8% in 2000. At this point we should be asking whether or not these statistics reflect society's move toward both materialism and individualism, or whether there is a deeper reason, which involves the nature of the church and the expression of spirituality. This question becomes more urgent when we find that there is a growing awareness amongst all people of 'spiritual experiences.'

When the church is regularly accused of being irrelevant to most people's lives, we need to demonstrate in our own lives the enriching and transforming impact of Jesus Christ in the busy and complex, hopeful and desperate, stress-laden and material world of everyday routine. The dualism between church and world, belief and life, that is a feature of so much Christianity leaves the church out of touch with our neighbours. There is a need for the church to engage the world and through apologetics, provide a demonstration that the Gospel is reasonable to accept for people living at the beginning of the twenty-first century. Once more we need to think about being 'outside-in'.

A resource page of world beliefs produced in the BMS World Mission magazine[26] showed that Christians made up some 33% of the world's population in 2000. However there were projections of significant changes in the distribution of Christians, worldwide, over the next 20 years. In 2005 approximately 37% of Christians lived in western countries and 62% in Africa, Asia, and Latin America, but by 2025 it is estimated that 70% will be living in these southern continents and only 30% in North America and Europe, including Russia. These changes have already been reflected in the presence of missionaries from the southern continents coming to Europe and North America.

The late David Bosch in his seminal work *Transforming Mission* helpfully argues for a new mission paradigm in a postmodern world.[27] Over the 2000 years of church History the missionary idea has been profoundly influenced by the cultural context. Today we live in tension between the Enlightenment and postmodern paradigms. The narrow Enlightenment perception of rationality has been found to be an inadequate cornerstone for life. Third World Christianity is growing with an interest in 'narrative theology'—symbol, ritual, sign—and we must recognize that true rationality involves experience. The church must recover its role as the Body of Christ building community.

Bosch is correct to argue for a new missionary paradigm; a move from 'church-centred mission to a mission-centred church.' We must re-emphasize the mission of the church, which entails going into all the world, as against a programme of seeking to attract outsiders into the church. Such journeying involves crossing cultural as well as geographical frontiers if we are to engage with people outside the church. This is not simply a matter of using data projectors, videos and the Internet within church services and meetings in an attempt to mimic or reflect the world. We need to focus on finding new ways of expressing the Gospel which are culturally relevant. This will come through listening and observing our friends and neighbours in every aspect of their and our own lives, and helping them to address questions about meaning and purpose, promise and fulfilment.

For most people belief belongs to their private world and is not often expressed in the daily routine of living. Grace Davie sub-titles her book, *Religion in Britain since 1945*, 'Believing without Belonging', recognizing the belief that exists outside the church, and also the unbelief expressed by some church attenders. For many there are common misunderstandings that being a Christian is a matter of being good and doing good deeds; that religion is essentially a private affair, which is between the individual and God; and that experience is more valuable than belief. The result is that the church seems to be a world apart, having little use or relevance in a modern fast-moving, technological world. We may well fear for such a church, which remains conservative and does not engage with society, where the insiders are comfortable because nothing changes, and where there is an emphasis on the buildings and the clergy.

In addressing this situation it is helpful to consider the variety of alternative models of church that are springing up, as described by Cathy Kirkpatrick, Mark Pierson and Mike Riddell in their book, *The Prodigal Project*.[28] They present a picture of post-modern society and a post-modern churchgoer that readers of Dave Tomlinson's *Post Evangelical*[29] will find depressingly familiar. They ask, 'Could the confusion and discomfort and yearning that are rumbling in the hearts of so many actually be the stirring of God? Could the straining towards new ways of being church together be the call of the Spirit?'[30]

Alternative models of being church often include a variety of features such as: joining with a group of like-minded friends; enjoying food and beverages (usually wine) as part of their gathering together; telling stories, and a willingness to be vulnerable and honest with each other; constant reflection on what has been experienced in life and work, and its expression in worship; and often prayer, laughter and tears. Such alternative models will provide the institutional church with challenges, pointers and inspiration in its desire to be relevant in the twenty-first century.

I have enjoyed attending such fellowships of believers, but the fact that the atmosphere is conducive for the expression of the faith of those who attend does not mean that it will be attractive to those outside of the present faith communities. Moving churches into cafés or cinemas, and replacing pews with small tables and chairs may make outsiders feel more insecure, as the experience they are being given is disturbingly different from what they expected to find in a church service. We can sometimes change the appearance of the church and its services, but still find that visitors, and even invited guests, feel like outsiders. We may simply have changed the form, but left the way of being church unchanged. Many people, both outside and inside the church, are often unimpressed by verbal presentations of the Gospel. They look for relevance and reality, and for people who are living the Gospel in an authentic and holistic way, involving their relationships and the whole of their lives.

We must recognize that general social rules often apply to churches as well; for example, smaller congregations tend to be friendlier and have a greater cohesion and commitment. Such churches are places where social interaction is more likely to take place—it is easier and is more difficult to avoid. We should also recognize that religious similarity is an important criterion of attraction. Social groups are usually constituted of those who share a common social identity and regard themselves as belonging to the same social category. In the church growth movement this is exemplified through what has been called the homogeneous unit principle. Laurence Brown expresses an important psychological insight that:

> Language, religion and ethnicity (often aligned with religion) are robust personal identifiers and explicitly support the social cohesion that flows from sharing experiences, perspectives, and such things as dress or diet, and from explicit signs of having been initiated into membership, e.g. circumcision .... Since a religious identity is an important component of the self concept, many who are religiously inactive retain a religious identity that they switch on in appropriate situations, while the clergy and other church officials are expected to maintain that identity consistently.[31]

However, increasingly we find that those who are marginal to religion, or who have no contact, are often unsure of the norms that they should observe, as can often be observed at such events as church weddings. Another challenge for church leaders is that the un-churched also expect church services, music, language, and architecture to remain unchanged. Those who have not been to a church service in the last 30 years (which includes almost all young adults) will have gained their understanding from national church services or soap opera presentations of church shown on the television. Attending services, especially in many Afro-Caribbean, Baptist, evangelical or new churches, will make such people feel like 'fish out of water.'

We need worship leaders who will provide a space in which people can encounter God and where God can encounter the people. We need fellowship times where people can find acceptance and build relationships, and where people will care and pray with them in their doubts, failures and struggles with temptation. We need preachers and teachers who will address the questions and issues that are common amongst their congregation and community. All of this takes time as leaders build up an atmosphere of trust; such alternative worship will not solve the church's problems overnight.

A vital part of any new model of being church will be the relevance of those things done in worship and fellowship to the congregation's daily life and work. A common problem that we face is the persistence of a Platonic dualism in church and congregation thinking that separates faith and reason, spiritual and material. The result is that work and life beyond the church, including sexuality and family, are devalued. We need to emphasize the Hebrew worldview, which unites the spiritual and created realms. Placing emphasis on personal—that is individual—salvation when the church gathers for worship is an error. We need to hear Paul's challenge to worship expressed through the whole of life (Romans 12:1-2; Ephesians 2:8-10), and with him we need to hear the cry of all creation (Romans 8:18-22), recognizing the God who is immanent in the created universe. We might take Genesis 1-11 as our foundational text, where the created spheres for human beings include marriage, family, power, politics, work and the whole of the natural world. As Christians we affirm that it is through Christ that all creation is brought into being, and that Christ, who is in all, restores all things (Colossians 1:15-20). The 'all things' that Christ, and his body the church, reconciles include marriage, family and work.

In the UK the traditional denominational churches are largely in decline, some dramatic and some even terminal. There is a need to recognize the issues noted above and to explore fresh and radical approaches to mission. Congregations need to be equipped and resourced so as to be able to give an intelligent and realistic account of the faith they profess. The future of the church is dependent upon a message centred on the Cross, which takes the Bible seriously; and which lives out the truth of the Gospel in community, empowered by the Spirit. The church must be culturally engaged, with a willingness for change, which demonstrates an openness to the world and to the Holy Spirit.

In the past it was Christians who were at the forefront of social action, with the provision of healthcare and education, and with social reform in areas such as slavery, working conditions and employment. But in recent times we will often find that it is those with a humanitarian concern or a Marxist philosophy who lead the way in commitment to the needs of the developing nations, or to the care and protection of the global environment. For the church to become relevant in our society we need to regain the cutting edge of those who speak prophetically in the name of Christ, and who dare to think and act radically.

Church and world

The present day is seeing great changes in the ways that people perceive the world; these changes in thinking are frequently referred to as post-modernism. Modernity has seen the development of the nation state, the industrialized society, urbanization, and the rationalization and secular-ization of society. But confidence in the Enlightenment, with its rejection of religious authority in favour of scientific reason, has steadily waned since 1945. For example, the environmental debate has not only shown up science's failure to solve ills, but has shown that it actually creates them.

There have now been three global summits addressing the concerns of the environment: atmospheric, and oceanic pollution; destruction of the bio-environment; exhaustion of non-renewable resources, especially energy; and the unfair distribution of technology and wealth.[32]

In September 2002 the third Earth Summit was held in Johannesburg, entitled *World Summit on Sustainable Development*. Environmentalist Jonathon Porritt commented about the first summit, 'I went to the Earth Summit in Rio de Janeiro with low expectations, and all of them were met!'[33] Porritt comments that in the ten years since Rio, only the UK can claim to have taken any steps in addressing the environmental and fair trade issues, and the UK has done only a little. The heart of the problem was summed up by George Bush Senior's comment in the light of the Rio declaration: 'The American way of life is not negotiable.' Unfortunately, you could put almost any nation in place of America, and discover the major problem at the heart of world environmental and justice issues.

The emphasis should not be on the security of the way of life for richer nations, but on the fact that a fifth of the world's population still lives on less than 67 pence a day per person. A change of heart is needed. But the view of Andrew Hewett of Oxfam International on the approach of world leaders to the earth summits was that 'most of them lacked the guts and will to achieve a brave and far-reaching agreement that might have effectively tackled the problems of poverty and the decaying environment.'[34] A similar comment might be levelled, with some justice, at the various G8 summits that have taken place since, even those which have addressed issues of international debt, aid and trade. As human beings, we are created with an ability to influence events in the natural world, with a freedom and power given to us by God. The question that remains is our response. We have the ability, but do we have the will? We are brought face to face with God who, in his self-limiting love, gives freedom of choice to his creation, but we are accountable for the choices we make.

We live in what is frequently described as a 'postmodern' world. In such a world there is an increasing distrust of organizational structures, whether in government, industry, or law. Instrumental reason is being challenged, something reflected in a cultural openness, an emphasis on information, and a growth in consumerism. While the church can exploit the cultural openness of the present times together with the cultural rebound caused by modernity's failure to deliver utopia, postmodernity is nevertheless a threat to the church because of its rejection of absolute truth and its tendency toward individualism and materialism. I believe that John Seel[35] was right when he warned the church that uncritical acceptance of the good gifts of modernity has left us blind to the dangers: the material rewards and technological benefits of our modern culture claim to replace our need of God. He notes that there are similar dangers for the church in taking up some of the aspects of the postmodernity that pervades our society and which is represented the world of Disney, McDonalds and MTV. In such a society everything is for sale. The principles of the fast food restaurant are becoming the dominant criteria—technique, presentation, efficiency and programme. Images and pictures that entertain are replacing words. The church thus needs to take a critical look at itself and ask whether organizations and activities such as church growth, Willow Creek, tele-evangelists, and marketing of Christian music, books and events, are simply a copy of the world's methods and values. The church needs to hold to one of the European Reformation maxims, *ecclesia semper reformanda*, 'reformed but always in need of reforming', and so involve itself in the task of reformation and renewal of the whole of life, rather than becoming another isolated consumer centre in a fragmented society.

Near Cerne Abbas in Dorset, my family and I came upon an Anglo-Saxon church built in the centre of an ancient British earth ring. On closer examination it became clear that the altar in the church was placed over the centre of the ancient circle. Now I have no idea what the beliefs of those who built this earthen ring were, or what rituals were practised there, but I do know that those who built the church were shouting loud and clear, 'Jesus is Lord!' They were also saying that his sacrificial death, celebrated in bread and wine, was superior to any pagan sacrifice offered in that place. This was good news of liberation and life in Christ that freed the previous generations of the people of Cerne Abbas from ancient superstitions, and gods who had to be appeased through sacrifice.

We rightly declare the lordship of Christ; that there is life and contentment to be found in him. There is Good News to declare. But what does it mean to say 'Jesus is Lord' and why should that be good news, light and hope for the communities where we live? We can find one clear answer in Luke's account of the Gospel. Luke begins his account with the promise that he has carefully investigated the sources and interviewed the witnesses in writing his story (1:1-4). In chapter 9, verse 20, Peter declares that Jesus is 'God's Messiah.' In the preceding chapter Luke brings together four events in the ministry of Jesus that he himself thinks paint a picture of who Jesus is, so presenting an important message for the first Christian disciples and a message for the church. We read that Jesus calms a storm (8:22-25), exorcises a demon (8:25-39), heals a woman of her menstrual haemorrhage (8:40-48), and raises a child from death to life (8:59-56). We see that in these stories Jesus is revealed as Lord of the physical world, Lord of the spirit world, Lord of the world of disease, and Lord of the world of the dead. He is Lord of all.[36]

We watch our television screens, we read the newspapers, we reflect on our own lives and those of our families, friends and neighbours, and we immediately realize that for most people life is not a bed of roses. The true picture of your life and my life is a mixed one: doubts and certainty, joys and suffering, successes and failures, pleasures and pain. This is true of the Christian life: following Jesus does not lead to a cosy cotton-wool protected existence. Much of the Gospel narrative concerns the ministry of Jesus out on the road. He walks from Galilee to Jerusalem, through the desert and the villages, with the ordinary people and their leaders, accepting the praise of the crowds together with their rejection and disbelief, experiencing hospitality, laughter and the cruel pain of crucifixion. In his three years of ministry he calls twelve disciples who will share his life, and who will learn about God's mission 'on the job'. Jesus takes his disciples into places where they are forced to face the reality of life, and the reality of Jesus' mission to the world. As Luke points out in his summary chapter, they encounter the violence of nature, the frightening experience of demon-possession, the constant concern of ill-health, and the universal fear of dying. They are frightened, annoyed, amazed, perplexed, over-joyed. Then the disciples are sent out on Christ's mission in the world. As we join their story we have to ask: how will we face the reality of the world in which *we* live?

It seems that Luke's account is full of 'happy-ever-after stories' — in the presence of Jesus and his miracle-working ministry, tribulation is overcome. But who overcomes? It is not the disciples, but Jesus. The closest the disciples get to having any part at all is to cry out for help, which only leads Jesus to question their faith. The disciples are observers of these miracles. It is Jesus who overcomes, and it is to Jesus that the church and we must look. Even when we have set up all our personal safeguards, support structures and church counselling practices to address life's problems, ultimately we rely on Jesus. He is Lord of nature, the demonic, sickness and death.

The disciples had an important lesson to learn They were going to face the reality of life in the world—with all its ups and downs, its praise and persecution, its frightening experiences and their own failures. This would happen immediately as Jesus sent them out, as Luke records in 9:1-6, and it would happen later on, when Jesus was betrayed, arrested, tried, and executed. Through Jesus' presence with them, they would be able to overcome, and live through each and every situation. We, too, live in the real world, with all the experiences, good and bad, that all people face.

In the real world, even many people who regularly attend church find that services are irrelevant and therefore boring. Men are less tolerant of what seems a meaningless church service. Young people are being brought up to analyse what is going on around them and so if it is incomprehensible or illogical they will have no time for it. The clergy are criticized as being unreal and distant, and the church is seen as full of yesterday's religious artefacts.

People do not leave their emotions and feelings at home or at the church door. Boredom in the church comes from a lack of awareness of people's actual needs, a lack of spiritual vitality, and a lack of creative imagination. According to Leslie Francis,[37] a survey of church-going 16-20 year olds revealed that they had had little opportunity to discuss the issues that were important to them in a church setting. The interests that were high on their agendas were: relationships, sex, marriage, racism, law and order, Third World, work, the environment, and pop music. Issues that also concerned them but which were regarded as of lesser importance were: the occult; AIDS, cults, TV, politics, prayer and (last) the Bible. This survey confirmed that relationships and family life are felt to be vitally important to people today. In the light of this, it is significant that a survey carried out in 1997 revealed that in the previous 3 months 56% had been stressed; 48% had consumed enough alcohol to be drunk; 38% had been lonely; 36% had intentionally hurt someone emotionally; and 9% had attempted suicide.[38]

Michael Fanstone[39] surveyed 500 people who had returned to church, and asked why they had left the church in the first place. In answer to the question, 'Why did you leave the church?' 62% identified issues of relevance: they felt that the world of work and the world of faith had been held worlds apart. 44% named personal issues: there was a lack of care, support or help offered by the church. 27% raised issues of leadership—'I didn't like/get on with the minister'—and only 7% issues concerning God—'God wasn't there when I needed him.' Other investigations[40] have suggested that alternative ways of thinking and believing, and the relevance of the faith proclaimed in the church to the life experience of the congregation, are major factors in decisions to leave. If Christian ministry concentrates on doctrines of God and church, we may well find that we are scratching where very few folk are itching! These surveys are a timely reminder of the need for an emerging missionary church that is just as concerned with what happens to those who are already in the church as it needs to be with strategies for bringing people into the life of the church.

The central claim of secularism is that the Christian faith is not credible as an explanation of the world in which we live. The church is perceived as a private club with its own private set of beliefs, which the rest of the world finds unacceptable. The church has tended to collude in this by the way in which it conducts itself and portrays its message. Those who are under 35 years of age are more likely to be concerned about the way the church does or does not address the concerns of their cultural context than with church structures and pastoral practice. We need to think much more carefully about how we can evolve new forms of being the church, which will address much more directly the themes of relevance and direction.

After a number of years of running 'Agnostics Anonymous' at Spring Harvest (the annual Christian family conference, jointly organized by the Evangelical Alliance and Youth for Christ) I realize that before people ask about becoming a Christian there is a wide chasm called 'questions' that has to be bridged. Some of the questions are: why should I believe in anything at all? It doesn't matter what you believe as long as you're sincere! What about suffering and war? Hasn't science done away with the need for God? The bridge over this chasm is relevance. This was clearly demonstrated by a survey carried out by Altrincham Baptist Church in the mid-1990s. When they asked 500 people in their town why they did not attend church, they didn't get the answers they expected: 78% of those questioned replied, 'Why are you asking the question?' or words to that effect.[41]

The world is changing rapidly and we need to keep in touch with the issues that deeply affect people. In the highly successful Alpha Course, developed by Nicky Gumbel,[42] the author has focussed on a number of issues that he has discovered are important to people seeking faith. These are: suffering, other religions, sex before marriage, New Age spiritualities, homosexuality, the relation between science and Christianity, and the idea of the Trinity. An ITN survey conducted at the end of the twentieth century revealed the top issues on people's agenda as being: the environment, poverty, unemployment, parenthood, crime, and war. We should probably add terrorism to the list in the first decade of the twenty-first century. These are all issues that the media are constantly dealing with, and so heightening the community's awareness of them. But how often does our preaching or Sunday worship address these issues? When did you last hear or give a sermon on one of these issues? The Bible has a great deal to say—but do we allow the people to get out of God's word what God has put into it?

The Apostle Paul was 'all things to all people', although the Gospel was fixed (1 Corinthians 9:22). He adapted his approach and method of communication to suit the culture and background of his hearers. Similarly, in a pivotal chapter recounting the development of the early church, Acts 10, Luke records how Peter's Jewish sensitivities and traditions were turned upside-down in the cause of the Gospel. Christian disciples have two needs that should be met through church membership: first, support for their living of the Christian faith, and second, opportunities to contribute to the church's understanding and expression of the Gospel in today's world. If we focus on church buildings and organizations we may simply confirm to those outside that we lack mobility and flexibility, and that we are more concerned with ritual than with relationships.

The tragedy is that for the majority of people, the church provides no adequate support to work out the implications of the Gospel in their particular context. To respond to this challenge we must address some of the hindrances that the very nature of the church presents, such as: being rooted in church buildings rather than in the communities where the church members actually live, work and socialize; running programmes that have their focus restricted to the congregation, rather than responding to needs in society; and having a leadership confined to pulpits and church programmes, interested more in increasing numbers than with growing people and building community.

The church and its leadership can become insular because they feel intimidated by a secular and pluralist society. Leaders often feel that they do not have the knowledge and experience to operate on the frontiers of faith in an unchurched mission environment, and are therefore unable to equip their congregations to operate outside the church context. Church members are endeavouring to live out their faith and bear witness in a world, which operates on a very different value system, and so there needs to be a training in the necessary apologetic and evangelistic skills. Unchurched people hold all sorts of views, which are often mutually incompatible, without any contradiction being recognized or any consideration of consequence. To be relevant the church needs to be in dialogue with the world, observing and listening before seeking to make comment or to respond.

There needs to be a paradigm shift with the church organized *outside-in*, where the gathering of the congregation will be to celebrate what God is doing through them in the world, and to respond with Gospel answers to the questions that their life in the world is raising. The church therefore needs to provide support systems to facilitate witness in society—to be an incarnate community of witness. The contextualization of biblical and theological insights will take place is an area where 'lay people' are the experts. We can start with small groups of people committed to mission, where we can seek to develop contextualized approaches to witness in various spheres of influence, identifying these people in terms of their knowledge and experience. Worship will seek to reflect and celebrate what is happening at the cutting edge, in the worlds of work, leisure and family life. As the gathered church in our groups and our worship services we equip and enable the congregation in their life as the scattered church.

Exercise 2.3

a. What are the questions about life or belief that are important to the people you work or live with?

b. If you had to select the three most important features of the lives of people in your community, what would they be?

c. How could the church address these?

Training in understanding our world

The beginning of a new century sees a western church in severe decline and with little influence on society or culture. However, in parts of Africa, South America and Asia we find a rapidly growing and vibrant church. We recognize that Christianity is a world faith and that we have much to learn from other continents. We need a strategy to reach the unchurched, which recognizes that church members are the ones who have contact with the outside world. The church must break out of its own alien culture and equip its members to live their daily lives in the world. The church is itself a sub-culture in society and so we recognize that mission to the unchurched will be cross-cultural, even when people inside and outside the church belong to the same social grouping. At the same time we will want to find ways of helping people in their Christian discipleship which do not entirely remove them from their own culture into a church culture. Therefore, we become involved in exploring new ways of living out the Christian faith that makes sense of, and answers, the questions posed by the world in which we live.

Such an approach for our ministry and mission requires church leaders who can encourage, empower and draw on the experience of congregation members. Such an approach will be the mark of church education and small group programmes. The emphasis for training leaders will take account of this and focus on such aspects as: spiritual development, giving confidence and security to people in their faith; and the practical aspects of ministry and mission, producing those capable of vitalizing the local church in relevant mission. In the training of church leaders there is a need to combine good biblical and theological foundation with cultural awareness, theological reflection, pastoral effectiveness, and relevant communication. It is a matter of enabling the church to be Christ in and for the world, engaging with all aspects and groupings within society.[43]

We look for leaders who are able to lead the community of the faithful in mission, and who will understand the church as community rather than as institution. These leaders will envisage the church as being a sign and sacrament of the Gospel, and a demonstration of Christ-like servant-love. They will enable all God's people in the task of doing theology, living out their faith in Christ, wherever they live and work. This will involve a shift of power that some may find painful, whereby pastoral ministry will involve helping believers understand and interpret the biblical text in ways which resonate with their daily experience, helping believers bring their successes and failures, ambiguities and insights into the life, worship, and support of the gathered community.

We must develop creative programmes that will help all God's people to discover the value of their own experience and learn to relate their faith and life. Many Christians experience a dichotomy between the 'Sunday world' of faith, which tends to be black and white, and the 'Monday world' of their experience of life and work, which tends to be various shades of grey. We can learn from the experience and approaches to theo-logical education and discipleship that we find in many of the churches of the developing world. Here we are challenged by their understanding that the realities of life precede theology. From this position they bring their experience as questions to the Bible, and develop their theology out of such reflection, with action following.

If we take seriously the view that our Christian discipleship includes all our experiences, we will place acting out faith and being Christ's fol-lowers at the centre of learning. Many of our church activities will need to be examined in the light of this perspective. The challenge is to link the always-relevant Jesus event of twenty centuries ago to the future of the promised reign of God, for the sake of meaningful activity in the present. The mission of God is what constitutes the church. It constantly needs renewing. The church is love incarnate, in community, and for the world.

Notes

[1] http://news.bbc.co.uk/1/hi/england/merseyside/4740095.stm; accessed 03.08.05

[2] http://news/bbc.co.uk/1/hi/england/merseyside/4736955.stm; accessed 03.08.05

[3] For an exploration of the ways in which children and adults develop in their perception of the world, see: Erik Erikson, *Childhood and Society* (New York: Norton, 1963); *Identity, Youth and Crisis* (New York: Norton, 1968); Lawrence Kohlberg, 'Stage and Sequence: The Cognitive Developmental Approach to Socialisation' in David A. Goslin (ed.), *Handbook of Socialisation Theory and Research* (Chicago: Rand McNally, 1969); Jean Piaget, *Six Psychological Studies* (New York: Random House, Vintage Books, 1967); Jean Piaget, *The Child and Reality* (New York: Penguin Books, 1976); James Fowler, *Stages of Faith* (San Francisco: Harper, 1981; 1995).

[4] Weaver, *Earthshaping Earthkeeping, A Doctrine of Creation* (London: Lynx/SPCK, 1999).

[5] Anne Hope and Sally Timmel, *Training for Transformation—A Handbook for Community Workers* (Harare: Mambo Press, 1984), Book 2, p.3.

[6] See John Daines, Carolyn Daines & Brian Graham, *Adult Learning, Adult Teaching* (Nottingham: University of Nottingham, Continuing Education Press,

1993, 1996); Hope and Timmel, *Training for Transformation,* Book 1; Jane Vella, *Learning to Listen, Learning to Teach: The Power of Dialogue in Educating Adults* (San Francisco: Jossey-Bass, 1994); Frances Ward, *Lifelong Learning: Theological Education and Supervision* (London: SCM, 2005).

[7] See footnote 3 above.

[8] See the works quoted in footnote 3.

[9] Jack Dominion, *Make or Break* (London: SPCK, 1984) pp. 48-50. Here Dominion recognizes three phases of marriage, and within each of those phases he considers the social, intellectual, spiritual, sexual, and emotional dimensions in which couples relate to each other. He identifies the *First Phase* as the first five years. This is the crucial phase when relationships become established or not. 30-40% of breakdowns take place during this period. He recognizes important areas as: self-worth, belonging, expectations and experiences. Added to this are separation from parents, having to be an 'adult,' children, housing, money, work, leisure, and sexual intimacy. 12-18% of couples admit to difficulties in this part of their relationship. His *Second Phase*, age 30-50 years, spans the period of children growing up and leaving home, and onset of the menopause for women. Spouses find their own authentic life during this period, as the fears and doubts of youth are shed and they discover what they want from life. This leads to problems when the spouse does not fit with these 'grown-up' expectations, which leads to what is called 'mid-life crisis.' Strains on the relationship result from one partner's ambition or success, or from disruptive factors such as alcohol abuse, illness, or unemployment. Functional problems in sexual relationship become more common, as do affairs. His *Third Phase*, 50 years to death of partner, sees the departure of children, which may lead to further breakdown. The positive aspects can be: grandchildren, leisure, financial security, and a rise in sexual activity with freedom from the anxiety of procreation. The downside may include: unemployment, thwarted ambition, ill health, depression, or increased impotence with the resulting stress through the loss of being able to share affection in a sexually intimate way.

[10] Dean Brackley, 'The Christian University and Liberation: the Challenge of the UCA', *Discovery* 2 (Jesuit International Ministries, 1992), pp.13-14; and my own conversations with Dean Brackley at University of Central America, San Salvador in April 1995.

[11] Denham Grierson, *Transforming a People of God* (Melbourne: The Joint Board of Christian Education, 1984).

12 Martin Robinson, *The Faith of the Unbeliever* (Crowborough: Monarch, 1994).

13 Quoted by Mark Greene, 'Imagine. How we can reach the UK', *Idea*, (Evangelical Alliance), March/April 2003, p.12.

14 For an account of the history of the project see: Adele Blakeborough, 'Responding to Drug Users', in Eric Blakeborough (ed.), *Church for the City* (London: Darton, Longman and Todd, 1995), pp. 75-90; for further information contact: Kaleidoscope Project 40-46 Cromwell Road Kingston Upon Thames Surrey, KT2 6RN.

15 See Elizabeth Kubler-Ross, *On Death and Dying* (London: Tavistock, 1970 / Routledge, 1992).

16 For a detailed exploration of church leavers and the leaving process see the works of Alan Jamieson, *A Churchless Faith. Faith Journeys beyond the Churches* (London: SPCK, 2002) and Philip Richter & Leslie Francis, *Gone but not forgotten. Church leaving and returning* (London: DLT, 1998)

17 Cf. Jamieson, *A Churchless Faith*, pp.145-51.

18 Dan Brown, *The Da Vinci Code* (London: Corgi Books, 2003). Film by Sony Films, May 2006, starring Tom Hanks, Audrey Tautou and Ian McKellen In March 2005 Cardinal Tarcisio Bertone, Archbishop of Genoa, spoke out against the controversial book. Its story about the Church suppressing the 'truth' that Jesus had a child with Mary Magdalene has convinced many fans. The Cardinal told an Italian newspaper: 'It astonishes and worries me that so many people believe these lies.' The book's central claim is that the Holy Grail is really the bloodline descended from Jesus and Mary Magdalene—which the Church is supposed to have covered up, along with the female role in Christianity. Cardinal Bertone hosted a seminar called *Storia Senza Storia* (Story Without History) to rebut the claims. The BBC news website (http://news.bbc.co.uk/1/hi/entertainment/arts/4350625.stm; accessed 26.08.05) noted that as well as the original novel by Brown, another ten books have been written to debunk its claims and a booming tourist industry has sprung up around its sites.

19 In 1996 the Walt Disney Company faced a threatened boycott from the Southern Baptist Convention and its more than 15 million adherents in the USA over its company policies with regard to gay and lesbian employees. The company issued a statement saying, 'We find it curious that a group that claims to espouse family values would vote to boycott the world's largest producer of

wholesome family entertainment.' Angry at the company's provision of health insurance to the domestic partners of gay employees, as well as the use of Disney theme parks for 'gay days,' the Southern Baptist Convention told its members 'to give serious and prayerful reconsideration to their purchase and support of Disney products and to boycott the Disney theme parks and stores if they continue this anti-Christian and anti-family trend.' In response, Disney said, 'We question any group that demands that we deprive people of health benefits and we know of no tourist destination in the world that denies admission to people as the Baptists are insisting we do.' This advised boycott was not withdrawn until 2004.

[20] See the discussion of the influence of television in Tom Davies, *The Man of Lawlessness* (London: Hodder & Stoughton, 1989).

[21] It should be noted, however, that at the beginning of the twenty-first century there appears to be a move, on the part of the British Ministry of Education, back to 'teacher-centred' or 'teacher-led' education, and away from experiential education, in Primary Schools.

[22] 'Belief and Church Attendance', *Quadrant* (Christian Research Association), July 1997.

[23] Brent Cross is a large, purpose-built, out-of-town shopping centre (mall), situated away from central London, adjacent to the North Circular Ring Road.

[24] Quoted in John Bowden, *Honest to God 30 Years On* (London: SCM, 1993), pp. 57-8.

[25] Grace Davie, *Religion in Britain since 1945* (Oxford: Blackwell, 1994), pp. 105-6.

[26] *Worldmission* (BMS World Mission), July/August 2005, p. 26. Sources quoted include: Missionfrontiers.org; and *International Bulletin of Missionary Research*, Centre for the Study of Global Christianity.

[27] David Bosch, *Transforming Mission—Paradigm Shifts in Theology of Mission* (New York: Orbis, 1991).

[28] Cathy Kirkpatrick, Mark Pierson, Mike Riddell, *The Prodigal Project* (London: SPCK, 2000). This book includes a CD-ROM with additional information and various alternative church websites. See also: James Thwaites, *The Church Beyond the Congregation: The Strategic Role of the Church in the Postmodern Era* (Carlisle: Paternoster, 1999); Eddie Gibbs & Ian Coffey, *Church Next—Quantum Changes in Christian Ministry* (Leicester: Inter-Varsity Press, 2001).

[29] Dave Tomlinson, *Post Evangelical* (SPCK/Triangle, 1995), where one of the central themes is the dissatisfaction felt by many evangelical Christians with the forms of service and nature of preaching in their churches.

[30] Kirkpatrick, Pierson, Riddell, *The Prodigal Project*, p. 37.

[31] Laurence Brown, *The Psychology of Religion: An Introduction* (London: SPCK, 1988) p. 69.

[32] I have sought to address these issues elsewhere: see Weaver, *Earthshaping, Earthkeeping,* chapters 8 and 9.

[33] Reported by Anthony Browne in *The Times* (London) Newspaper 31 August, 2002. see also Andrew Hewett's Oxfam Press release, 3 September, 2002.

[34] See footnote 33.

[35] John Seel, 'Modernity and Evangelicals: American Evangelicalism as a Global Case Study', in P. Sampson, V. Samuel & C. Sugden (eds), *Faith and Modernity* (Oxford: Regnum Lynx, 1994), pp. 287-314.

[36] Here I have developed some of the thoughts expressed by Michael Wilcock, *The Message of Luke.* Bible Speaks Today (Leicester: IVP, 1979), pp. 99ff.

[37] Leslie J. Francis, *Teenagers and the Church: a Profile of Church-going Youth in the 1980s* (London: Collins, 1984).

[38] 'Right from Wrong', *Quadrant*, Autumn 1997.

[39] Michael Fanstone, *The Sheep that Got Away—Why Do People Leave the Church?* (Tunbridge Wells: MARC, 1993).

[40] See Jamieson, *A Churchless Faith*; Gordon Lynch, *After Religion: 'Generation X' and the Search for Meaning* (London: DLT, 2002); Richter & Francis, *Gone but not forgotten.*

[41] Information provided by Revd Roger Sutton, Altrincham Baptist Church.

[42] Nicky Gumbel, *Searching Issues* (Eastbourne: Kingsway, 1994); also see by the same author: *Questions of Life*; *A Life Worth Living*; *Telling Others: the Alpha Initiative* (Eastbourne: Kingsway, 1993-1995) and many further publications. For more information on Alpha, contact the Alpha Office, Holy Trinity, Brompton, London, SW7 1JA.

[43] See Peter Brierly, *Act on the Facts –Information to Steer By* (London: MARC Europe, 1992) pp. 190-1, and Ian Bunting, *The Places to Train* (London: MARC 1990) pp. 54-5.

3
Analysis: Foundations Explored

Following his brutal, racially motivated murder, Anthony Walker's mother said: 'I am sorry for the people that have done it, and if you know anyone then come forward, they don't deserve to walk the streets.' At the scene of Anthony's death, the mother of murdered black teenager Stephen Lawrence said she hoped his family would have justice. 'I'm only hoping that this time justice will be done and seen to be done, because Stephen's killers are still walking free and I'm hoping that Anthony's killers will be brought to justice. I think he deserved that; his family deserve that.'

The entrance to McGoldrick Park, where Anthony was killed, was transformed into a sea of flowers with messages from well-wishers. One message left on a bouquet seemed to capture the mood better than the rest. It read: 'I just hope people see Huyton through the example Anthony set rather than the murderous scum.' On the estate where Anthony grew up neighbours spoke highly of a friendly young man and their feelings were expressed by Joyce Turner, who said: 'We have lost a good citizen of Huyton—many of us feel ashamed that this is happening where we live.'[1]

In 2000 there was another violent death that shocked the British people. Victoria Climbié was tortured and murdered after being sent to Britain from the Ivory Coast in the hope of a better life. Victoria died as the result of the neglect and the vicious beatings meted out by her great aunt, Marie Therese Kouao, and her boyfriend Carl Manning. But she was also failed by social workers and others who could have stepped in to protect her. Victoria died of hypothermia in February 2000. She had 128 injuries. In an interview Victoria's mother Berthe Climbié opened her heart over the murder that shocked Britain—the brutal torture and death of her eight year-old daughter.[2] Berthe Climbié revealed that despite her pain and suffering, she forgave Carl Manning, who was sentenced to life behind bars for the murder. But Berthe said the lack of remorse shown by Marie Therese Kouao meant she could not be forgiven.

In discussing the work of the Truth and Reconciliation Commission in South Africa, John de Gruchy states that we must never deny the reality of what people have experienced. He goes on to ask: are we speaking about reconciliation in order to forget the past, or in order to deal justly with its legacy? Dare we proclaim such a message if in doing so we reinforce structures of injustice and undermine the will to resist and transform? How dare we speak of reconciliation in a world in which there is little justice for the victims of oppression, an immodest haste to forget atrocities and forgive perpetrators of their crimes?[3]

A military chaplian described a discussion that developed during his work. 'During a recent presentation of the Just War theory to a group of soldiers, one of them asked, 'How can justice have value in a country full of hatred like Northern Ireland?' The soldier went on to question the idea of forgiveness within the Province and the contribution the church can make to the process.[4] We recall, as we think of his reaction, that Northern Ireland has witnessed over 3,600 people killed in the last 35 years, mostly civilians, and 1,800 of them are unsolved murders.[5]

What is true of divisions between people groups, or in extreme circumstances of individual violent deaths, also points us to the dynamics of relationships within families and within the church. What can we say about forgiveness and reconciliation there, closer home to us? As part of a first year course in Practical Theology at Cardiff, I spent two hours exploring some of these issues and feelings with a group of eleven Anglican, Baptist and Methodist ministerial students. The following are some of the thoughts that developed from our discussions.

We took as our starting point Paul Fiddes' exploration of the Christian idea of Atonement in his book *Past Event and Present Salvation*. Jesus' death for the world is expressed in terms of forgiveness. While some people illustrate the meaning of the cross with the image of God's 'royal pardon' for a condemned prisoner, we realize that a pardon does not necessarily change the prisoner's attitude to the judge, the victim, or to the offence committed. Fiddes states that forgiveness must be more than mere pardon; it is a shattering experience for the one who forgives as well as for the one who is forgiven:

> This is because forgiveness, unlike a mere pardon, seeks to win the offender back into relationship. . . . Reconciliation is a costly process because there are resistances to it in the attitude of the person who has

offended; the one who sets out to forgive must aim to remove those blockages and restore the relationship. Forgiveness then involves an acceptance which is costly.[6]

Thinking about this, we recognized that forgiveness in seeking to create a response would always be a time-consuming, expensive effort, involving difficult and painful emotions and attitudes of the will. While the refusal of a royal pardon by a prisoner would make little sense, a human lack of response to the grace of God in Christ is not so surprising when we realize that we are talking of forgiveness. It is hard to accept forgiveness, as this requires a personal response, which necessitates repentance. In exploring repentance we recognized that this also included emotional and volitional energy and pain. We were struck by the image that Fiddes offers, of forgiveness as a painful and costly journey of experience, on which both forgiver and offender have to embark. We produced a provisional diagram with two equal and opposite journeys, one of forgiveness and one of repentance, both of which declared the same message, namely, that what had occurred was wrong.

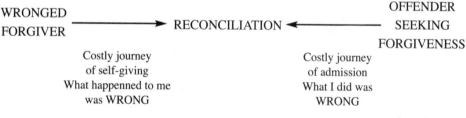

WRONGED FORGIVER ———————▶ RECONCILIATION ◀——————— OFFENDER SEEKING FORGIVENESS

Costly journey of self-giving What happenned to me was WRONG

Costly journey of admission What I did was WRONG

figure 3.1

Fiddes, in his careful exploration of forgiveness and reconciliation helpfully draws out the implications for us:

We notice that in any act of forgiveness there is a change that takes place in both the participants, in the forgiver as much as in the one who is forgiven. For true reconciliation there must be a movement from both sides. Naturally the offender has to move in sorrow and repentance towards the person he has hurt, but the forgiver also needs to move and experience change within himself, even when he is totally willing to forgive.[7]

This change, explains Fiddes, is a journeying empathetically into the experience of the offender, seeking to understand at the deepest level why he or she said or did what they did; this is a sharing of experience that is bound to affect the one who engages in it. But only this will move the offender to repentance. Forgiveness is thus an act that enables people to be fulfilled, an empowering of life in its God-given fullness (John 10:10). This is God's act in Christ, taking the painful journey into the depths of human alienation. From this position we began to explore the model of forgiveness, repentance and reconciliation exemplified in God's act of grace through the cross of Jesus, and our response.

Paul Taylor and Michael Barton were sentenced to lengthy jail sentences on 1st December, 2005 after being convicted of Anthony Walker's murder. But for the Walkers, anger gives way to sorrow as they consider his killers—two boys who attended the same school as Anthony and his siblings. While they will never forget, his mother Gee and sister Dominique said they had certainly forgiven.

> 'Why live a life sentence? Hate killed my son, so why should I be a victim too?' said Mrs Walker.
>   'Unforgiveness makes you a victim and why should I be a victim? Anthony spent his life forgiving. His life stood for peace, love and forgiveness and I brought them up that way. I have to practice what I preach. I don't feel any bitterness towards them really, truly, all I feel is . . . I feel sad for the family.'[8]

Lack of forgiveness will affect the quality of living. What the Chinese proverb says about revenge is also true of forgiveness: 'Whoever plans revenge should dig two graves'.[9] But how can we begin to explore such situations of human evil and misery, where justice is not always seen to be done, and the innocent continue to suffer the pain and heartache of the crime? How can we accompany those involved on the journey of forgiveness? Here I have begun this chapter with the example of one situation that needs to be analysed and explored—that of forgiveness—but we shall be thinking about a range of circumstances as the chapter progresses.

In the second phase of the pastoral cycle, learners must bring careful analysis to their experiences. What social and psychological factors can be discerned at play in the situations that have been described in stage 1? What complexities need to be explored here? What theological insights can be brought to bear on them, and in particular where does a study of the Bible impinge upon them? Only when we have explored the foundations of a situation like this can we draw the provisional conclusions that will take us on to a further stage.

The Bible as story which engages with our lives

The Bible has been described as a story with two characters: the reader (you or me) and God. The narrative parts of the Bible are stories of God's dealing with people and of their experience and understanding of him. Narrative has a narrator, characters, plot, and resolution or revelation. Stories and narrative have an important place in the patriarchal sagas and in the Deuteronomic History. There are also parables in the Old Testament, for example Nathan's story of the poor man's sheep, as a challenge to David's adultery with Bathsheba (2 Samuel 12:1-10). There is a power in parables; whether told or acted, they communicate God's message to God's people. Jeremiah observes an acted parable at the potter's house (Jeremiah 18), and Ezekiel acts out a parable with his demonstration of siege and exile (Ezekiel 4, 5 and 12). But perhaps we feel that it is with Jesus, his words, his actions and his life that we find the clearest portrayal, not only of God's message, but also of the very nature of God. Jesus is the storyteller par excellence, offering the profound timeless truths contained in the parables and other proverbial sayings.

Jesus' method of teaching was like his healing (for example: Mark 10:51—'What do you want me to do for you?', or John 5:6—'Do you want to get well?'); there was no imposition of his will on others. A good example of Jesus' approach is found in his resurrection appearance to the two disciples on the road to Emmaus (Luke 24:13-35). First of all Jesus gets alongside and listens. He then asks them to tell their own story, which they do including all their dashed hopes. Then Jesus begins to explore their story in the light of the scriptures and the promises concerning the Messiah. Finally he sits down to a meal with them, where they recognize him and respond by returning to Jerusalem to share what they have learnt with the rest of the disciples.

When speaking of forgiveness, Jesus not only calls us to forgive (Matthew 6:14-15; c.f. 18:21-35), but demonstrates his forgiving love in the midst of his death (Luke 23:34). Jesus also presents us with the offer of the forgiveness of God and a pattern for us to recognize and take to heart.

When one of my former students asked me to preach at her ordination and induction, I followed my usual practice and invited her to suggest a text. Jean's email reply read as follows:

> 'Dear John, my favourite passage of the Bible is John 8:1-11 (about the woman caught in adultery) but that probably isn't appropriate on this occasion and some might well read more into it than is actually there! Seriously though, I love that passage simply because of the way Jesus acts—it probably has influenced the way I think about ministry more than any other passage. It certainly gives us all hope.'

I took Jean's request seriously. I gave a great deal of thought to this passage and came to the conclusion that it is a most appropriate passage for an ordination and induction, as indeed for any service. This passage gets right to the heart of the Gospel and right to the heart of the church's mission and ministry to a world which struggles with fear, failure and guilt. Here Jesus faces the judgmental attitude of self-righteous people. It is so easy to recognize failure or sin in others, so easy to feel strong about those things that do not tempt us. Many people fear being found out and fear losing the material things that they have accumulated and which are so important to them. Tabloid journalists excel at exposing people, accusing people, and being moralistic and self-righteous, even when they have no grounds for being critical of others.

This event takes place after Jesus had attended the Festival of Tabernacles, which was the most popular of all the Jewish festivals. It took place over a period of eight days, celebrated the harvest with thanksgiving, and looked forward to the new year with hope. Central to the festival was the image of life-giving water, which Jesus identifies with the

Holy Spirit whom believers will receive after the crucifixion and resurrection (7:38-39), and following all this they bring the woman caught in adultery to Jesus.

After the Jewish leaders have pronounced the sentence of death by stoning, Jesus is silent and writes in the dust. Again the sentence is read out and the penalty of the law defined. Jesus stands up. His words are significant, 'If anyone is without sin.' He is not suggesting that only the morally perfect can pass judgement, but rather that we need some honesty in the way we pass judgement. In passing judgement we judge ourselves (Matthew 7:1-5). The impact of Jesus' challenge is overwhelming—they all drift away—and I like this touch, 'the eldest first'. Amongst the oldest would have been the Sanhedrin members, the very ones who had the duty to throw the first stone. But the older we get the more personal experience we have of struggling with conscience, temptation and failure. Jesus, once more, writes in the dust. They all slip away and Jesus is left alone with the woman. Her accusers have left and Jesus will not accuse her. Instead he offers acceptance, forgiveness, and a call for a new beginning.

The religious folk made their judgement concerning one law and its penalty, but Jesus presents us with God's perspective, which encompasses the whole of life—our total relationship with God. Jesus' words are not 'Let those who have not committed adultery, cast the first stone,' but rather *let those without sin*. No one was without sin—that was why the Day of Atonement came around with predictable regularity every year. They always stood at a distance from God, aware of their sin. But now in Jesus the relationship is restored. 'I do not condemn you, go and sin no more.' In this sentence is the heart of the Gospel, with our liberation and hope. We tirelessly declare the reality of God's forgiving love. While in this story there is a self-confessed sinner, we recognize that today most people will *not* feel guilty about what the church calls sin; they are far more concerned and fearful of being found out. However, here is also someone who has been found out, and Jesus offers her acceptance and a new beginning.

Jesus summons the woman to a new obedience—she is freed to follow the Jesus way. Forgiveness is not conditional on repentance, but repentance is the natural outcome of Christ's offer. This restoration of our relationship with God is not easy; there is no cheap grace. The path of forgiveness is costly, it is all the way to the cross, and it shouts out to us that our lives in rebellion against God are wrong. The very act of forgiveness thus awakens our awareness of what we have done.[10] The path of repentance is also costly as we admit to all that is wrong in our lives, and we understand that the cross is the place where God restores our relationship with him, and gives us the opportunity of living life to the full. This is life as God planned and designed it to be; this is resurrection life in the power and presence of the Spirit—fulfilled, a satisfied, a contented life.

In this kind of way we can take our experiences of life and relate them to the biblical stories because each is a human experience. We are dealing with the same human condition, and with the same creator God who cares about the human condition, and who in Jesus was incarnate in that humanity. We should, therefore, not find it surprising that Jesus' stories are our stories. Indeed the story of Jesus' birth, life, ministry, and death is an all too human story and it is in the Resurrection that the human story finds hope. It is this hope that makes doing theology worthwhile: the difference that Christian theology has to offer is that it is the God of hope who shares our lives, and who is the ultimate end of our human story.

The church re-enacts the central motifs of the New Covenant, through its participation in the death and resurrection of Jesus, celebrated in the Lord's Supper. Some churches also re-enact the Christmas, Palm Sunday and Good Friday events. We enter into the story at this point, in the same way as Jewish communities reaffirm their identity by retelling the Passover story from Exodus. In the Old Testament we find that the Passover becomes real in its re-enactment. People participate in the story as they re-tell it; they become the covenant people who receive God's promise, law, and land. Through the reigns of David and Solomon the celebration of the Passover story was neglected, being replaced by the focus on the temple in Jerusalem. But when Josiah rediscovered the Torah (the written account of God's laws for human life), he also rediscovered and celebrated the Passover (2 Kings 22 & 23). The Lord's Supper, instituted by Christ is a similar celebration: living out the death and resurrection of Christ is important as we celebrate being the New Covenant people of God. Andrew Walker helpfully observes that

the early Christian liturgies were a retelling of the divine drama of salvation, centred upon a re-presentation of the main events of the life of
Christ, the apostles, and the patriarchs and prophets of old. This drama
was housed in the appropriate 'theatre', which was reflected in the very
architecture of the church building . . . being in church, with its food,
smells, lights, body language, Bible stories and homilies, was rooted in
the material world with its linear time and structure. And yet the liturgy,
with its many component rites and customs, was seen in itself to be a
living symbol of God's Kingdom.[11]

We need to rediscover the nature of the church as a pilgrim people
who tell, listen to, and live the ongoing story along their way in life.
Indeed, the recovery of 'narrative theology' has helped us to explore the
journey of faith. David Gunn and Danna Fewell rightly note that narrative
interpretation does something different from historical criticism: 'we read
these narratives as we might read modern novels or short stories, con-
structing a story world in which questions of human values and belief
(and theology) find shape in relation to our own (and our readers')
world(s).'[12] The power of stories is that they speak about events and situations that we recognize and to which we are able to relate. We use our
experiences as real people to relate to the characters in the story. Hence
the concern that audiences have with the marriages or deaths of characters
in television soap operas—they become real people and floods of sympathy or congratulation cards pour into the television studios from the
audiences. The text, as narrative, comes alive when we engage with it.
The text is always more than a mere vehicle of a message.

Many people have asked about the place of the sermon or the word-
based presentations of much of our church services in today's
communicative environment, where TV, film and increasingly computers
appear to dominate.[13] Jolyon Mitchell suggests that preachers can learn
from radio, which is exclusively a medium of the spoken word.[14] By making pictures through telling stories, the speaker engages all the
imaginative senses of the audience. His underlying theme emerges as a
principle of 'embodiment and translation', which is at the heart of
Christianity.

We are a culture that 'veggies out' or 'chills out' after a day of stress, which appeals to the television or video/DVD: 'Entertain me.' With the rise of a hedonistic entertainment culture, we have become soaked in image and narrative. We are familiar with stories, pictures and icons, while the sermon has tended to concentrate on precepts and concepts. Preaching needs to adapt to an environment where many listeners are becoming used to interactive and audio-visually based means of communication. The preacher seeks to locate God in everyday stories and the language of the marketplace, drawing on pictorial language, and recognizing that 'signals of transcendence', as Peter Berger calls them,[15] are to be found in everyday life. The observant reader will recognize a pattern set in the Gospel by Jesus.

There is no need for the preacher to fear a multi-media society, for while television and film make images for us to watch, the spoken word enables us to make our own. This is why radio plays are often more frightening than television dramas—our imagination can produce more terrifying pictures than any director. Sermons must be rich in narrative and image, creating pictures in the listener's mind.

In preaching we will also be wise to use the language of the street, be natural, be ourselves, and demonstrate personal integrity. Our style will be relational and conversational, person to person and inclusive, using the form 'we' and not 'you.' The trouble is that the pulpit tends to strangle the natural pastor Jeckyll, who knows all about life, and changes us into the saintly Reverend Dr Hyde, who is ponderous, academic and strangely judgemental.[16] To overcome this we should ask questions and paint word pictures, and in doing so allow our audience to be free to make their own decisions and come to their own conclusions. Psychological research has some useful insights here, identifying four subjects which are of immediate interest to most people: *security*—for my job, my family, and my work; *achievement*—since nobody wants to fail; *inquisitiveness*—new ideas and creativity are attractive; future destiny and *decision*—motivating hearers to do or become something new.

Holding interest will require a great deal of preparation. We learn from the description of a good novel as a 'page turner.' One author placed the following words at the top of her typewriter: *Will the reader turn the page?* Therefore we can use incomplete narrative, for while stories remain unfinished the interest remains acute. The bottom line is the fact that the medium is the message. In the first few minutes the audience will ask: Do I like this speaker? Does this speaker like me? Is this speaker being honest with me and with himself or herself? How am I and the speaker alike?

Stories from everyday life will disclose the things of God, as the stories of Jesus in the Gospel demonstrate. Modern church leaders stand in the tradition of a Galilean storyteller, who translated his message into accessible pictorial language and parables. Storytelling is important, for without images and senses we are left with a colourless form of Christianity. We recognize God's communication through the incarnation, and his communication with our senses through the visible signs of bread and wine, which are felt and tasted so that the story of the past comes alive in the present.

Story, in fact, is a basic means by which we can understand our circumstances and experiences, more effective often than abstract analysis. Our response to stories is never neutral. Stories are told for effect. The Bible readings produced in the Central American base communities crucially use the stories to open up an understanding of the contemporary social situation of the readers.[17] Every real parable can be recognized both as a story in its own right, but also with a further meaning, which can be applied to or engages with the listener in their situation. It is certainly possible for the hearer to follow and appreciate the former meaning without at first having the slightest inkling of the application. We see this with the parable of the ewe lamb in 2 Samuel 12:1-14, which is deliberately intended to arouse the conscience of David and to convict him of his sin, but David thinks at first that it merely concerns one of his subjects. The effectiveness of the parable is in the response it produces — in this case David's moral indignation. The impact is realized when David is told that the story is about him.[18]

Such a story today might be applied to the dispossession of the land of the peasant farmers of North East Brazil by large agricultural combines, as illustrated in the stories of women struggling to remain on the land, recorded by Frances O'Gorman.[19] In our own country we might consider the impact of the supermarket chains on small retail outlets and on farm producers, or the undercutting by international airlines which has forced some smaller airlines into liquidation.

We are all shaped in our reading of the biblical narratives by our own worldview. Western thought, since the Enlightenment, has pursued truth as definable, locatable and agreeable. Western ideology has set an agenda that carries with it the cultural values of gender, race and class—predominantly male, white, and professional. This causes Gunn & Fewell to ask some important questions:

> What if we find ourselves identifying with the Canaanites who must forfeit their land to the Israelites? (The story recorded in the Book of Joshua). This is certainly where South American Indians, Aboriginals, and many Palestinians find themselves today. Or what if we find ourselves relating to the patriarch's wife, whose sexuality is pawned to strangers because of her husband's cowardice? (Genesis 12:10-20).[20]

The Bible is itself a product of culture, with particular notions of politics, nationalism, race, class, gender and ethnicity, which may well be different from our own. It ranges over at least 1,000 years, in which the people involved move from nomadic tribes to slaves, to settled farmers and city dweller, to exiles, and to a conquered nation with an army of occupation. There are a wide diversity of situations and cultural views. We also need to recognize the honesty with which the Bible reports situations and describes the main characters. It does not set us up with characters who are models for us: they are far too ambiguous, as we see for example with David, Saul, Moses and Abraham. We ourselves cannot be objective readers of the text. We view the biblical characters through the lenses of our own cultural, gender, and social values. Therefore it is important to discuss the stories with other people, especially those with a different cultural or ethnic background to our own, as this will help us to gain fresh insight.[21]

If we realize that the world of the Bible is a broken world (a fallen world), that its people are human and limited, and that its social system is flawed then we may recognize our brokenness, limitations and flawed society and become agents of change. We can learn to recognize our own world in the stories and attempt to relate to all the characters and not just the heroes. We can listen to more than one voice and particularly to those faint, niggling voices that whisper 'all is not right with the world.'[22]

We are rightly charged by critical biblical study to take the cultural milieu of the Bible seriously. As the cultural picture moves over time from nomadic tribe to an occupied state, particular views emerge about many issues—for example, about the spiritual world of the demonic. We also recognize the different genre of the literature with poetry and history, law and story, sermon and theology. Yet underlying all of these differences the scriptures are a record of human responses to the revelation of God recorded by the community of faith. Sometimes, then, we may sense the challenge of the Spirit through the text as it stands, without literary interpretation. The role of the readers in giving meaning to the text, rather than passively receiving it, is important here. So we interact with the text, reflect upon it, and respond to it in active discipleship.

The Bible: a book of the community of faith
We need to wary of seeking to establish one correct meaning of the text. When we attempt to do this we impoverish our understanding. For example the New Testament presents us with Matthew's understanding of Isaiah 7:14 (Matthew 1:23), and Paul's use of God's promise to Abraham (Genesis 12:1-3; 15:1-6) in his account of justification by faith (Romans 4; Galatians 3). But these texts in the Old Testament have their own meaning and importance. We must not make monochrome readings of scripture; the texts are far richer and demonstrate a repeated process of interpretation and re-interpretation. We start from finding accounts of Israel's history, and of the life, death and resurrection of Jesus, but then we move on to explore how the Jewish and Christian communities of faith understood these texts and the events in which God revealed himself. Stephen Barton helpfully observes that the Gospels are classic expressions of Christian spirituality, being shaped through and through by a sense of the presence of God in Christ. The Gospels are to be seen as faith documents from start to finish. Barton does not believe that a historical investigation of the Gospels takes us far enough. He says that 'In particular, it tends to pay insufficient heed to the fact that the gospels are documents of the canon of Christian scripture held as sacred within the communities of Christian faith which scripture sustains and nourishes.'[23]

A historical and literary approach to scripture is certainly highly illu-
minating, seeking to detect its historical context and to discern the variety
of forms in which it has been written, for a variety of purposes. For example, it seems that the books of Esther and Daniel, ostensibly set in the
Jewish exile, and probably drawing on actual experiences from this
period, are stories to encourage a second century Jewish audience facing
occupation and oppression by the Seleucid Ptolemaic heirs of Alexander
the Great's empire.[24] But the danger of this approach is that other possible
ways of listening to the texts are neglected, and interpretation is left in the
hands of the biblical scholars. We need to remember that these texts originated in the life and experience of people who were reflecting on their
experience of God as the covenant God who loved, protected, and walked
with them. It was out of this experience that they wrote of God as the creator of the universe, the beginning and end of all life.

The Gospel story, like the Old Testament stories, is reflected upon
within the community of faith today, as it has been throughout the history
of the church. Stephen Barton begins his study of the four canonical
Gospels by stating that 'because the gospels are written from faith for
faith, it seems legitimate to try to grasp what they are saying about life
under God or life lived in response to the sense of the presence of God—
specifically, the presence of God revealed in Jesus Christ through the
Spirit'.[25] We therefore need to find ways of closing the gap between the
reader and text so as to find insights for the life of faith. The ethical and
theological concerns of the community are lost when we concentrate on
an historical-critical examination of the text. Important as this is, the key
to our engagement with the text is the way in which it becomes part of our
lived experience of God, especially as we seek to allow our faith to
address our whole life and for our lives in the world to bring questions to
our Bible study and worship.

Asking questions of the text may be a useful approach: how would a
Jewish rabbi have understood this event or situation? What would a
teacher in the early church have made of this? For example we can look at
the first sign that John records in his account of the Gospel, where Jesus
turns water into wine (John 2:1-11). This is far more than a miracle, it is a
sign of who Jesus is and of what he will do. John records this event at a
private marriage feast in a Palestinian village, before Jesus' public min-

istry began, because, from the other side of the crucifixion and resurrection, he could see the far deeper significance.

But how would a rabbi, a Jewish biblical scholar of Jesus' day, have understood these events? He would have seen a great deal of significance in them. There was a wedding—a bridegroom and his bride—an event which speaks of the Old Testament picture of God in his desire for a faithful relationship with his people Israel, and which also recalls the darker picture of Israel in its disobedience as an adulterous bride (see, for example, Hosea 1-3). This was a wedding where the wine runs out, where the source of joy and festivity dries up. Israel's life with God had run out, and come to an end, through its lack of trust and obedience (see the Song of the Vineyard in Isaiah 5:1-7). At this wedding there were stone jars for the water of ritual purification—not to clean dusty and dirty feet, but for the ritual hand washing, symbolizing a constant need of cleansing from contact with a sinful life in a sinful world. These jars were empty and would need refilling—a reminder that they always had to wash, for they were never clean. It was a constant reminder that no one was worthy before God: they had to stand far off, constantly offering sacrifices for their sin.

Now enter Jesus. How would these events be seen by a Bible scholar in the early church, after the death, resurrection and ascension of Jesus? Jesus the bridegroom comes to meet with his bride, the church, and looks for a response. He cares and loves all whom he meets. He will change water into wine. He will take their empty watery life without God, or far apart from God, and transform it with the richness of his life and presence. The water of ritual cleansing is transformed into wine—the substance of joy. It is the seal of the New Covenant, or the new marriage relationship of God with his people, through the wine of forgiveness, the blood of Calvary (Matthew 26:28). Those who shared in the *agape* meal of the church of Christ would see the significance here. And no one reading this story in the light of the resurrection would miss the significance of John's opening line: *On the third day ... a wedding took place* (2:1).

In his book, Stephen Barton explores the spiritual implications of the differing emphases of each account of the Gospel. In Matthew he identifies the God who is with us, so that we are to be light in the world. In Mark he finds the forsakenness of the Cross, with our call to follow the way of the Cross. In Luke there are signs and wonders, leading us to repentance and to faith in the power of the Spirit. In John the emphasis is on the witness to glory, and our experience of being 'born from above'. Matthew is biblical and traditional in its shape and texture, which makes it a good starting place for the disciple, especially one who comes from a Jewish background. Mark on the other hand presents a dark, strenuous spirituality, a Gospel of the Passion, with little humour or joy. This is a Gospel for the martyr. Barton notes that Matthew ends with Jesus' eternal presence, whereas Mark ends with Jesus' absence. Luke-Acts is seen as an antidote to despair, but with its unabashed supernaturalism it has a tendency towards triumphalism. John's account is a place to reflect on our response to the gospel. As the fourth account it sums up and gives an authoritative interpretation to the message of other three, stressing that coming to know Jesus is the most vital thing in life. Each of the Gospel writers is addressing a particular Christian community, which has specific questions and needs.

All this raises, for me, the question of whether we can use the different accounts of the gospel to reflect upon and analyse different aspects of the Christian journey of faith. Does Mark, for example, offer an account for the stage in discipleship which follows the enthusiasm of the beginning? Is the Gospel according to John the account for the mature believer, who will reflect more deeply upon the faith? The gospel accounts mutually reinforce and correct each other, as do different periods in our experience of discipleship. They must become part of our growth as the community of faith, as we, in our turn, reflect on the words and stories of Jesus and make them our own. Central is the crucified Christ with the message of forgiveness, reconciliation and renewal. The gospels are fundamentally for the pastoral care of the church.

The teaching of Jesus and the human situation

To set Jesus' words and stories in the context of the development of his own life, we might take a brief survey of the opening chapters of the Gospel according to Luke. At twelve years of age Jesus is taken to the temple in Jerusalem for the first time; from then on we might suggest that he remains 'in his Father's house' (cf. John 5:19ff. and 14:1-3) doing 'his Father's will'. For the first seventeen years of his adult life (13-30), from his *bar mitzbah*, when he became a son of the law, he grows in spiritual as well as physical maturity, in wisdom and understanding of the law (Luke 2:42; 3:23). This is seventeen years of life among ordinary people, sharing the common life of the village community of Nazareth, perhaps occasionally journeying to a family celebration in another village, for example a wedding celebration at Cana (John 2:1-11), or the annual pilgrimage to Jerusalem for the Passover or other major Jewish religious festivals.

The picture is of village life: a small local synagogue, obedience to parents, and work in the local building and furniture trade as a carpenter alongside his father. This was not a significant place to grow up from a worldly point of view as Nathaniel was quick to point out to Philip: 'Can anything good come out of Nazareth?' (John 1:46) But from our point of view this upbringing was extremely important. This was self-emptying (Philippians 2:7); this was the place where Jesus learned about people and life in the raw; this is where Jesus entered into the people's stories; this was Jesus' own 'immersion experience' (see chapter 2 p. 50). Jesus is obedient and committed to God's self-emptying, incarnation among ordinary human beings, and at his baptism in the Jordan receives his Father's affirmation: 'This is my beloved son with whom I am well pleased' (Luke 3:22). This commitment to God's way is re-emphasized in the temptations when Jesus faces the alternative ways of economic, religious and political success.

Putting these temptations behind him Jesus lays down his radical manifesto, the declaration of the Year of Jubilee, prophesied by Isaiah (Luke 4:18-19 cf. Isaiah 61:1-3). In the call of the first disciples they are also summoned to put the whole of human life under obedience to God (Luke 5:1-11). When they land the fish, they leave boats, fishing business, and family behind, and follow Jesus. This is the setting into which Jesus tells his stories—stories about people and life, which open up windows into understanding about God and the way in which he acts in the world and in individual human lives. This is God's down-to-earth religion in Jesus.

The main source of Jesus' teaching are the words recorded in the four accounts of the Gospel. There were clearly a number of collections of Jesus' life and teaching in existence from an early date, certainly by the time Paul wrote to the church at Corinth (1 Corinthians 7:10; 9:14). But as Anderson helpfully suggests[26] rather than speaking of *ipsissima verba* (the actual words) of Jesus, we should recognize the 'sense' and 'voice' of

Jesus' teaching—*ipsissimus sensus* and *ipsissima vox*. It is likely that much of the accounts of Jesus' teaching and ministry were first heard as sermons, where it is probable that it was tailored to specific audiences. Jesus' teaching arose from personal encounters, challenges or questions, and from the varied occurrences of everyday life. He often used hyperbole and paradox, and we would do well to 'hear the twinkle in his eye.' Jesus used his own understanding and experience of farming, weather, village life, and the concerns of the people, together with knowledge and understanding of the Old Testament scriptures.

The material in the Gospel stories was selected because of its relevance to the life and problems of the church. We must always keep in mind that these accounts belong to the communities of faith in which they came to birth. But this should not lead us to think that their words cannot be understood and applied in the twenty-first century. The Egyptian grain harvests affected the Roman world in much the same way as Middle East oil affects our world today, and Jesus' teaching on divorce is as applicable within today's world as it was in the first century. The wars, rumours of wars, famines, volcanic eruptions, hurricanes, typhoons, earthquakes and tsunami are as common today as they were then (see Mark 13:7-8). The teaching of Jesus is only difficult and unacceptable because it runs counter to our individualism and hedonistic lifestyle, which the twenty-first century has in common with the first century.

Donald Kraybill underlines these thoughts when he says that Jesus' 'words and insights bring a note of judgement on our affluence, war-making, status-seeking, and religious exclusivism.'[27] The values of the world are turned on their head in the Kingdom of God. The life and teaching of Jesus shows us the shape and form of the Kingdom. We need to break free of the values, beliefs and norms of the society in which we live and ask why? for Jesus presents us with parables and sermons where, to use Kraybill's words, 'the good guys turn out to be bad guys.'

When we consider Jesus as a storyteller, there is no feature of Jesus' teaching more striking than the parables. They have provided inspiration for poets, artists, and writers, and they have entered into common usage, for example 'the return of a prodigal' or someone described as 'a good Samaritan.' The various groups of parables in the New Testament have been discussed at length by a variety of authors,[28] but it is sufficient to note here that through them Jesus reflected on actual situations of the life of the people he lived with, and presented a single message of challenge or correction. It is also important to hear the caveat offered by Christopher Rowland and Mark Corner,[29] that the parables are meant to be understood in terms of a particular social context, both in their writing and reading, and are not universal truths that have been handed down from on high. We have to recognize that we do not receive the parables in their original form or setting, as they were modified, expanded, allegorized in relation to the church's experience of living between the cross and final appearing (*parousia*) of Jesus.

They were presented in a form to be understood by the particular audience. For example, in the parable of the wedding banquet Mark 13:35 has the Roman division of four watches of the night, whereas Luke 12:38 has the Palestinian three. The church related parables to its own concrete situation; so, for example, the parable of the nocturnal burglar ends with a reference to the *parousia* they were expecting—'Be ready when the Son of Man comes' (Matthew 24:43f; Luke 12:39f). Jesus' parable refers to an actual burglary—a day of terror—whereas the *parousia* will be a day of great joy for the disciples of Jesus. But for both the situation of Jesus and the early church it could still offer a warning of eschatological catastrophe (c.f. Amos 5:18, Matthew 24:37-39, Luke 17:28-32). Jesus addressed this parable as a warning to the crowd about an impending crisis that might befall them, while in a church waiting for Christ's return, it becomes a word of challenge for its lifestyle. We must also recognize that Jesus himself may well have used the same story on different occasions and with differing applications. It is therefore important for us to seek to hear what the message was for the first hearers, before seeking to gain an understanding for our contemporary church.

Mark brings together a collection of stories about sowing and harvest, in which Jesus links the Kingdom with the Word of God which is like the seeds.[30] These are stories of encouragement, assurance and challenge, when we recognize Jesus' main point. How do we understand the parable of the sower? If we begin by asking, 'what are the different soils, and what or who do they represent?', then the parable appears to very negative. But Jesus was saying something positive.

The thrust of his message is that some seed always falls into good soil, where it will produce a rich harvest (Mark 4:1-20). How then are we to understand the parable of the sower? It is about the proclaiming of the Good News and the results of that proclamation—there will be rich results when God's word reaches receptive hearts. Here is encouragement: there will always be results. Despite repeated failure and rejection (in Jesus' own mission) Jesus urges joyful confidence, because God has made a beginning and will bring a harvest beyond asking or conceiving.

What is the impact of your church on your community? Does it seem somewhat small? Jesus says that the Kingdom of God is like the seed, after it is sown—there is an unceasing growth (even if we cannot see it) until the harvest time is reached (Mark 4:26-29). The earth produces because the seed and the soil were made for each other. People who are created in God's image are the perfect soil for God's word, and we can take confidence in this. In answer to doubts concerning his mission, Jesus assures his disciples that God's hour will come unimpeded: he has made a decisive beginning in the world. We can be assured that God is at work to bring about his harvest.

What is your view of the significance of the local church in your community? We often seem insignificant. There is a problem of wasted seed, of a long period of waiting, but also our own depression at being an overlooked minority. The seed we have seems so small and contemptible to the world with its science, technological developments and education. Standing up for Christian values today often meets with sarcasm or dismissive attitudes.Think of the people around Jesus—partly discouraged, partly antagonistic, partly excited and expectant. Someone could drift up to the edge of the crowd and listen sympathetically—it cost nothing, and if the going got tough, one could always leave. But the disciples had given up their jobs and committed their whole life to following Jesus. They'd staked everything on Jesus, and what would the outcome be? Not much, it seemed. True, a few folk had been healed, some amazed, but the religious and political leaders had taken little notice, and as far as the Greeks and Romans were concerned, it was no more than a storm in a Galilean tea-cup. Jesus had asserted that the Kingdom of God had arrived, but where was it? The results looked pretty meagre. The church today often feels like this, asking 'have we believed for nothing' 'Is it all really true?' The disciples must have had the same sense of discouragement. So Jesus takes a tiny seed, which in due course will produce a mighty plant, up to three metres high (Mark 4:30-34). Leave the seed in the packet and there will be no growth, but let it get to human lives and it will bring transformation. So the message is: be encouraged—God promises a harvest and is at work to bring it about.

Parables call us to a better life and challenge us to a deeper trust in God. They have a single purpose, which is to show what God is like and what we might become in Christ. We recognize that the life of Jesus, therefore, is perhaps the clearest parable that we have. This must move us on to consider our own response to the life and stories of Jesus. Where does our life fit into this picture and how are we living as Christ's disciples? Human experiences and human relationships are opened up, and the true motives of work, employment and religion laid bare. It should not surprise us to find that there are resonances in our own stories and our own experiences. But we face an ever-present temptation to avoid the message by thinking it to be culturally bound in rural Palestine, 2000 years ago; or by adopting a 'spiritual' meaning to Jesus' words which leaves out the practical ethics; or by allowing Jesus' teaching to affect our personal character and personal morality but not our social ethics.

Parables must be read not only in terms of the social and political situation of the text, but also that of the reader. For example, the parable of Dives and Lazarus (Luke 16:19-31) is a challenge to the rich. Dives is not said to be bad or ungenerous, he simply does not see the needs of the poor. This is a challenge not only to the West, where the rich get richer and the poor poorer, but also for the view that charitable giving by the rich answers the needs of the poor. Pious comments about its being our *attitude* to money that really matters, loses sight of the experience of being poor. The parables are stories deliberately earthed in the material circumstances of their time, and to understand them we allow them to address our lives rather than form the content of an abstract Bible study. After understanding the story in its first century context we ask where the story connects with our experience today.

We might also encourage people to become involved in the experiences of their community. John Reader suggests a four-fold structure for tackling community issues: listening to the local stories; drawing on contemporary analytical frameworks such as sociology and psychology; drawing on Christian sources; and then direct engagement with local issues and needs.[31] An important fact that emerged from such involvement was that a thoroughly secularized community is no longer familiar with Christian ideas and biblical stories. Their natural narratives may relate to explicitly local events, for example, the closure of factories or schools. However, such shared stories become even more problematic for those who have moved around the country or the world and have never been anywhere long enough to become part of a particular locality in this way. For them, their stories may be more personal, based on their family or on an individual's experience. The way in which theology needs to be done, therefore, will vary according to social circumstances. Here we may recognize the pattern that has already been set for us in the ministry of Jesus—taking the local stories and experiences and teaching Gospel truth through them.

Exercise 3.1

The story of the Good Samaritan:

a. Read the story in Luke 10:25-37.

b. Find contemporary stories in the newspapers of people who have done surprising things.

c. What do we learn from such stories, and how might we respond to the words of Jesus (Luke 10:37) in such contexts?

Learning lessons from the Third World

At El Cordero de Dios Baptist Church, San Salvador, at 9.30 on a Sunday morning the Bible study considers John 19:25-30—Jesus' mother at the foot of the Cross and Jesus' last cry: 'It is finished.' Present at this service, I find the perception of the people in linking this Bible story to their own lives to be challenging. Lucy speaks of the lives of the street people, especially the prostitutes who sit at her fruit and soft drinks stall in the park. They are abused by their clients and violated by their pimps. Naomi talks about the reality behind the new act to authorize the death penalty—more legalized oppression and violence. Tony draws on the story of a man carrying a float with the statue of Christ in an Easter procession, which is hit by a car. The concern of the people is for the statue rather than the man. What emerges from this sharing of these stories is a fresh understanding of God's suffering with the people.

Our primary concern will be to ensure that the biblical stories engage with our stories in a way that takes both the text and our reality seriously. In a 'liberation theology' approach, reflecting on the world of real life takes first place, with reference to the Bible and church traditions coming as the second stage. There is a prior political and ethical option for the poor, stemming from an understanding of the Gospel as essentially good news for the poor. This determines the social context, where a sociological analysis is used, based on an interweaving of action and reflection. The hermeneutical approach to scripture that is employed is not a concern for the extraction of abstract principles, but engagement with the specific situations of people. The questions that arise from these situations are put to the revelation of scripture, and the answers from those scriptures bring insight and illumination to the situation. The test of this approach is the effect it has in people's lives; there must always be pastoral action.

Such an approach has been the mark of base ecclesial communities of Latin America. These communities have arisen from grass roots; they are born out of a reading of scripture; they realize a new way of being church, in terms of community; they celebrate faith and life together; they are the context of theological reflection; and they exercise the gifts of ministry (*charismata*) which demonstrate the body of Christ. They have developed in rural areas and on the margins of the cities and are small groups of ordinary people, often the poorest, who share a close fellowship.[32] For example, the farm workers and labourers bring their experiences of helplessness and oppression, and their sense of the unjust gap between rich and poor, when they come together for Bible study. They discover their story in the Bible stories. The text is questioned from their situation; the meaning of the text is sought from someone trained in scripture, the meaning in the biblical situation is considered, and then their own situation is confronted by the biblical situation. Thus the Gospel is reflected upon.

Maria Isabel and Maria David, who have been involved in the establishment of base communities in El Salvador since 1972, describe them as
going through a number of stages: the flowering of community with signs
of the Kingdom; the persecution that resulted from the prophetic voice of
these communities in challenging the injustices of society's dealings with
the poor; and the present struggle against hierarchical conservatism
within the church, which wants to withdraw from grass roots expressions
of community.[33] The establishment of each community typically began
with visits over a period of about three months to people's homes as
expressions of friendship. Often people were sick, or they had bad family
relationships, and these visits demonstrated care and began the process of
building new relationships. Barriers were broken down and friendships
developed within the community. There was then a period of nine months
during which people were invited to a monthly study on concrete life
issues through the Bible. The first three themes were injustice, evil and
death. The emphasis was on participation, in which everyone's view was
valued. Isabel and David recall that:

> We wanted to learn to interpret the Word of God from our reality.
> Illuminated by our reality we became a new church in which we all par-
> ticipated—a new model, rather than listening to the priest as expert. We
> looked to cultivate the values of the Kingdom—awakening an interest
> for our neighbours meant love in solidarity, concern, and in living
> together.

After this first year they held a number of retreats designed for the
deepening of spirituality through three kinds of encounter: with other people, with oneself, and with Christ. Alongside these 'deepening' retreats
were two others—for 'initiation' and 'confirming'. This led to committed
community and, through witness, to the multiplication of communities.
Fasting during Lent enabled money to be saved, which was presented to
other communities as a gift. One community obtained a connected elec-
tricity supply through the giving of another; such was the sacrificial nature
of these groups. A young woman from one group was tortured and jailed
when she failed to reveal the names of other members of her church,
showing the commitment that had developed to these communities.

Perhaps, in response to the above example, we should ask whether the outposts of the early church (see the closing greetings of Paul's letters) were the same sorts of community as these base ecclesial communities. Can we learn something from the issues that were discussed? We catch a glimpse—for example—of discussions about eating meat that had been offered to idols and then sold off cheaply in the market, or about men sleeping with prostitutes, or about what sharing of belongings might mean. But, sadly, the early church quickly lost the concept of holding all things in common (compare Acts 2 with 1 Corinthians 11). Maybe we have to be poor to share together in the ways in which the first Christians did, and as many congregations in the Third World do now.

The popular reading of the Bible within local congregations composed of 'lay' members appears to be a most productive activity, as the reading and interpretation of scripture is owned by the group. They recognize that there is a source of authority, which can speak into their situations, and they find a prophetic voice in their world. The themes of everyday life, of work, land, health, family, sex, education, and festivity are constantly reflected upon in the context of their faith, and this often involves story telling, symbols and myths.

An example of this group reflection is outlined by Latin American theologian, Carlos Mesters.[34] He describes how a group of illiterate farmers, in Brazil, meet to discuss their life. They ask Mesters many questions, such as:

- What about these community activities we are engaged in? Are they just the priest's idea or do they come from the Word of God?
- What about our fight for land? What about our labour struggles and our attempts to learn something about politics? What does the Word of God say about all that?
- What about the Gospel message? Does it have to do just with prayer, or is it something more?
- The other day, in a place where there was a big fight going on between the landlord and his tenants, the priest came, said mass, and explained the Gospel in a way that made the landlord right. Then the local priest of the parish read the same Gospel and explained it in a way that made the tenant farmers right. So who was really right?

• The landlord gives catechism lessons that teach subservience and bondage. In our community we have catechesis of liberation, and the landlord persecutes us for it. So how do we settle the matter and figure it all out? We want to know whether the Bible is on our side or not.

Mesters outlines three elements in the common people's interpretation of the Bible: the Bible itself, the community, and reality—both of the people's situation and that of the surrounding world.

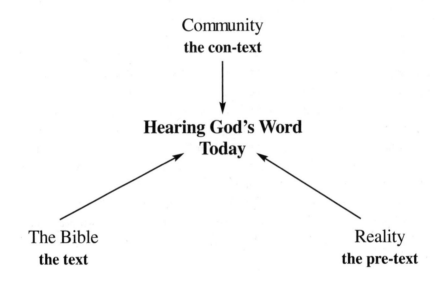

figure 3.2

Mesters maintains that when the community takes shape on the basis of the real-life problems of the people, then the discovery of the Bible is an enormous reinforcement. We can start with the Bible, or with the given community, or with the real-life situation of the people and their problems. While the Bible is the text and the community is the context, the reality of life is there ahead of any reading of the text (the 'pre-text'). The important thing is to attempt to include all three factors. God's Word is heard when people read the Bible together in the light of the everyday things that happen to them and to other people in the situations in which they live and work.

For such base communities the Gospel is gradually becoming a day-to-day reality in their life and thinking, liberating and transforming those who tend to be the voiceless. Such experiences should be a challenge for the development of all church communities, whether rich or poor, First or Third World. There is a vital connection between knowledge of God and discipleship, and through active obedience we experience the presence of God (see John 14:23). We have to question pronouncements of truth that fail to make the connection between ways of thinking and ways of doing (James 2:14-26). We have to recognize, however, that our hermeneutical stance is shaped by our own social and cultural position, and therefore also be aware that we run into danger when we seek to draw universal conclusions about the Bible from our position. We are forced to ask: what world does the interpreter inhabit? With Theo Witvliet we question whether the God of the Conquistadors was the same as the God found by the Indians; or when slave and owner sang 'Amazing grace' whether they were singing the same hymn; or during the years of apartheid in South Africa whether Vorster and Botha were praying to the same God as Tutu and Boesak.[35] We can at least conclude that their *images* of God were very different, shaped by their different contexts. Similarly, if the Bible read by liberation theologians and by middle class western Christians is the same book, which at times seems difficult to believe, we must recognize that each reading has its inevitable bias.

John Levenson, for instance, is critical of the kind of exegesis of the Exodus story that finds its original reality in a class struggle, with an underclass breaking free from slavery in Egypt. This exegetical approach suggests that succeeding editors, for whom the monarchy and nation state or priestly ruling class were seen as positive, have sought to disguise this original story. Levenson comments: 'I suspect many of those Soviet Jewish emigrés, those Vietnamese boat people, and those Cuban refugees would indeed find their own experience in the book of Exodus . . . except that they would see in [the] Communist revolutionaries not Moses but Pharaoh.'[36]

Communities are about people and at best are characterized by love, accountability, acceptance, dealing with conflict, and building strong relationships. But we recognize that even in such groups there is a danger of letting our own experiences swamp the biblical stories rather than allowing the Bible to interpret our situation and our situation to inform our understanding of the Bible. An interpretation of the text that begins with the community's experience can have a feet-on-the-ground realism about it, but this may lead to a 'blind alley' exegesis. It is only when we have taken care to let the Bible speak for itself, that there will be left an important and necessary difference of perspective between the interpretations of different communities. This is what will add to our richness of understanding of the Word of God.

Jesus' parables were an invitation to change according to God's justice and goodness. It was not surprising, in the first century, that the powerful who ran things did not like Jesus' stories. This may explain why the parables of Jesus often resonate with the experience of many peoples in the developing world. They read the Bible in the light of their journey of faith in the often harsh realities of life. Such an engagement with scripture was identified by Gerhard Von Rad as happening within the Old Testament itself, noting of its developing theology that 'the process is in reality a sign of the living force with which the old message was handed on and adapted to new situations.'[37] Each community of faith studies the scriptures within the light of its own experiences and situation and seeks to discover God's enlightenment through the Spirit.

Questioning the way we live

There are lessons for western churches coming out of the experience of Third World theologies and communities. A privatized conception of salvation, where redemption is exclusively connected with the relationship of the individual to God, is challenged by a messianic liberation approach which embraces the whole of life. Ours is a holistic Gospel. We find new insights in our understanding of the scriptures, when we look at them through the eyes of people in another culture.

In an interview with Rosino Gibellini, Gustavo Gutierrez comments that European theology is concerned with the problem of atheism, while the theology of liberation is concerned with the problem of idolatry, expressed in terms of money, which puts profit before people. Mammon is the idol, putting riches in place of God. This leads on to the exploitation and oppression of the poor in many parts of the world and indeed in all societies. Gutierrez goes on to reflect that in Latin America they experience the negation of life, and therefore reflection on God develops not as a confrontation with disbelief but as a dialectic of life and death.[38]

The key difference being articulated here is between people as non-persons rather than as non-believers. And yet the latter situation is now surely as true of twenty-first century Western society as it is of Latin America. Clodovis Boff states that 'First World theologians have also woken up to the confrontation between the Christian faith and the contradictions specific to so-called advanced societies.'[39] Liberation hermeneutics has brought us back to a true understanding of scripture, using the Gospel stories to ask questions of our experience and story.[40] Liberation theology is not a movement but is theology in movement. There is a new way of doing theology here. It takes place along the way of life; it is on the move, it involves continual reflection, and it is always reforming. Liberation theology has redefined who does theology; why, where, and how it is done; and what is its agenda. Western scholarship has accepted the Enlightenment dichotomy between dogma and ethics and so tends to be abstract; as a result, it fails to translate into active commitment. Liberation theology's basic impulses, on the other hand, arise from the biblical reflections of Christian grass-roots communities, removing the dualism between theory and practice.

Recent years have seen the flowering of liberation theology in the Western world, for example in black theology and feminist theology. There has been a new recognition of responsibility of the First World toward the Third World, and the need to address the 'new poor' such as drug addicts, the elderly and migrant workers. These issues are also being raised in the UK. For example, Stephen Pattison[41] in his consideration of patients in mental health care believes that pastoral care, which seeks the well being of people, needs the method and critique that liberation theology provides to enable it to challenge unjust systems. It helps us to break free of a 'therapeutic captivity',[42] forcing us to seek justice for the patient even if this means coming into conflict with health-service institutions, through practice-focused critical methods and theological reflection. He challenges theological education that avoids the socio-political issues, and encourages the church to use the tools of the social sciences. Otherwise we may find ourselves tackling symptoms without addressing the cause.

The division between personal salvation and social transformation is a false one. The Gospel has become hijacked and spiritualized by those who do not want their comfortable lifestyle challenged. There is a danger of finding ourselves in the position outlined by Amos (5:1-27) of looking forward to the Day of the Lord, while neglecting the poor, the abused, and the disadvantaged in the world around us (cf. Luke 16:19-31; and Matthew 25:31-46). Following Jesus is a life of righteousness, which exceeds that of the Pharisees (Matthew 5:20), a righteousness that is deeds and not merely words (Matthew 7:20), deeds that are not religious rituals but acts of mercy and loving kindness (Matthew 9:13; 12:7). The religiously correct Pharisees are criticized for talking about theology but never lifting a finger to help (Matthew 23:3f). Jesus points to two kinds of life: listening, or listening and doing. Like building on sand or rock, one way leads to catastrophe and the other to safety (Matthew 7:24ff). In Matthew 25:31-46 Jesus speaks of the finality of judgement, where, again, two kinds of life are identified—there is knowing what God requires, and there is knowing and doing what God requires. We are challenged to follow Jesus' example in a caring love that goes beyond words. We find in the Gospels that Jesus did not preach at the poor and oppressed; he did not tell them what he would do for them; he did not impose himself upon them; rather he asked, 'What do you want me to do for you?'

The focus on mission will always include reading both the newspaper and the Bible. Faith in Christ is not a step beyond humanity and the world, but towards them. In Christ we demonstrate what it means to be fully human. The church is the church when it witnesses to God's saving activity in Jesus Christ in liberating people to become the children of God. In this context, as Jon Sobrino suggests, the rich find salvation through the ways in which they address the needs of the poor.[43] The church is the fellowship of those who embrace this task, in the freedom of God's forgiveness and renewal, who engage in concrete celebration of this freedom, reflection upon it, and its proclamation. It is only as Christians together seek to make this commitment that the nature of Jesus Christ and his Gospel become identifiable in the world.

The Third World view of the challenge of the non-person, as opposed to the non-believer, is increasingly true in our own society: those treated as non-persons include the factory assembly-line worker, the unemployed, the homeless forced to beg for money on our streets, the handicapped, the elderly, the young, and the mentally ill. People feel increasingly powerless and voiceless and cut off from relationships with others or any kind of real community—and this is not confined within the lower social strata of society. We recognize that there are more fundamental questions about what a non-person might be, and, indeed, about what church should be. We may find some answers as we explore our stories, the scriptures and the ways of working out theology within our own communities. We are embarked on a journey, which is theology in movement, striving for orthopraxis and orthodoxy rather than orthodoxy alone. I believe that when we have the courage to allow all people to discover their special place within the community life of Christ's church, then we will find liberation.

We can suggest the following characteristics of a church that lives and proclaims a holistic Gospel:

- having a freedom to explore what faith means in the world of everyday experience;
- questioning the political, social and economic decisions of government and industry;
- understanding the nature of community and family, and focusing on building strong relationships;
- freeing the Bible from captivity within church services and letting it shape our daily living;
- having a freedom to explore and question the scriptures, to learn about prayer, and to celebrate life and work in worship;
- having a freedom from intellectualism, but not from understanding;
- recognizing and reaching the poor and the powerless in our communities, and addressing the needs of the socially deprived and the socially inadequate.

Exploring the complexity of the issues
When the church does address the issues facing its community or the wider world, it is often accused of meddling in things it knows little or nothing about. The Bishop of London, Richard Chartres, noted that the

church of England *Faith in the City* report failed to make a political impact and was criticized by politicians because it was built on poor economic thinking. He says that 'Church leaders must be aware of the complexities involved in making choices about social provision when resources are finite and they must not be trapped into the dangerous luxury of simplistic calls to increase funding to defend the *status quo*.[44]

Mike West, from the Industrial Mission in South Yorkshire, makes a similar point when he recalls the statement in 1944 of the first industrial chaplain appointed to Sheffield; at that time Bishop Leslie Hunter said that 'the church was trying to tackle the issue of an industrial world with the tools of a pre-industrial one, though the two hardly touched.'[45] Ever since then industrial missions have claimed that their task includes developing Christian thinking and practice through the industrial realities that they are involved with. This is also the activity of the whole church, in all walks of life, and should not be restricted to industry and commerce. Everyone will have experience as worker, manager, consumer and member of a community.

The primary question for the church, when addressing industrial issues theologically will always be: can we return to the problem with new ways of seeing it and new possibilities for resolving it? We can then push our considerations further and ask whether such new possibilities are consistent with the Lordship of Christ, and whether they allow us to deepen our understanding of the ways in which God acts in the world. But before moving on to such theological reflection there will need to be analysis aimed at understanding the issues. Facing up to the facts of a situation may be difficult and even threatening as controversial issues are raised. However, if we are to deal with what are often complex and interconnected issues such analysis is vital. In the analysis of a company, an industry or the community in which it is set, our analysis can be divided up under a number of headings.

• Historical overview: how have we got to where we are now? This may indicate where the unit or community may be going and what might be possible for the future.
• Geographical overview: what does the area look like? What are the factors that exercise control on future development?

- Social analysis: who holds power and who makes decisions? How do the people involved relate to each other?
- Economic analysis: where is the wealth located and what is the influence of money?
- Cultural analysis: what are the cultural and racial mixes? What religious influences can be identified?

The results of this analysis will inform our discussions of the identified issue and will serve as a control as we seek to reflect biblically and theologically. Our reflection will often point us toward the appropriate action.

Let me take an example which is close to my expertise and to my present pastoral concerns. When considering the South Wales Valley communities and the impact of the closure of coal mines in South Wales we find both positive and negative features. We can begin with our experience as those actually living in such an area:

- closure of the mines;
- the resulting demographic changes with outward movement of skilled labour;
- the effects on the communities;
- declining influence of chapels and declining church attendance;
- lack of leadership in community and in churches, the more able having moved to jobs elsewhere.

We can then make an analysis of the reasons for the closure of the mines:

- distance to markets;
- geological issues—the nature of the rocks;
- availability of other fuels for power stations—especially the increased use of gas from the North Sea natural gas field;
- the impact of the global market—cheaper fuel from abroad;
- the influence of the green movement—favouring a move away from use of coal, to lessen sulphur dioxide in the atmosphere and resulting acid rain;

- the danger of global warming—concern for build up of greenhouse gases, especially carbon dioxide from the burning of fossil fuels.[46]

We should consider sociological and psychological issues involved:

- a lowering of self-worth among the unemployed;
- depression;
- increased risk of suicide;
- increased risk of alcohol and drug abuse;
- increase in domestic violence and dysfunction in families;
- poor record of juvenile behaviour and school attendance and attainment;
- increase in very young parents and single parents;
- increase in crime;
- the results of all this in a poor image of community, a loss of hope and a despair about the future.

In summary, we notice that the degradation of the Coal Industry has both positive and negative social results:

Negative
- unemployment;
- degradation of communities;
- loss of self-worth for people;
- resulting social problems;
- resulting psychological problems.

Positive
- an end to poor working conditions;
- better health;
- government and European Union action to fund new industry and employment opportunities;
- improved physical environment;
- increase in commuter population with an accompanying rise in some house prices.

Some initial theological points now need to be addressed, which will assist us with both the *analysis* of the situation and the *integration* to which this leads (see further chapter 4):

• a theology of work needs to be developed;
• likewise, we need a theology of wealth creation and distribution;
• this theology must be for community and for society;
• yet we must not lose an emphasis on the value of each individual;
• prophetic insight must be gained into the situation, and a prophetic voice raised.

Out of this analysis and reflection come specific issues for action for the church (see further chapter 5):

• How should we support the disadvantaged?
• How should we approach the disreputable?
• How should we engage the inadequate?
• What do we say to the local government and national government?
• What local organizations should we join with?
• Are there political and pressure groups whom we should support?
• Are there local groups whom we should oppose?
• Are there developments that we should celebrate through the life of the church?
• Are there projects that we should initiate?

The complexity of many situations that the church will want to comment upon, both in its local community and in the wider world, demands adequate research, detailed information, and sometimes professional guidance. Only after these steps have been taken will theological comment and proposals of action be advisable.

Different ways of learning from experience

The church is more than the community that hears the word preached; it is the community that makes a response to the preaching of that word. So we must ask whether the ministry of preaching and teaching within the church is giving insights to the congregation as to how they might live for

Christ in the midst of the actual struggles, temptations and suffering of their lives in the world.

A few years ago I was speaking with a young Baptist youth worker from Moscow, who was in a class of students I was teaching in Budapest. She told me that her fiancé, conscripted into the Russian army, had recently come back on leave from Chechnya, and that he was deeply troubled. She told me something that neither she nor he were able to share with their pastor: he had discovered that he enjoyed killing people.

Here is another experience of war. As I write this chapter I have been speaking with a military chaplain soon to join his unit in southern Iraq. He has trained with them; he has thrown live hand grenades and fired automatic weapons on the firing range. He told me that he understands the seduction of the power of such weapons, but also recognizes the horror and fear that awaits them under fire.

Nearer to home, a young minister recently discussed with me a problem that many of his male church members were having at work. In the lunch breaks their office colleagues gathered around a computer to look at pornography, and as their minister he was unsure about how to advise them to address the situation.

Our approach to learning will need to recognize such real experiences, as we attempt to understand the relevance of our beliefs for our life in God's world. Whether we are talking to children or to adults, to Christians, interested enquirers, or uninterested outsiders, we need to start where people are, with their experiences and their understanding of them. A key aspect of such a process is our openness and honesty in working and learning with each other. We are not doing things for, or to, people but we are learning with others. It is important to recognize the principle of the incarnation, of God with us, revealing God in everyday experiences of life. The first church was based on community living, on shared experiences and believers' reflection upon those experiences.

The majority of people who make up the congregation of the local church do not find it easy to live as a Christian in the world they inhabit. Many will wonder where their faith fits with the daily news from around the world. Most will have important questions to ask and vital issues to share about their own lives, but find no place or opportunity to raise them. Services of worship may be lively, enjoyable, challenging and instructive, yet leave the concerns of the congregation unaddressed. Parents will be concerned about such things as vaccinations, potty training, schooling, discipline, friendships, relationships, alcohol, sex and drugs. Those caring for elderly relatives will be worried about their strength to care, having enough patience, and dealing with their tiredness, irritation, and anger; they will be anxious about their charges' senility, lack of mobility, weakness, and incontinence; they will be concerned about the National Health Service's provision of respite care, hospital beds, place in a nursing home, and questions of pain management and euthanasia. Those in employment, both employees and employers, are concerned about money, job security, disputes, redundancy and government policies. By contrast, many less well-off people are only concerned about food on the table, clothes for their children, and keeping out of debt. There must be space for people to express these concerns, discuss their faith (both doubts and certainties), find biblical and spiritual direction for their lives, and know the love and support of the Christian community.

Do we acknowledge the difficulties that members of the congregation face in the engagement of their faith with their work? Do we provide support for, and training in, this aspect of Christian discipleship? Are the leaders of our churches aware of, knowledgeable about and sensitive to, the daily contexts of in which the congregation work, live and engage in leisure activities? Do we encourage the development of a network of small groups personally supporting each other in their calling in the world?

We will want to affirm that human experience is many-faceted, and that the rich well of experience that is represented in the lives of most congregations will be a source of powerful creativity for the church. In shaping Christian disciples and in being church our theological assumptions will influence not only the content but also the way we lead, teach, support and guide people. Do we allow people the freedom to take the initiative? Do we believe that God may be disclosed to us through the insights and lives of others? Do we encourage adults to use the gifts that may take us in new directions? Such questions are the basis for a group to reflect theologically on a situation, in order to see where it fits into the mission of God. Ballard and Pritchard maintain that 'there is nothing difficult or elusive about this activity. It simply brings together the practice of ministry with the rich resources of the Christian faith and allows the interaction to guide what we do.'[47] We each bring our knowledge of faith, our grasp of the Bible and our expertise in other disciplines, and from our critical discussion of experience we find new understanding of the ways in which God is active in the world. Such meetings will be a place where we covenant together in open and trusting relationships.

In exploring experience and investigating complexities, different styles of learning will suit different people, as a number of authors have observed;[48] we will therefore need to provide a variety of styles and activities within the church's programme. For example, a highly analytical approach, using steps of logic and critical appraisal, will not appeal to someone who tends to work on an instinctive, intuitive level. Four general learning styles have been recognized: activist; theorist; reflector; and pragmatist. People who have different ways of thinking will favour these different styles. The activist learning style uses participation in activities, and learns directly from experiences and the problems these throw up. The theorist approach is theoretical and explores the methods and assumptions behind the activity; it is intellectually stretching. The reflector learning style concentrates on observation, research and an analytical response. The pragmatist style emphasizes technique and performance; it provides an immediate opportunity to grapple with real problems.

It has long been recognized that the left and right sides of the brain control different aspects of thinking. Right hemisphere thinking is reflective rather than analytical, and is synthetic, imaginative, holistic and metaphorical. Such thinking seeks by imagination and intuition to grasp the webs of significance that hold the meanings of events for people. Michael Polanyi emphasizes the primacy of the creative imagination.[49] He maintains that the creative imagination is that capacity of the human mind which effects the integration of the parts into a coherent whole, and thereby calls into being new possibilities of thought and action. On the other hand, left hemisphere thinking tends to be rational and analytical; it is logical thinking that follows a linear progression.

People who favour different styles of learning will respond differently to differing models of religious education. Yet whatever the preference, we will want to encourage a participative approach where all members of the congregation seek to bring about transformation in the light of God's call for justice for all people. Such education will be a means of social transformation.

Paulo Freire[50] has sought to develop the key principles for this radical style of education. He proposes that we should identify the issues which are of relevance to people in their lives; adopt a problem-posing approach, which involves active participants; make dialogue a central element, where all persons bring their own perceptions based on their experience; follow an action-reflection/learning cycle model; and aim to see a radical transformation, which actively involves the whole community. Such principles provide a most useful model for the church to adopt in helping its members to relate life and faith. But such an approach requires more than words. I agree with Anne Wilkinson-Hayes who states that adults learn principally through involvement. She maintains that:

> only when people are face to face with a homeless person do the issues of homelessness and housing really begin to impinge and become more of a priority in church life. Only when people share in the staffing of a night shelter do they begin asking why there isn't more affordable social housing. Engagement in practical concern results in politicization.[51]

By moving beyond providing mere aid or a service, to empowering oppressed groups to take greater control of their own situation and to work for change within it, we naturally run some risks. We shall find that those whom we work alongside are being enabled to ask challenging questions not only of the authorities, but also of the church.

Exercise 3.2
a. Where, how, and what do we enjoy learning?

b. How then should the Christian church teach about the Christian faith and lifestyle in the world of today?

Some pictures to think about
Picture a scene in the year 2003. The place is a city centre church, and the occasion is the welcome service for a new minister. The opening prayer focuses on the 'glorious radiance of God's eternal throne', while the guest

preacher outlines the new minister's role as 'preaching the Gospel of redemption to the heathen.' He urges that 'we will all stand before God's awe-full throne of judgement' and will be found wanting unless 'we have been washed in the precious blood of the Lamb of God.'

I was present at this service, and I hope that I will not be misunderstood by my readers. I found little to disagree with in the doctrine of the preacher's message; what made me feel uncomfortable was the fact that we were meeting in the centre of a cosmopolitan city, where over 93% of the population are unchurched. Language and content of both the worship and the preaching made contact with few except the older members of the congregation, who had been Christians for forty years or more. Points of engagement with the world and the local context were almost totally absent. The text and context of our preaching and teaching must be relevant, must be in touch with social reality as well as the scriptures, and must invite a response.

This experience brought to mind Stella Gibbons' parody of 1920s rural melodramas, *Cold Comfort Farm*, where at one point in the story Amos Starkadder, the local preacher, is asked about his church and style of preaching by the heroine, Flora Poste.[52] Cousin Amos preaches twice a week at the 'Church of the Quivering Brethren, a religious sect which had its headquarters in Beershorn.' On the way to the service Flora remarks, 'It must be so interesting to preach to the Brethren, Cousin Amos. I quite envy you. Do you prepare your sermon beforehand, or do you just make it up as you go along?' Amos is upset by such a godless thought, emphasising that the word falls from heaven 'on me mind like manna.' So Flora, growing in interest says, 'Then you have no idea what you are going to say before you get there?' To which Amos replies: 'Aye . . . I allus knows 'twill be summat about burnin' . . . or the eternal torment . . . or sinners comin' to judgement.'

A similar picture is drawn by John Grisham in his autobiographical account of 1940s mid-west United States, *A Painted House*, where at one point he recalls a typical Baptist sermon.[53] He comments that Brother Akers 'was angry as usual, and he began shouting almost immediately. He attacked sin right off. . . . We sinners drank and gambled and cursed and lied and fought and killed and committed adultery because we allowed ourselves to be separated from God. . . . Gran closed her eyes, and I knew she was praying—she always was. Pappy was staring at a wall, probably thinking about how a dead Sisco [a local petty criminal, who had been killed in a fight] might affect his cotton crop. My mother seemed to be paying attention, and mercifully I began to nod off.'

Contrast these pictures with the Archbishop of Canterbury's New Year message on 1 January 2004, when Rowan Williams spoke about the meaning of trust over background pictures of families learning to ice skate. Or picture a sermon on peace in Christ set against video images of the Iraq War, the Twin Towers on 9/11, and street violence in the UK. Or consider a Christmas poster of a mother sitting by a Calcutta roadside, trying to breastfeed her starving child, with the questioning caption: *the Word became flesh?*

Returning to that joyful occasion in the city centre church, what might the new minister have been encouraged to achieve in his preaching and teaching? To open up a Bible that addresses the human condition, and to demonstrate that Christ makes sense of our daily lives. This is to present good news and the offer of a new beginning.

Exercise 3.3

a. Suggest ways in which the daily concerns of the congregation can be addressed through the worshipping community of the church.

b. If Ephesians 4:11-16 is a pattern for the church today, where and how does the equipping, building up, and growing into the maturity of Christ take place in your church?

Notes

[1] http://news.bbc.co.uk/1/hi/england/merseyside/4739569.stm; accessed 03.02.05.

[2] http://www.blink.org.uk/pdescription.asp?key=2742&mid=&grp=56&cat=296; accessed 03.08.05.

[3] John W de Gruchy, *Reconciliation. Restoring Justice* (SCM: London, 2002), p. 16.

[4] From an MTh essay, Cardiff University, June 2004, by Revd Christopher Broddle, used with permission.

5 A great deal of theological exploration has been carried out by ECONI (Evangelical Contribution on Northern Ireland) as demonstrated in their pack, *Forgiveness Papers.* See also Mark Amstatz, John Brewer, Cecil McCullough, Duncan Morrow, *Forgiveness: making a world of difference* (Belfast: ECONI, 2002).

6 Paul S Fiddes, *Past Event and Present Salvation. The Christian Idea of Atonement* (London: Darton, Longman and Todd, 1989), p. 16.

7 Fiddes, *Past Event and Present Salvation*, p. 173.

8 http://news.bbc.co.uk/1/hi/england/merseyside/4471440.stm; accessed 15.12.05.

9 Chinese proverb quoted in Johann Christoph Arnold, *The Lost Art of Forgiving* (Farmington/Robertsbridge: Plough Publishing, 1998), p. 15.

10 See Fiddes, *Past Event and Present Salvation*, pp. 174, 176.

11 Andrew Walker, *Telling the Story* (London: SPCK, 1996), pp. 27-9

12 David M Gunn and Danna Nolan Fewell, *Narrative in the Hebrew Bible* (Oxford: Oxford University Press, 1993), p. 9.

13 See, for example, David Day, Jeff Astley & Leslie Francis (eds), *A Reader on Preaching. Making Connections* (Aldershot: Ashgate, 2005); Alec Gilmore, *Preaching as Theatre* (London: SCM, 1996); Calvin Miller, *Marketplace Preaching. How to Return the Sermon to Where it Belongs* (Grand Rapids: Baker Books, 1995) and Miller, *The Empowered Communicator. 7 Keys to Unlocking an Audience* (Nashville: Broadman & Holman, 1994).

14 Jolyon P Mitchell, *Visually Speaking* (Edinburgh: T&T Clark, 1999).

15 Peter Berger, *A Rumour of Angels. Modern Society and the Rediscovery of the Supernatural* (Harmondsworth: Penguin Books, 1969, 1971).

16 For a full discussion see Calvin Miller, *Marketplace Preaching.*

17 For example, see E. Cardenal, *The Gospel of Solentiname*, 4 volumes (New York: Orbis, 1977-1984), and more generally Christopher Rowland & Mark Corner, *Liberating Exegesis. The Challenge of Liberation Theology to Biblical Studies* (London: SPCK, 1990).

18 The Christian writer Adrian Plass has written a poem called *The Nathan Rap*, which retells the parable that Nathan told to David. It is produced in his book *Clearing away the Rubbish* (Eastbourne: Monarch, 1988), pp. 183-5.

19 Frances O'Gorman, *Down To Earth—101 women from rural areas of Brazil tell their struggle to stay on the land* (Rio de Janeiro: CEAR [Ecumenical Centre for Action and Reflection], 1987).

20 Gunn & Fewell, *Narrative in the Hebrew Bible*, p. 193.

[21] Such fresh insights, for example, are found in: R S Sugirtharajah (ed.), *Voices from the Margin. Interpreting the Bible in the Third World* (London: Orbis/SPCK, 1995).

[22] Gunn and Fewell, *Narrative in the Hebrew Bible*, p. 205.

[23] Stephen Barton, *The Spirituality of the Gospels* (London, SPCK, 1992), p. 3; see also R. E. Clements' comments on the Old Testament in *Old Testament Theology—A Fresh Approach* (London: Marshall, Morgan & Scott, 1978), p. 12.

[24] For a further discussion of the setting of Daniel see Ernest Lucas, *Daniel* (Apollos Old Testament Commentary; Leicester: Apollos/Inter-Varsity Press, 2002) and Lucas, *Decoding Daniel. Reclaiming the Visions of Daniel 7-11*, (Grove Biblical Series B18; Cambridge: Grove Books, 2000).

[25] Barton, *Spirituality of the Gospels*, p. ix.

[26] Norman Anderson, *The Teaching of Jesus* (London: Hodder & Stoughton, 1983), p. 26.

[27] Donald B Kraybill, *The Upside-Down Kingdom* (Scottdale: Herald Press, 1978), p. 10.

[28] The following are a selection: Michael Ball, *The Radical Stories of Jesus. Interpreting the Parables Today* (Oxford, Regents Park College/Macon: Smyth & Helwys, 2000); C. H. Dodd, *The Parables of the Kingdom* (London: Collins, 1935, 1961); Ruth Etchells, *A Reading of the Parables of Jesus* (London, Darton, Longman and Todd, 1998); Joachim Jeremias, *The Parables of Jesus* (London: SCM, 1963); T.W. Manson, *The Teaching of Jesus* (Cambridge: CUP, 1948); David Wenham, *The Parables of Jesus. Pictures of Revolution* (London: Hodder & Stoughton, 1989). For a very different approach to parables in which young people create parables for their time see: Geoffrey Barlow (editor) *Young People's Parables* (London: Quartet Books, 1983).

[29] Rowland and Corner, *Liberating Exegesis*, p. 8.

[30] I am indebted to Donald English, *The Message of Mark*. Bible Speaks Today (Leicester: IVP, 1992), p. 92ff, for some of the ideas I have developed here.

[31] John Reader, *Local Theology: Church and Community in Dialogue* (London: SPCK, 1994), p. 16.

[32] See Theo Witvliet, *A Place in the Sun. An Introduction to Liberation Theology in the Third World* (London: SCM, 1985), pp.139-140. Witvliet comments that 'word and reality, action and meditation, liturgical celebration and political action are not detached, but interrelated and held together by the group as such, operating as a collective subject.'

[33] Based on my conversation with Maria Isabel and Maria David, during two months that I spent in Nicaragua and El Salvador with BMS Worldmission missionaries in Spring 1995.

[34] Carlos Mesters, 'Bible Study Centre for People's Pastoral Action (Brazil): The use of the Bible among the common people' in F. Ross Kinsler (ed.), *Ministry by the People. Theological Education by Extension* (Geneva: WCC/New York: Orbis, 1983), pp. 78-81.

[35] Witvliet, *A Place in the Sun*, p. 37.

[36] Jon D. Levenson, The Hebrew Bible, the Old Testament, and Historical Criticism: Jews and Christians in Bible Studies (Louisville: Westminster/John Knox, 1993), pp. 127-59.

[37] G. von Rad, *The Message of the Prophets* (London: SCM, 1968), p. 27.

[38] Rosinio Gibellini, *The Liberation Theology Debate* (London: SCM, 1987), p. 84.

[39] Leonardo Boff and Clodovis Boff, *Introducing Liberation Theology* (Tunbridge Wells: Burns & Oates, 1987), p. 81.

[40] For further discussion see Gordon Spykman (ed.), *Let My People Live— Faith and Struggle in Central America* (Grand Rapids: Eerdmans, 1988), pp. 235-6.

[41] Stephen Pattison, *Pastoral Care and Liberation Theology* (Cambridge: CUP, 1994)

[42] Pattison, *Pastoral Care and Liberation Theology*, pp. 209-11.

[43] Jon Sobrino, *The Principle of Mercy. Taking the Crucified People from the Cross* (New York: Orbis, 1994).

[44] Richard Chartres, 'Church Ministry in London', in Eric Blakebrough (ed.) *Church for the City* (London: Darton, Longman and Todd, 1995), pp. 25-6.

[45] Mike West, *Doing Theology—a Model Examined* (Paper to the Mission and Economy Conference, Sheffield, 1994).

[46] For a full discussion of renewable and non-renewable forms of energy and of the impact of fossil fuels on the environment, see my paper: 'A Theology of Energy', *Baptist Ministers' Journal*, 284 (October 2003); available on CD-ROM from the *Methodist Church Energy Pack*, Methodist Publishing House, 2003.

[47] Paul Ballard and John Pritchard, *Practical Theology in Action: Christian Thinking in the Service of Church and Society* (London: SPCK, 1996), p. 118.

[48] See the works of: Paul Ballard and John Pritchard, *Practical Theology in Action*; Yvonne Craig, *Learning for Life: a Handbook of Adult Religious*

Education (London: Mowbray, 1994); P. Honey and A. Mumford, *The Manual of Learning Styles* (1992) available from Dr. P. Honey, Ardingley House, 10 Linden Avenue, Maidenhead, Berkshire SL6 6HB; Sheila Mayo (ed.) *Living with the Story: Bible Studies for Group Participation* (Swindon: Bible Society, 1994); Jack L.Seymour and Donald E.Miller (eds), *Theological Approaches to Christian Education* (Nashville: Abingdon, 1990). The Myers-Briggs Type Indicator (MBTI) also sheds light on people's preferred learning style.

[49] Michael Polanyi, *Personal Knowledge* (Chicago: Chicago University Press, 1958); Polyani, *The Tacit Dimension* (New York, Anchor Books, 1967).

[50] For the main works of Paulo Freire see: *Pedagogy of the Oppressed* (New York: Seabury Press, 1970); *Education for Critical Consciousness* (New York: Seabury Press, 1973); *Pedagogy in Process* (New York: Seabury Press, 1978).

[51] In Steve Finamore (ed), *On earth as in Heaven: a Theology of Social Action for Baptist Churches* (Didcot: Baptist Union, 1996), p. 4.

[52] Stella Gibbons, *Cold Comfort Farm* (London: Penguin Books, [1932], 1987), pp. 84-9.

[53] John Grisham, *A Painted House* (New York: Dell Publishing, 2001), pp. 103-5.

4
Integration: Examples of Practice

When her younger brother Anthony was killed with an axe in a racially motivated attack, Dominique Walker commented that 'We have to forgive' the gang who took his life. Quoting from the Bible, she said: 'Seventy times seven we have to forgive, that's what Jesus said. So we have to, we have to forgive.'[1] Hearing what the Bible has to say and letting it shape our lives is often a difficult exercise. In the situations like the one that took place in Liverpool in July 2005, it seems to become almost impossible.

The Gospel is about overcoming alienation and estrangement between each other, and at root between us and God. Reconciliation has to do with the healing of relationships, but it also includes the doing of justice. The Christian doctrine of atonement is an important basis for developing forgiveness and reconciliation in pastoral relationships, through our understanding of God's act of forgiveness and reconciliation in Christ. S.C. Guthrie clearly focuses our understanding: 'The biblical doctrine of the atonement teaches that it is God who initiates and fulfils the reconciliation between sinful humanity and God. God is the subject, not the object, of what happened on Good Friday'. And he goes on to emphasize that 'It is not the guilty but the injured party who acts to restore the broken relationship. . . . It is not God who is reconciled to us but God who makes peace with us. This is what the death of Jesus is all about.'[2]

Here we see a clue to forgiveness in the doctrine of atonement: it is the one who has been sinned against who takes the first step across the gap of alienation. Another clue lies in the perception by John de Gruchy, who notes that in the New Testament the words for 'reconciliation' are compounds of the Greek *allasso*, to exchange, and this in turn is derived from *allos*, meaning the other. 'The words thus carry with them the sense of exchanging places with "the other", and therefore being in solidarity with rather than against "the other".'[3] This accords with the Gospel, which has representation at its heart. De Gruchy maintains that it is when we recognize the 'other' that we hopefully come to *know* the 'other.' The next step is a willingness to listen to the other's story. The critical step in reconciliation is to put ourselves in the place of the other. Reconciliation is always located in the particular. He suggests that

> there comes a point in the process when reconciliation becomes a reality, when the conversation reaches a new level of commitment, embrace and shared hope. This is the point when marriage partners are able to heal their failing relationship, and a country decisively breaks with its oppressive and divisive past and embarks on building a new future.[4]

However the seriousness of sin cannot be overlooked, for to do so would deny our God-given free will, which is able to respond to God's love. De Gruchy rightly states that 'the reality of the world reconciled by God in Christ does not mean that the world has become good, that all evil has been eradicated, or that the reign of God has come. Quite the contrary, for the world remains the world because it is the world which is loved, condemned and reconciled in Christ.'[5]

We can explore forgiveness through figure 4.1, which focuses on our reconciliation with God through the cross of Christ (see 2 Corinthians 5:19; Colossians 1:20).

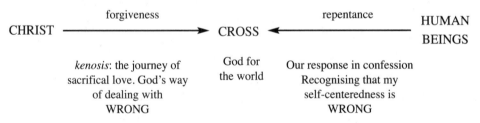

figure 4.1

God, in Christ, has made the painful and costly journey of forgiveness, encountering us with the offer of acceptance, mercy and love. The focus of this offer of forgiveness is seen in the cross. The Gospel is not sentimental words of forgiveness but has the cry from the cross, the abandonment of Christ by God, and the descent into hell in order to redeem the world. There is no cheap grace here. For reconciliation to take place we too must take the painful journey to the cross. This will be costly in terms of self-denial and admission of guilt. The journey of Christ to the cross is a statement that our way of life is not as God desires; it is wrong. Our journey of repentance is the confession that we know that much in our lives is wrong.

Paul Fiddes expresses something of the enormous depth of God's grace as demonstrated by the following:

> Though himself living in tune with the Father's mind, he [Christ] consents to participate in the alienation which is the lot of humanity which has lost communion with God. He stands with the guilty under the weight of the verdict which God passes upon rebellious human life. . . . The plea 'Father forgive them' does not conflict with the awful cry 'My God why have you forsaken me?' but brings out its meaning, since forgiveness is nothing less than a voyage into the dark void of the guilty life.[6]

Human alienation and broken relationships are taken into the very being of God and addressed through *kenosis* and sacrificial love. There are enormous pastoral implications and applications here, especially as a challenge to all our relationships and the way in which we view forgiveness. In imitation of God, we too make a journey of empathy into the lives of others, putting ourselves into their shoes, even when thy have hurt us badly. As our relationship with God is restored, our relationship with others is challenged. As Paul expressed it to the Corinthian church, we who have found reconciliation now offer reconciliation to the world (2 Corinthians 5:17-21).

Reconciliation lies at the very heart of life, but perhaps we can refresh what sometimes seems an over-religious concept with the term 'integration'. Integration, or a making whole, points us both to the healing of relationships and to a theological method which may help us to reach this wholeness. In the third phase of the pastoral cycle, learners take experiences and situations they have described and analyzed, and aim to integrate their theological reflections upon them into the ongoing course of their daily lives, today and tomorrow. If this is to happen, scripture must be thoroughly contextualized, in a way that connects with the culture and society in which the reader lives. The Word of God will be heard in scrip-

ture, the Christian community and in the world. Principles for action will
be formed which will take us forward into appropriate responses.

In this chapter I want to consider how integration can be encouraged
in a number of areas and settings—in Bible study, in preaching, in exploring pastoral problems, in considering social behaviour, in watching films
and television, in thinking about work and employment, and in facing
issues of politics and power. In six of these areas we shall look at just one
example in detail: a Bible study on the Samaritan woman, a sermon on
the transfiguration of Jesus, the pastoral issue of cohabitation, the social
issue of genetic selection of embryos, the film *Hotel Rwanda*, and the
results of a survey on Christians in work. Finally, to illustrate the possibilities of Christian engagement with politics and power I want to refer to
two examples from Northern Ireland.

Bible studies that integrate with life

In studying the Bible we are always faced with the question of whether
our own context or that of the original writer should take precedence in
our interpretation. The more we learn, the more we recognize the need of
an expert in aiding our interpretation. But then we also recognize that this
expert will be inevitably viewing the scriptures through a lens taken from
his or her own context. It is for this reason that Craig Blomberg[7] urges a
comparison of the exegesis that comes from different traditions and world
cultures. He believes that we will then come to the text with a fresh set of
questions, which are not normally asked by our own tradition. He says
that immersion in the poverty of the Third World makes the point for him:
'A traditional Gospel of merely spiritual salvation lacks credibility in situations of intense physical suffering, while an offer of merely physical
help, when many will die anyway, leaves people without hope for the
eternal fellowship with God which far more than compensates for even
the greatest suffering of this life.'[8]

The biblical writers were, like us, also engaged in a dynamic and creative exercise. Laurie Green[9] rightly notes that they selected from the
living stories that were held in the community of faith and drew ideas
from them that seemed appropriate for the situations in which they lived
and into which they wrote. These writings were always within the checks
and balances of the understanding and experience of the community of
faith. The first Christians were Jews who had heard and seen Jesus living

their life in their land, facing and addressing the very same issues that they faced. The second generation of Christians were forced to ask if there was anything in their recollection of the sayings of Jesus that was applicable to the situation that they were facing. They could then reflect on their own experience and link it to that of Jesus. We find ourselves in this position as we seek to find guidance from the stories of Jesus in our reflection and questioning of our experience of the world.

There will therefore be the need for exegetical work, as Ian Fraser recognizes:

> Once Christian communities today can talk not simply about Jesus and Zacchaeus in face-to-face encounter, but about the church of Luke and the context (rich Christians wondering how they get into the Kingdom of God, where Jesus says "Happy are the poor") which gives point to a specific story or parable of the gospel, the imagination of all kinds of ordinary people can be brought into play.[10]

This understanding allows people to take the Bible story into their own context and bring their own questions to it. We need to bring together the resources of the scholars and people's expertise in living. A helpful approach to Bible study that enables a group to discover meaning for themselves in a narrative passage of scripture, makes use of four simple questions: what do we hear, feel, imagine, conclude?

The following is the record of a church group studying John 4:5-26. The passage from the Gospel according to John was read to the group in a dramatic way, so that the full picture of Jesus' encounter with the Samaritan woman might emerge. The group were then given time to re-read the passage for themselves, after which they were invited to close their Bibles. After this the group explored together what they had heard, felt and imagined as they read the story. The following insights arose in a mixed age group of ten Christians and were written out on overhead projector transparencies, so that the group could see the discussion develop.

What did you hear? What was the story about?
Jesus was tired and thirsty, and sat down.
A woman was coming to collect water but in need of much more.

'Give me some water,' says Jesus.

'Jews and Samaritans don't drink or eat together,' replies the woman.

'I have the water of eternal life'.

'I'd like some of that for then I wouldn't have to bother with coming to this well every day.'

'Go and get your husband.'

'I've not got a husband.'

'An honest reply—You've had five husbands and the man you are now living with is not your husband.'

'You're a prophet! But Jews and Samaritans worship in different places'.

'The time is coming and has now arrived when all people will worship God in spirit'.

'But that will be when the Messiah comes'.

'I am the Messiah.'

'Could this be the Messiah?' says the woman to the people of the town.

What did you feel? What were the woman's and Jesus' emotions?

The woman was shocked, surprised, threatened by the situation; maybe touched by the fact that this man speaks to her. She feels bitter and angry about her life; she feels rejected by the other women of the village. She is coming on her own at noon to the well; is she an outsider if not an outcast? Is she frightened, confused, guilty? Perhaps she feels used by men, rather than guilty.

After her encounter with Jesus she feels accepted, disturbed, excited (wanting to tell others) and has a new courage to communicate with those who have rejected her.

Jesus is tired, hot, thirsty; yet he has a readiness and willingness to engage in conversation with this Samaritan woman, who has been ostracized by the community.

Jesus has compassion, is sad for her situation, has patience and understanding. He is ready to help her and reach out to her.

What did you imagine? What pictures formed in your mind?

Jesus sitting against the side of the well—it's hot, hazy, and dusty; grey and white rocks lie around.

The woman is a lone figure crossing a dry, stone-strewn piece of land with the white walls of small houses in the background. The scene is empty apart from the woman.

The woman is dressed in a Palestinian black garment, with her head and face covered. Jesus is sitting calmly while the woman walks around him in an agitated fashion. Above all, the woman appears to be lonely.

What did you conclude from what you heard, felt and imagined?
The argument and discussion between the woman and Jesus develops into a revelation of who Jesus is.

The woman is a rejected outsider, who has been abused by a male dominated society, where divorce for men was easy and women were totally dependent for their existence upon men.

The woman is a lone figure in this encounter—there is an emphasis on her position as an outcast from society and her resulting loneliness.

Jesus felt compassion and offered acceptance to the woman. The woman in return felt accepted by Jesus. Jesus revealed himself as the Messiah to this outcast, Samaritan woman.

We can now ask two further questions:

What other Bible stories or church traditions/doctrines come to mind?
• Zacchaeus—an outcast accepted by Jesus.
• Matthew—a collaborator welcomed as a disciple by Jesus.
• The woman at the home of Simon the Pharisee.
• The woman with the haemorrhage.
• The revelation of the Messiah's birth to the shepherds—also a lowly despised group in Palestinian society.
• The very choosing of Mary to be the mother of the Messiah.

We see the unconditional approach of Jesus to an individual and the unconditional acceptance of an individual, whatever the human judgement of that person's character might be. We find that God shows himself in unexpected places and in unexpected ways to people.

What new insights do we have for our lives as disciples of Christ?
• We all have value.
• The gospel is for everyone, whoever they are and whatever they have done.
• We should not allow prejudice and human judgements to become barriers to the gospel.
• Maybe we should begin to expose such barriers and injustices in our society.

   This record of what the group discovered demonstrates the value of this approach. The group have made the discoveries for themselves and have related the story to their own feelings and experiences. The result is that they own the conclusions that they have come to and have a new and richer understanding of the passage. This was confirmed for me, when two and a half weeks later the minister of the church preached from Luke 7:36-50 about the woman who washed and anointed Jesus' feet at the home of Simon the Pharisee. Three of the Bible study group came up to me after the service and excitedly discussed the relationship between that passage and Jesus' encounter with the woman at the well at Sychar.
   It is not only in Bible-study groups that we tell and re-tell the story of Jesus. We should be conscious of re-telling the death and resurrection of Jesus at every communion service and service of baptism. Each time we hear the words of Jesus, break bread and drink wine, we enter into that story and make it our own once more. In baptism the believer participates in the story—dying with Christ, buried with him (beneath the water) and rising to new life in the power of the Spirit. It is here that we begin our discipleship (see Romans 6:1-14), but to live the Gospel means that we will have to work away, with each new experience, in each new place and at each new time, at re-telling the story persuasively and so naming Christ in the power of the Spirit. We re-contextualize the text again and again.

Preaching that engages with the congregation
Preachers must take the trouble both to understand and to address the forces that shape the lives of those who make up their congregations. They must seek to understand the local context and the important issues that arise within it. The description of Christians as salt, light and yeast

underlines the interaction of believers with their surroundings and emphasizes that the mission of the church is to be good news within a specific
set of human circumstances. The church must never be isolated from its
context. Andy Bruce is right to conclude that 'Churches which fail to
interpret and apply the gospel contextually not only seriously diminish the
word of God, they also frustrate God's mission. Far from affording shelter, Christian commitment should lead to a heightened exposure to the
elements.[11]

It is important that preaching gets to grips with the realities of life,
demonstrating a love and respect for people, living and working in the
world. The members of our congregation are communities of the Word,
who have the responsibility of speaking and sharing the Word. The church
is the Word made flesh, incarnate in the world.

It is thus important that we find ways of enabling our congregations
to tell their own stories and to examine the ways in which their stories
interact with the Gospel story. Alongside the interactive Bible study,
described above, there is the interactive sermon, where members of the
congregation are able to contribute their insights to the questions raised in
the biblical passage. The following is an account of working through a
sermon based on the Mount of Transfiguration narrative taken from the
Gospel according to Luke (Luke 9:28-48) with the fellowship of a Baptist
church on the occasion of their church anniversary.

Introduction
We're going to do something dangerous this evening — I'm going to let
you speak during the sermon!

We're going to think together about the story of the Transfiguration of
Jesus and what happened afterwards, when Jesus and his disciples came
down from the mountain.

Let's read Luke 9:28-36. Jesus has stilled the storm, he has healed the
demon possessed at Gerasa where the pigs rushed into the sea, he has
healed the woman with the menstrual haemorrhage, and he has raised
Jairus' daughter from death to life. Jesus is Lord over nature, Lord over
evil and the demonic, Lord over sickness, and Lord over death. Following
this Jesus asks who they think he is, and Peter answers, 'You are the
Messiah.'

Now, for the three disciples, Peter, James and John, there is an impressive confirmation of Peter's declaration. They get a preview of the future: the glory to come, and the confirmation of God through a voice from heaven.

How did the disciples feel on the mountain that day?
The following are the answers given to that question by the congregation, and written down on an overhead projector slide:
• happy
• excited
• scared, afraid
• bewildered, confused
• amazed
• wanting to stay there—to keep the enjoyment
• wanting to keep near to God
• wanting to preserve the experience—build shelters
• unsure of their response
• out of control
• feeling must do something
• not understanding
• perhaps expectant
• Peter has to say something or do something—this is his vulnerability

Comment by the preacher
Peter's idea was fair enough. He saw three men, each one a manifestation of divine glory and he wanted to capture this fleeting and wonderful moment, this tremendous experience. He would build a tabernacle for each, just as the people of Israel had built a tabernacle in the wilderness to enshrine God's glory. Moses had spoken with God face to face, Elijah was the champion of God, both his beloved servants. But Moses and Elijah, like John the Baptist were part of the old order—they vanish and Peter hears the voice from heaven, the now: 'This is my beloved Son, listen to him!' (c.f. Hebrews 1:1-3).

Jesus fulfils the work of the others. He is the prophet who is to be heard and heeded; he will stand for God's truth; he will provide the church with all that it needs in following him; and he is the servant who treads the path of suffering.

What have been our significant spiritual experiences?
Here are some of the answers offered by the congregation:
• God's closeness in times of need
• baptism
• the assurance of the Holy Spirit
• sunset
• knowledge of God's love for us
• talking to God
• seeing miracles
• the birth of a baby
• conversion
• a wedding
• the faith of a dying person
• answers to prayer
• experience of God in worship

How have we reacted to these?
To this, the following answers were given:
• tears of joy
• a prayer of praise
• amazement at God's activity
• the experience changed me and changed my view of God
• wanting to share, wanting to tell others
• desire to repeat the experience
• overwhelmed: joy, tears, excitement
• challenged: felt uncomfortable
• felt privileged
• became despondent about the real world

What happens next? What did the disciples and Jesus do?
It's time for the disciples to come down from the mountain and accompany Jesus, their glorified Lord and Messiah, into his continuing ministry among the people of Israel. Let's read the rest of the story: Luke 9:37-48.

Now the congregation draws out some of the key points in the story:
• back into the world
• failure
• misunderstanding
• confronted: with people, with themselves, with sickness and evil
• they feel inadequate
• facing the cost of discipleship
• facing everyday realities of life
• Jesus' ministry continues
• the glory is no longer visible
• they show a lack of understanding and faith
• distance between disciples and God
• despondent and disillusioned

Comment by the preacher
They come down from the mountain, into the world of the ministry of the suffering servant; and they fail. They have already seen so much of Jesus' power—to heal, to exorcise demons, to raise the dead, to feed the 5000, to still the storm. They themselves have also experienced this when Jesus sent them out in mission. But they are still immature, still having so much to learn about Jesus and about themselves. A distracted father brings his son to Jesus—the disciples have been unable to cure the boy's epilepsy. Having rebuked them, Jesus heals the boy and all are amazed at the greatness of God.

Then Jesus speaks once more of his passion. They are unprepared for this; they are reluctant to ask him about it; and they did not begin to understand what he is talking about until after the crucifixion and resurrection. Instead of asking Jesus about his passion, they ask each other about their relative importance. It seems incredible that a band of grown men, still more Christian disciples, could argue openly about who was the top member of the group. Their childishness is shown when Jesus takes a child and stands it in their midst and rebukes their lack of humility. To follow means to do the grown-up thing—to serve.

As Christian disciples, we need to think about what it means to follow Jesus today. We need to seek to grow into the maturity of Christ, in humility looking to the needs of others before our own interests.

So what does tomorrow hold for you?

Every member of the congregation was able to contribute an answer to this question. The following is a sample:

• Monday morning
• school
• playgroup
• Christmas shopping
• picking up a pram for my daughter
• celebrating a birthday
• family day
• 'real world'
• family needs
• caring for relatives
• grocery shopping
• cleaning

Conclusion

Special times of encountering God are very important to us; special days and special services or anniversaries are important in our Christian life. But we must not try to preserve them, or simply long to repeat them. We have to live with the daily reality of our lives. This is our journey of faith; this is our daily worship of God. We come together on Sunday as the gathered church to encourage and equip each other for being the scattered church, during the rest of the week. We remember the special times and draw strength from them, just as Peter did, when reflecting upon his experience of the transfiguration (see 2 Peter 1:16-19). Peter says, this is what it was like for me on the mountain with Jesus, Moses and Elijah, and this is how I now live in its light. We go out from here to live for Jesus, to serve him in the world, through the power of the Holy Spirit, always remembering that the God who has encountered us in the past and today, goes ahead of us and is with us until the end of time.

The advantage of this form of sermon presentation is that the congregation have, in part, written the sermon, and will as a result both own it and remember the message more clearly. This method is far more risky for the preacher and demands a greater amount of preparation. The risk is the result of not knowing, exactly, the direction that the sermon will take, hence the need of preparation. It will also require additional skills on the part of the preacher: choosing clear and simple questions, which all can answer; non-judgemental responses to the contributions that are made; careful re-directing of the course of dialogue, when it is running down blind alleys or diverging from the theme of the biblical passage; and sensitivity to the place and timing of the proclamatory aspect of the sermon.

All members of a congregation can respond from their own experiences to the questions posed, and so this is not restricted to the more intellectual members of churches or to those with a great deal of biblical knowledge. Exciting insights often arise from unexpected people. On one occasion I was using this approach in considering Paul's testimony to his encounter with the risen Lord Jesus on the Damascus Road, before King Agrippa (Acts 26). I asked the congregation what they thought Paul would have felt when he discovered that he was persecuting the Messiah. One middle-aged church member, who has learning difficulties (a mental age of about 10 years), was first to answer: 'Betrayed,' he said.

'By whom?' I asked.

'By God,' he explained.

Such experiences of using this approach have increased my confidence in its value for presenting the Gospel.

Exploring pastoral issues

Applied theology is talk about God in the human context. The absolute importance of the application of theology goes without saying for those who are engaged in the mission and ministry of the church of Christ. Doing theology in a pastoral setting is a dynamic thought process involving analysis and insights, the application of resources from faith, and making a practical response. An important fact emerges from such engagement: it becomes clear that a thoroughly secularized community is no longer familiar with Christian ideas and biblical stories. People's natural narratives will probably relate to explicitly local events or to more personal events, based on their family or on an individual's experiences. Here we may recognize the pattern that has already been set for us in the ministry of Jesus—taking local stories and experiences and teaching Gospel truth through them. This may counter the widely held view that the church's answers to contemporary issues no longer convince because they seem to be divorced from experience. However, we need to be aware that any approach that builds on the experience of a group of people runs the risk of being human-centred, and therefore must be placed within our understanding of Christ-centred living.

Christianity is an ethical religion, but it is also a faith that combines mercy and justice. There is a tendency in our modern world to minimize the ethical dimension, which is seen by many people to be judgmental. An emphasis on private morality, 'what's good for me', and on the wide variety of views and accepted standards of behaviour has led to values and practices that are detrimental to society. Common sense is not always the best guide; for example, because most teenagers and young adults agree that sex before marriage with a variety of partners is all right, it does not mean that it may not damage the potential for stable family relationships.

The ethical dimension within pastoral theology questions our norms and values and challenges accepted behaviour patterns. It asks what ideas are being fostered in counselling, questioning whether the stress lies entirely on the individual or whether there is also a consideration of the effects on others. It prompts us to form an approach to such issues as abortion and euthanasia that we might otherwise avoid.

In pastoral encounters we might adopt the pragmatic approach of situation ethics, asking what is demanded of love and justice in a particular situation, regardless of any universal principles; but this is often inconsistent and unreflective. Another unhelpful approach can be an emphasis on love and acceptance which disregards moral standards. In short, there is a need for the church to integrate ethics with acceptance. This form of approach would be one of ethical confrontation within a context of acceptance, with an invitation to explore a better way. In this we avoid a judgmental or repressive approach in favour of finding ways of helping people to discover a better way for themselves. Here we might consider the method adopted by God's prophet Nathan, who told a story to David (2 Samuel 12:1-7) and let it make its own impact, as we saw in Chapter 3. We should allow people to draw their own conclusions and answer their own questions, as Jesus did in telling the story of the Good Samaritan (Luke 10:25-37). In adopting this approach, pastoral practitioners will find themselves challenged to face their own values, and to reflect on their own beliefs and practice as part of a learning cycle.

In considering the Christian lifestyle we cannot separate discipleship from discipline. Church discipline needs to be exercised over Christian character and witness, both of individual members and of the corporate dimension of the church's life and mission. That is, in its teaching, preaching and fellowship the church will seek to encourage nurture and growth, as well as seeking to prevent wrong behaviour. The development of the church's spiritual life through spiritual guidance is vital for growth. Many people have found the support of a spiritual director an important part of their discipleship. In all of these areas of Christian lifestyle and in the various areas of personal, social, business and medical ethics, the Bible will play an important role in our reflection. In the epilogue to his book on pastoral ethics, David Atkinson provides a helpful guiding principle: 'Throughout we have tried to allow the word of God as revealed in the scriptures to illuminate our minds, give us criteria for selecting relevant empirical facts, guide our choice of moral priorities and tune our pastoral responses to the themes of the Gospel.'[12]

When we consider the place of the Bible in our approach to Christian lifestyle, we will recognize the dangers of a biblicism that merely appeals to proof texts and will seek to discern theological guidelines instead. We should encourage the finding of a Christian lifestyle that belongs within the whole framework of the Gospel message, rather than being attached to a few texts, and for which God's character of love will be the overriding principle. In developing guidelines for behaviour, we must thoroughly consider the biblical perspective to each life issue, together with historical responses within the church tradition, relevant factual information and secular views and understanding. This will result in a coverage that is comprehensive, but not always clear-cut for those who would like to have easy answers to complex issues. When church leaders or church groups consider situations of Christian lifestyle they will need to recognize that to embark on such discussions will involve a great deal of time and tough thinking, sometimes accompanied by painful readjustment.

We might take as an example of a vital pastoral question the place that cohabitation has within the church's teaching about marriage. This is an issue that affects both young and old, inside and outside the church. The factors involved are complex and need time for investigation and discussion by the church. I have explored this subject in detail elsewhere[13] and offer the following as a summary of the areas in which research will be required, and of the theological issues that may arise.

The importance of such discussion by the church is raised when it faces a particular pastoral situation such as that of Rachel and Patrick (not their real names) who come to ask to be married in church. Rachel, the daughter of committed church members has been living with Patrick for over two years. They are committed to each other, have bought a house and are carefully building a home. They now believe that it is the right time to get married, their relationship having been 'tested' through living together. Rachel has been brought up in a Christian home and has an understanding of the Gospel and wants God to be a part of her future life with Patrick. Patrick is from a non-Christian background but is sympathetic to Rachel's wishes and is willing to discuss the implications of the Christian Gospel for his life. Rachel's parents have 'fallen over backwards' in not putting pressure on the couple.

What should the minister say? What will the church say to such a situation? Before these questions can be properly answered, others need to be asked. What are the facts about the society in which we live? What was the situation in the first century when the church was founded? What does the Bible have to say? What has the church practised through the years?

When we refer to the current state of society, we find that Government surveys define cohabitation as 'a co-resident man and woman living together within a sexual union, without that union having been formalized with either a civil or religious ceremony.' For marriages that took place in 1987 58% of men and 53% of women claimed to have lived with their future spouse prior to marriage. The 2003 UK Government General Household Survey states that 25% of all men and 27% of women aged 16-59 were cohabiting. The highest figures were recorded for men 25-29 at 31% and women 25-29 at 32%, but when this included those who were separated rather than single or divorced the numbers increased to 39% for men and 49% for women aged 25-29.[14] Figures produced by Anglican parishes in London reveal that in 1993 up to 90% of couples seeking marriage were living together. We are living in the midst of a sexual revolution brought about by advances in medicine, changes in society's attitudes and teaching, economic pressures (e.g. the high cost of housing), and the influence of a high divorce rate leading couples to embark on 'trial marriages.' Cohabitation is essentially a private arrangement, in contrast to marriage, where the public witnessing is an important element.

When we turn back to first-century society, we see Jesus attending a marriage at Cana in Galilee (John 2:1-11), but all that is recorded is a party, where the wine ran out. We need to investigate the marriage practices in Jewish society, the Hellenistic world, and in Roman society. The early church does not seem to have held a religious ceremony, perhaps recognising that commitment to marriage was within the new covenant community (see Paul's teaching in 1 Corinthians 6 & 7).

The foundation for our understanding of marriage is to be found in the opening chapters of the Bible (Genesis 1:26-27, 31). The goodness of creation, including sexuality, affirmed there is underlined in Song of Songs 4:1-5; 5:10-16. Genesis 2:18-25 declares the relatedness and oneness of human sexuality, and the story of the creation of the human being in Genesis 2:7 shows the interdependence and interwoven nature of male and female. The domination of women by men lies after the fall of humanity (Genesis 3:16). In Christ we thus affirm our full sexuality: love's intensity, restraint, mutuality and permanence. A word of Jesus tells us that lust creates bad sex (Matthew 5:28), and he declares the original design of God for committed relationship, affirming the life-unity of one flesh (Matthew 19:4-6). Yet we note Jesus' attitude toward those in a cohabiting or adulterous relationship (John 4:16-26; 8:1-11), who were neither rejected nor condemned, but rather invited to find something new in Christ.

As we look over two thousand years of church history, we see that a nuptial mass first appeared in the fifth century. Monogamous life-long union dates in Europe from the twelfth century. In 1175 the Council of Westminster decreed the need of a statement of consent for the marriage to be valid. Luther considered marriage to be a civil contract requiring no church involvement, but we should recall that at this point society was considered to be 'Christian' and so, as in the Jewish society of the New Testament, such marriages would be within the covenant community. In 1753 the Marriage Act was passed, which stated that the only legal marriages were those conducted within the Church of England, with exception clauses for Jews and Quakers. All other marriages were 'Common Law' marriages. Cohabitation was fairly common, especially as a short term arrangement prior to marriage. Legal marriage reached its high water mark in 1950s.

In the light of all this, church groups may like to consider the following questions:

- Is cohabitation marriage in the sense of the creation ordinance?
- What is marriage? Is it the creation ordinance (Genesis 2:25); a civil or legal marriage; or Christian marriage and church ceremony?
- What difference is made to a Christian marriage by the vows that form a part of the service?
- What do the church community express by their presence at a wedding service?
- What then will the church say to those who cohabit?

A Christian, by definition, is someone who has invited Jesus to be the Lord of his or her life. A Christian marriage is where two such people have invited Jesus to be Lord of their married life together. When Jesus is invited into our relationships he brings his love, strength, faithfulness, courage, and peace (*shalom* means wholeness). This has got to be good news for all who cohabit. What is important is to move on from just living together to a marriage in which these qualities can be fostered. To those inside the church, in an area of widespread marital breakdown, we must then bring biblical teaching about marriage relationships. To those outside the church we will have to give an apologia (a positive defence of the Christian view in the face of alternative opinions in the world) for marriage, presenting God's better way. An excellent place to start might be the marriage feast described in John 2:1-11, presenting the transformation that Jesus can bring to any of life's situations.

Exploring societal issues
The possibilities that are now apparent for assistance with the conception and development of human life are enormous. Coupled with the delay in starting a family for many couples and the increased incidence of diffi-

culty in conception, interest in the whole area of the human genome and genetic engineering is growing.

In October 2000 great concern was expressed over the ethics of creating 'designer babies'. In the USA the Nash family were involved in the 'engineering' of baby Adam as an exact tissue match for his sister Molly, to act as a donor to save her from the genetic disease *Fanconi anaemia*. In the UK dozens of couples have already opted for pre-implantation genetic diagnosis (PGD) to avoid giving birth to children with serious genetic disorders such as cystic fibrosis and haemophilia.

A year later in December 2001 the UK Human Fertilization and Embryology Authority suggested that in some cases it might be acceptable for embryos to be checked to see if they are a tissue match for an existing child. This would enable blood from the new baby's umbilical cord to be used in bone marrow transplants. This decision implied that Raj and Shahana Hashmi, from Leeds, might have received the go-ahead to use only embryos that precisely matched the tissue makeup of their son Zain, who has *thalassaemia*, a potentially fatal blood disorder. (*Thalassaemia* is one of the conditions for which PGD can be carried out.) However, this suggestion raised strong negative reaction from pro-life groups. Initially, the HFEA, which regulates the use of IVF embryos in the UK, considered giving the Hashmis the green light, but said that future applications would be assessed on a case-by-case basis. In the final analysis, the permission of the HFEA was not granted to the Hashmi family.

In June 2003 this issue was raised again. Michelle and Jayson Whitaker's baby, Jamie, was genetically selected while he was still an embryo to be a near perfect match for four year old Charlie. The couple went to an American clinic for test tube baby treatment because the selection procedure is not allowed in the UK. The Whitakers bought treatment in the USA, while the Hashmi family are still waiting for a HFEA review of their decision so that they, too, can save their child, Zain. The *Observer* newspaper commented, in 22 June 2003, that few of us would want to deny this family the chance of saving their child's life.

New techniques offer great hopes but also raise ethical dilemmas, particularly in the emotive field of fertility. Is it right to bring a child into the world with a predetermined genetic make-up to offer a lifesaving cure for an existing child? And if so, is it also right for would-be parents to choose characteristics—blue eyes, for example—of an unborn child, the so-called 'designer baby?' If we just follow common sense, we might welcome the first, but oppose the second. We might reason that in seeking to avoid the trap of 'designer babies' we may prevent giving humanitarian aid to those parents who wish to save their children. *The Observer* in its article adds: 'No parents should have to nurse a dying infant knowing a technique exists to save their child.' It sounds a brilliant way of saving a child's life, doesn't it? But many people see this technique as the start of a slippery slope that leads to human cloning.

How shall we reflect on this issue theologically, and integrate our conclusions into our lives? For the sake of limiting the discussion to manageable proportions, we will concentrate on the production of babies, through IVF (in-vitro fertilization), in order to cure a genetically-induced terminal illness in a sibling.

On *Radio Five Live*, June 23rd, 2003, Professor Robert Winston expressed his view that the central issue is that such a child has effectively been brought into the world as a kind of commodity, and will know this. He posed the question of how this child will feel as it grows up, always knowing that it is the perfect organ donor for any problem that its sibling may have, and he expressed his fear that the child would be obliged to give other stem cells to a sibling later in life. He suggested that doctors should be focusing on finding realistic cures rather than a solution which he felt had little chance of working.

To Professor Winstone's questions we may add the following:

- For the scientist who has developed the technique the dilemma is summed up in the question: 'we can, but should we'?
- Doctors and clinicians find themselves wrestling with surprising non-scientific questions, such as: 'How do I feel when I can play God'?
- For parents, family and medical staff in a situation where one child is produced as a source of 'spare parts' for a sibling—even as just one reason for being born—the question arises: is this child being treated as second class?
- The wider scientific question concerns the human gene pool. If we move into the area of designer babies, where only the perfect are born, are we limiting the possibility of the unique, the genius, the novelty, the 'abnor-

mal?' Will we risk denying society of the inventive, the artistic, the creative and the eccentric?

- From a theological point of view we will want to stress that we are not captives of our genes. We have freedom of will, and we are all open to the transformation of the Holy Spirit.
- From a sociological perspective, the question is: are we in danger of moving into eugenics? Is this a return to the kind of medical experiments conducted by the Nazi party in Germany in 1930s and 1940s?

The diagram in figure 4.2 may help to focus our reflection.[15]

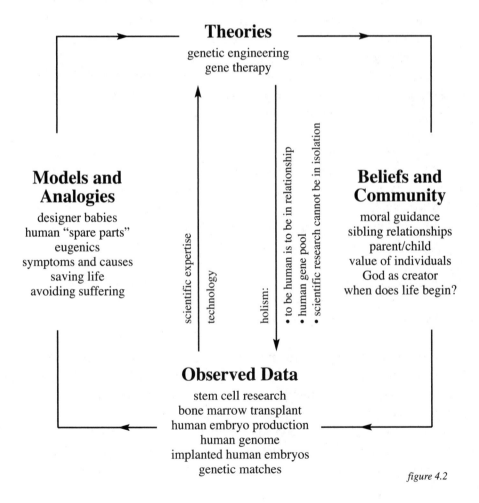

figure 4.2

We start with the *observed data*:

- Medical science is able to treat certain life-threatening disorders through bone marrow transplants and stem cell implants.
- Medical science has perfected the production of embryos in the laboratory.
- Medical science is able to identify and isolate individual genes in human embryos.
- It is possible for embryos of a specific genetic make-up to be implanted in a mother's womb.
- It is possible to produce a child who has the exact genetic match to be the perfect donor for a sibling with a life-threatening disorder

If we follow the vertical upward arrow on the diagram, that is of scientific materialism—asserting 'we have the technology'—we find ourselves in the position of being able to provide a potential cure for certain genetic diseases. This is the theory, at least. But we note the misgivings of Robert Winston, and his concern over possible success rates for the procedure.

We see the relevance of considering the left hand pathway on the diagram, where the observed data passes through the sharing of models and analogies, which evoke understanding and response. This is the area of imagination and leaps of sympathy. We will want to consider the following:

- Designer babies may be an ultimate end point of this process.
- One child might be reduced to being produced as 'spare parts' for another, and so a mere 'commodity'.
- There is an analogy with with 1930s experiments in eugenics.
- There is a trap in treating symptoms rather than seeking the cause and so a possible cure.
- But, positively, there is the possibility of saving life, and avoiding suffering.

Beyond this, it will be useful to explore the right hand side of the diagram and consider the influence of beliefs in both scientific and religious communities. Some of the issues we may identify as:

- The help sought by doctors' in ethical and moral guidance for the techniques that they are researching and perfecting.
- Inherited values about the relationship of siblings to each other, and of children to parents, which might be changed where it is known that one child has been produced for a particular reason.
- Belief about the value of each human life to God.
- Understandings of God as the author and creator of life.
- Differing convictions about when human life begins: fertilization, implantation, 'quickening', or viable existence outside the womb?

Finally we can consider the vertical downward arrow in the diagram, testing a theory or a practice through understanding persons and the world as a whole. First, what makes a human being human are relationships — with each other, with the whole created world, and with God. One must ask whether these relationships are in danger of being destroyed by genetic manipulation. There is, second, the state of the natural gene pool of which each individual is a part. When we restrict human reproduction, will we prevent novelty and diversity, which can result in genius? Theologically, too, we may be restricting God's grace in creation. Third, scientific research on human beings cannot act in isolation, as environmental science is helping us to understand the holistic nature of the whole of creation. Ecology is not a chain of cause and effect but a web of interconnectedness. 'Once we learn that the lives of snails and sparrows are linked to our own in a dozen ways, the meaning of ecology gradually expands to include every other aspect of human life and well-being.'[16] Theologically, we may envision this connectedness as the participation of creation in the life of the triune God who lives in communion.

We might now be in a position to pull all these factors together. Mechanical descriptions of genetic engineering do not tell the whole story. A merely rational and objective analysis fails to uncover a full understanding of the situation. Those involved in the process must be part of the truth of the situation. So we must take account of the experiences and feelings of the scientists involved. We must also recognize the effect on the values and beliefs of a society in which such procedures are allowed to take place. We must take account of the feelings within the family for whom this procedure is conducted; especially we should consider the relationship that will exist between the siblings. Finally, in our theological reflection we should consider the hidden relationships of Creator to creation.

Exercise 4.1
Consider elderly people nearing the end of life.
a. Read Ephesians 6:1-3; Acts 2:17; and Old Testament insights from Leviticus 19:32; Proverbs 16:31; 23:22.

b. Discuss questions such as: can we distinguish between pain management and euthanasia? Have people the right to die in the same way as they have a right to life? How strenuously should doctors seek to prolong life? Can we justify the expenditure for keeping people alive? Who decides on laws in this area: the public, the doctors, the government, or the church?

Issues portrayed in film and on television
One way in which congregations can be helped to reflect theologically on life issues is through the medium of film and television. A group may be invited to watch a film together, or agree to watch a television programme one day and discuss it on another, or use can be made of television advertisements.

Films can become a vehicle of the gospel, and I have used them with a variety of study groups. Having watched the film, discussion is facilitated by identifying significant questions raised by the film. I have found films such as: *The Mission, Witness, Kramer vs. Kramer, The Color Purple, Blade Runner, Cry Freedom, 1984, Schindler's List, Saving Private Ryan*, and *Bridget Jones' Diary* useful in opening up discussion.[17] Here I want to take as an example the film *Hotel Rwanda*, released by United Artists in December 2004 and directed by Terry George.[18]

The film uses the tag line: 'When the world closed its eyes, he opened his arms.' Don Cheadle stars in the true-life story of Paul Rusesabagina, a hotel manager who housed over a thousand Tutsi refugees during their struggle against the Hutu militia in Rwanda. His compassion, humanity and quick thinking allowed him to 'open his arms' and save 1,268 Tutsi refugees from being slaughtered during the 1994 Rwandan genocide. Paul Rusesabagina is not a perfect human being. As manager of the Belgian-owned Mille Collines, a luxury hotel in Kigali, the Rwandan capital, he knew when to bribe corrupt officials, to ease the smooth running of the hotel and his own comfortable life. However, these connections became his salvation when Rwanda descended into civil war, and Rusesabagina became an unlikely hero.

At the start of the genocide, Rwanda had a population of six million people, who were about 85 percent Hutu and 15 percent Tutsi. The primary cause of the conflict can be traced back to European colonialism. The Belgian rulers saw the tall, thin Tutsis as superior to the short, stocky Hutus, and tended to give them the main positions of power.

The Hutus naturally resented this favouritism and when Rwanda became independent in 1962, there was a Hutu dictatorship, who blamed the Tutsis for every problem. The civil war and genocide depicted in the film resulted from the assassination of the Rwandan president, Juvenal Habyarimana, a Hutu, on his way back from signing a peace agreement. His plane was shot down above the Kigali airport on April 6, 1994, an act blamed on Tutsi rebels.

Within hours Hutu militia began the genocide of all Tutsi citizens. The slaughter spread to much of the Rwandan countryside, where Hutu peasants were encouraged to kill their Tutsi neighbours. At its peak, the genocide claimed 8,000 lives per day, and in all some 800,000 lost their lives. The international community sought to avoid using the word 'genocide' lest they be obliged, under the UN Geneva Convention, to intervene.

Synopsis of the film

The scene is set in Kilgali, the capital of Rwanda, in 1994. Power is in the hands of Hutus, and we are told that the Tutsis were collaborators with the Belgium colonialists—collaborators and traitors. The hotel manager, Paul Rusesabagina is presented as a self-seeking man, trying to gain influence with the Hutu political leaders and the UN Commander. He wines and dines them at the hotel, where he is the manager. He is storing up favours, but the deadline for the signing of the UN peace agreement is approaching.

We are introduced to Paul's family: his wife, Tatiana is a Tutsi, while Paul is a Hutu. They see one of their neighbours being beaten by the militia, but Paul closes his high gate and says, 'Family is all that matters.' He hopes that the peace agreement signed by the President in Tanzania will mean that 'we all find peace,' and when warned of the danger of the Hutu militia, he says 'but the world press are watching.'

With the murder of the President by the Tutsi rebels there is fear, and violence increases into civil war. The cry goes up from the Hutu radio: 'Cut the tall trees (Tutsis) now!' We see militia on the streets and dead bodies on the lawns in front of houses. Paul and his family, and friends are escorted by his contacts in the army to the hotel. There is panic and all the foreigners leave the hotel and Rwanda. The situation is getting worse; a news cameraman brings video evidence of a massacre just 'half a mile down the road' from the hotel. The world must see it and intervene they say, but the cameraman explains the truth that they will see it over their cornflakes—they will be upset, but they will not intervene.

There is the promise of a multinational intervention force, but when it arrives only the whites are rescued. Paul recognizes that they've been abandoned. He says to his wife, 'I thought I was one of them [the rich and influential foreigners]—I've been a fool.' He assures her that he will never leave her.

Hutu soldiers arrive at the hotel telling everyone to leave—their massacre is imminent. Paul offers them beer and while they are drinking he tries to get hold of his friend the Hutu general, but with no success. Then he phones the hotel owner in Belgium, saying that they will all be killed: 100 staff and 800 guests (refugees). The hotel owner calls the UN and the Belgium Prime Minister, but Paul tells him, 'Get hold of the French Prime Minister, they supply the army.'

Meanwhile the Hutu soldiers want the hotel guest list. 'Get me the names of all the cockroaches (Tutsis) now!' shouts their commander. But before they can do anything, the soldiers are called away—'Who did you call?' he asks Paul. Seeing that the western governments will do nothing to help, Paul gets all the refugees to use the hotel telephones to call anyone they know in power, any government officials from their own African countries of origin. He adds that 'The fact that this is a four star hotel is all that is keeping us alive.' The Hutu general tells Paul: 'Your white friends have abandoned you.' But Paul continues to ask for protection, assuring the general that the rich Belgium hotel owner will reward him.

The UN commander arrives with the news that their telephone calls have worked, and he has exit visas for many of the families, but not all. As the radio reports that the death toll in the Rwandan conflict may have reached 500,000, Paul says goodbye to those who are left at the hotel. But then he changes his mind, he can't leave them—he asks someone to take care of his wife and children and shuts the lorry tailgate. But the convoy under UN protection doesn't get far before it is attacked by the militia. Fortunately Paul manages to notify the Hutu army, who rescue them and return them to the hotel. Paul has nothing else with which to bribe the Hutu general, who then says: 'No more police; no more protection!'

The hotel comes under mortar attack from the Tutsi army who are attacking the city. The UN commander suggests that they get to the other side of the Tutsi lines, where they will be safe. They leave in another UN convoy, with all the refugees from the hotel. They travel along the road toward the Tutsi lines with streams of refugees moving towards them, travelling in the opposite direction. Behind the refugees come the rebel army, who are being attacked by the Hutu militia. The convoy safely gets through the Tutsi lines and reach a Red Cross refugee camp. They are told by the UN commander, 'Buses on the other side of the camp will take you to Tanzania.' Many of the former hotel 'guests' thank Paul and his wife, who are re-united with their nieces in the camp.

Issues for reflection
This film is a *Schindler's List*[19] for the Third World. In the midst of the killing of almost one million Tutsis, Paul Rusesabagina saves 1268 through using the influence he has over corrupt officials and through further payment of bribes. We can consider a number of specific issues raised in our minds by the film.

First, there is the question of Paul Rusesabagina's character: is he a good man? In only three months, one million people were brutally murdered. In the face of these unspeakable actions, inspired by his love for his family, it appears that an ordinary man summons extraordinary courage to save the lives of over a thousand helpless refugees, by granting them shelter in the hotel he manages.

Is this the result of mere circumstances, or is there real goodness here? Paul is clearly presented, at the beginning of the film as self-serving, but as the film progresses he uses the influence he has contrived to gain through bribery to secure the safety of the refugees. Early in the film, Paul is told to kill the Tutsis in his group, including his own wife: 'Shoot them or die,' orders the Hutu army general. Paul pays bribes for his wife and family. Then he seeks to find bribes to pay for the lives of the rest. He gathers all the money they have, only to be told that it is 'enough for one. Pick one.' But Paul promises to get another 100,000 francs, and manages to get everyone to the hotel, where he is now left in charge. An International Red Cross worker arrives at the hotel with 20 children from the St Francis Orphanage, whom Paul accepts. He remembers being told: 'Never, never lower the tone of the hotel,' with the threat of losing his job; but now, he thinks, 'I have taken in orphans and Tutsis.'

Towards the end of the film we see the children playing around the hotel and everyone being fed. Paul's wife says: 'You're a good man, Paul.' She adds, 'We've had a good life. I thank God everyday for the time we've had.' So the film vividly presents us with the question: how do we define goodness?

Another key question is this: where was God in the Rwandan genocide? There are powerful images in this film that speak of the evil that human beings inflict on each other. On the way to a wholesaler to get food, Paul drives past burning houses and evidence of torture and massacre. The wholesaler says, 'Soon all the Tutsis will be dead.' Paul says, 'You can't kill them all,' to which he replies, 'We're half way there already.' The return journey at night is along a misty, strangely bumpy back country road that ends with Paul realising that he's bouncing over hundreds of dead bodies. We see a UN convoy carrying refugees from the hotel, which is forced into a stand off with a machete-wielding mob. The UN commander and a handful of Belgian troops fight to keep their human cargo alive.

Should we be warned by the challenging words attributed to the English jurist Edmund Burke 'The only thing necessary for the triumph of

evil is for good men to do nothing'?[20] But is God only to be found in the
courageous stance of a few good people?

Finally, there is the question of stewardship and responsibility in a
world of inequality, injustice and violence. By repeatedly emphasising the
failure of the West to send an intervention force into the troubled country,
Hotel Rwanda asks probing questions about the lack of willingness to do
anything to alleviate the suffering of the ordinary people of Rwanda. The
film makes some damning statements about the First World's racist foreign policy decisions. The UN has no mandate to intervene in the
massacres. 'We are peacekeepers, not peacemakers' says their commander. When the whites only are rescued, the powerless UN commander,
Colonel Oliver, tells Paul Rusesabagina in self-criticism: 'We think that
you're dirt,' and 'We're not going to stop this;' and he adds, 'You're not
black . . . You're African.'

Around one million Tutsis were killed by the Hutu majority over the
course of 100 days while the West turned a blind eye. This is a powerful
indictment of our culpability. One critic cynically commented that this is
cathartic cinema—watch it, feel bad, then go home and wait for the
sequel, 'Hotel Sudan.'

After the Holocaust, the international community pledged 'never
again' to allow genocide to take place. But it did happen in Cambodia, the
former Yugoslavia, and in Rwanda. Throughout 2004-2005 evidence of
genocide has been unfolding in the Darfur region of Sudan. That conflict
erupted in February 2003, when black rebels took up arms against what
they saw as years of state neglect and discrimination against Sudanese of
African origin. The Arab government, aided by a militia known as the
Janjaweed, cracked down on the rebels and their perceived supporters,
creating what the UN has described as the world's worst humanitarian crisis. More than 70,000 people have been killed or have died from hunger
and disease in the area, according to the UN, and another 1.5 million people have been displaced. How, then, do we exercise our God-given
responsibilities?

Here I have concentrated on a film as material for theological reflection. Television drama and the numerous 'soaps' provide further ground
for study, and perhaps an area that is overlooked is that of television
advertisements. These have the advantage of being easily accessible, con-

stantly repeated and short. Adverts give a snapshot of the ways in which people think (or at least how those who do the research for adverts believe that people think), and the things that are important for people. The groups of adverts that may be useful include: adverts for cars that suggest that they are more important than human relationships (Renault, Pergeot and VW adverts in particular); the growing number of adverts that indicate our preoccupation with money and pleasure (for example: financial loans, accident claims, and chat lines); and the general range of consumer durables that we cannot live without. For example, there was an advert screened before Christmas 2005 on behalf of Mastercard: 'Digital camera, £390; more food than you'll ever eat, £185; bibs, £11; Christmas with your first grandchild: priceless. There are some things money can't buy. For everything you need at Christmas there's Mastercard.' Adverts can be captured on video or DVD and presented as a montage for discussion.

Exercise 4.2

Choose an important life issue such as, relationship breakdown or divorce, 'falling in love', fear or concern for the future.

a. How is this aspect of life handled by advertisements or within the story line of a TV 'soap?'

b. Compare these representations with Christian understanding and the teaching of the church.

c. What insights can we find for our engagement in mission?

Exploring work and employment issues

Church members find themselves on the cutting edge of mission, but they often compartmentalize work, life and worship. Engaging our faith with our everyday activities can be very demanding and pose some uncomfortable and challenging questions. We may find that people would prefer that the church avoided too much teaching about the relation between faith and work. As we saw in chapter 1, many in society do not want Christian worship services and Bible studies that engage with their daily lives, because such ministry would confront the false values of careerism and consumerism on their own ground. Yet, Christian discipleship is a full-time occupation, seven days a week.

How do we react to the Liberation theologians' challenge that we should be more concerned for *orthopraxis* (right doing) rather than *orthodoxy*? Jesus (Matthew 7:15-27 and 25:31-46) and James (James 2:14-26) certainly underlined orthopraxis. Statistics suggest that 47% of Christians say that church teaching is irrelevant to their daily lives, and this is not a problem of form (contemporary versus traditional) but rather one of content. When asked the question: 'What work do you do for God?' many answer with their roles in church. What we do outside the context of church is not viewed as being 'holy' — it is simply a source of income.

There have been tremendous changes in the pattern of work. In the UK, jobs in the service sector increased by 36% from 15.6 million in 1978 to 21.2 million in 2000. During the same period jobs in manufacturing fell by 39% from 7 million in 1978 to 4.2 million in 2000.[21] In 1971 40% of workers were women, but by 2001 this had risen to 45%, and it is now approaching 50%. Part-time jobs for women have increased significantly during the same period. At the beginning of the twenty first century only 2% of the UK population work in agriculture and 16% in manufacturing. We are both a post-agrarian and a post-industrial society.

Opinion polls of people at work — whether in the UK or the USA — find that most people have taken on more responsibility, think that their workload has increased greatly in recent years, judge that their work interferes more in their home life than five years ago, and are concerned about the security of their job. One of the main reasons for these increases is seen as the pace of change in work.

A key question to be asked in reflecting on the world of employment is: what is to be counted as work? If I do my garden in the evenings or decorate the living room at the weekend it is leisure, but for a gardener or decorator it is work. I can play cricket or football as a leisure activity, but for a Michael Vaughan or a Steven Gerrard it is work. So, should we define work as paid employment? But if work is what is paid for, how shall we regard housework or caring in the family, especially in a society where we are often defined by what we do?

Do we work simply to earn enough money to live? In our modern society, with the growth of professions and choice in career, there is a demand that our work should be meaningful in itself. The result can be greater pain and more severe loss of dignity in being unemployed.

In our mobile society there is an increasing separation of the place of work from the area of community and home. On the other hand, with the increased use of the Internet, for some people the workplace can be too much identified with home, with all the tensions that this brings. There is also an alienation of workers both from their tools and from the finished product. The worker uses the firm's equipment and rarely works from the beginning to the conclusion of the job or product. This gives a sense of powerlessness.

Ann Bradshaw has helpfully explored another feature of work today, the move from covenant to contract in the caring professions. In her book *Lighting the Lamp: the Spiritual Dimension of Nursing Care*[22] she examines the way that being in covenant with patients and fellow-workers in giving care has been replaced by a contractual agreement with the employer to deliver a specific level of treatment. Teaching has made the same kind of move, from helping students to learn, to 'delivering courses'. Even pastoral ministry is in danger of moving from a covenant with the congregation (and God) to a contract with the local church government to fulfil designated tasks. Some ministers are also wanting to define contracted hours and time off.

There is no theological body of truth that we can apply directly to the complex situations encountered at work. There will need to be discussion and reflection as we look for responses and action. There is, however, a theological framework for thinking. We need to re-interpret our understanding of work in terms of the redemption brought through the cross of Jesus. The 'image of God' in which we were made, and which has been marred by human fallenness, is a sharing in the work of God as creator. The redemption in Christ restores the capacity of work to be *imago dei*, co-creative with God.

When we explore a theology of work, we can consider work as duty, vocation or service. The so-called 'Protestant work-ethic' presented the view that work was a *duty* we owe to God in response toward God's grace. But it was Martin Luther, at the birth of Protestantism, who suggested that all of life, including daily work, was to be understood as a *vocation* from God. The concept of the 'priesthood of all believers' gives a sense of all Christians having a calling, expressed in the workplace, the home, as well as the pulpit. Further, when we consider the action of Christ, who as servant, gave himself for the world, we can image human activity primarily in terms of *service* to God and others. Jürgen Moltmann adds that work needs to be understood in the light of the pain and struggle of the passion of Christ, whereby the work of redemption in Christ crucified sets all our work in a new context.[23]

The understanding of work as duty proves less than helpful in our modern context. Duty has become a powerful force in a secular capitalist system, becoming linked with notions of competition, profit and career achievement, which do not sit comfortably with a Christian understanding of love for God and neighbour. Even the idea of vocation needs modification. The flexibility and impermanence of career structure and work pattern means that we will need to conceive of vocations that shift and change in our world of redundancies, retraining and job-sharing. Service, however, remains a concept of permanent value in work today, as is recognized in secular management theory.[24]

Fundamental to a Christian view of work is the witness that Christians give through it. It is when we are at work in the workplace or in our own homes that people see us as we really are. They see the difference that Christ makes when we fail or succeed, when we are irritable and annoyed, when we deal with gossip and blame. Here they will see whether our honesty and integrity matter, whether God matters to us or not. In the UK Christians may only be 10% or less of the population, but they have a great potential for influencing others. The fact that many Christians spend some 40 hours a week with, on average, 50 other people represents a huge opportunity and challenge.

We are not instruments but persons, with both a reflective and performance aspect to our work. There must be space to reflect on who we are and what we have done, and are doing. Work should be limited so that there is space in our lives where we are free for God. That space can include leisure and play, or simply quiet and rest. We set ourselves free to hear God, and so this space will include prayer and worship, and enjoying the world and its creator. This can be compared with the picture that we find in Genesis 3:8 of walking with God in the garden in the cool of the evening.

A survey conducted in the UK in 1992-1993[25] of 368 Christians at work has revealed some challenging results for the churches. Seeking to establish some factual information, the survey asked five major questions:

- How did Christians, as Christians, view their working experience and the organizations which employed them?
- How did they engage and communicate as Christians with others in the workplace?
- How did the local church validate and resource its members in their working lives?
- How did the church as a whole draw on and make use of their experiences at work?
- What insights, skills and resources might Christians at work want to help them fulfil that aspect of their ministry?

The respondents were 60% male and 40% female, with a mean age in the mid-forties. 83% were managerial or professional, and expressed high job satisfaction. 92% saw their work as a Christian vocation, and 84% saw their work to some extent as part of the mission of the church; in addition they spent an average of four hours per week on church activities, many holding church offices. These people are then amongst the most highly committed of church members, which makes their responses all the more challenging to the church. The following are some of the issues and questions raised by the survey.

a. *Personal problems faced at work*

- Management issues: poor communication; low motivation; difficult decisions.
- Colleague issues: language, sexism; care; relationships.
- Nature of work issues: tiredness; stress; boredom; difficulty in establishing priorities.
- Resource issues: lack of resources; poor working conditions; non-payment of bills owed to the company.
- Personal issues: time away from home; uncertainties; difficulty in switching the mind off from work.
- Value issues: ethics; profit versus service.

b. *Questions that work raises about faith*
The following broad questions were raised. The percentage of respondents who identified the particular issue is also indicated.

• The relevance of faith and church to work: 30%.
• The conflict between business ethics and Christian principles: 23%.
• The desire for justice and the wish to be seen by others to be fair: 11%.
• Showing Christ in a multi-faith society: 10%.
• The difficulty of acting with integrity when in a position of authority: 8%.
• The creation of wealth, especially personal wealth: 5%.

c. *The place of the church*
Questions about the nature of the church's response to work issues received the following replies:

• Does the worship of your local church affirm you in your work? 35% little or not at all; 17% very much
• How could worship affirm work? Through knowledge of each other's work and life.
• How much do church members know of each other's work? 47% little or not at all; 5% a great deal.
• Does pastoral care support you in your work? 33% very little; 24% not at all; 9% very much.
• Do educational programmes in your church address your faith and work concerns? 50% very little or not at all; 3% very much.

Over a third of respondents felt that Sunday worship was separated from the rest of the week. They expressed a need for daily work to be valued in the worship, preaching and teaching programmes of the church. They placed the following as priority issues for those programmes: ethics, care, management, employment, ambition, wealth creation, justice and fair trading. The responses indicate both a do-it-yourself theology and the failure of two cultures—work and worship—to connect. The church appears to ignore the large issue of the relation between ethics and faith, while concentrating on private morals. There is a danger of emphasising values and virtues without understanding their basis in the doctrines of creation, incarnation and redemption.

It is clear that the church will need to develop a theology of work that will enable its members to reflect upon their own experiences in the light of their faith. The faith community will also need to give time to working through the ethical issues that are raised within the workplace, as well as those that arise as moral dilemmas in personal life. The role of the clergy will be vital, as new forms of leadership are required to enable such integration of faith and work to take place. Leaders will need to be able to create learning communities which will encourage the discussion of faith and ethical issues in the context of work, and to develop a theology of public life.

Just one model of learning that can assist this kind of reflection was developed by Ian Fraser in the 1970s, to be used in a course for Industrial Mission staff.[26] He offers a useful process for a group to work through a case study, which relates to a major issue in a particular firm or industry:

- Identify the most significant themes in the story of the case.
- Select a manageable number of these themes.
- For each theme list:
    the powers at work in it
    the human consequences.
- Identify Biblical and theological resources relevant to the most significant 'powers' and 'human consequences'.
- Apply this material to the original situation.

The integration of the results of this study into practical discipleship will involve a humility before God and before people; a recognition that God is present in his world; a holding onto the values of God's Kingdom in the face of the world's values; involvement with others who are seeking those values in our society; and an openness to work in the ways and in the places that God is working.

Politics and power

While care of the individual is an important task for the church and the pastoral counsellor, pastoral ministry has often fallen into the trap of thinking too narrowly. When people are allowed to tell their stories often a great deal of pain emerges. The problem is that the church as a social group either wants to deny the pain or to soothe it. There can thus be a conflict between the principles that motivate the carers and the behaviour of the institutions within which they operate.

Stephen Pattison provides six basic principles to move pastoral careers away from an individualistic and church-centred paradigm: analyzing the socio-political context; creating an option for the oppressed; becoming the organic intellectuals within oppressed groups; co-operating with such groups who are seeking to change society; realizing that this is an unfinished model; and determining that individual pastoral care will continue, but not as a denial of the wider reality.[27]

In his study of the prophetic voice in modern society, John Davies has commented: 'Any claiming of the prophetic tradition for our contemporary world would have to include a critique of our systems of taxation and land-tenure: nothing, surely, could be more fundamentally public and basically ethical. And yet how often do you see these subjects addressed in our standard dictionaries of Christian ethics?'[28] We might add, and how often do we hear them addressed in sermons and the teaching of the church?

Jesus faced temptations in the arenas of politics and power (Matthew 4:1-11; Luke 4:1-13). These present us with the reality of the temptations that also face us in our modern world. They each have social implications, as we see Jesus tempted to follow one of three options. There is the political option, as he is shown all the nations of the world, the religious option, of a miraculous demonstration in the Temple precincts, or the economic option, of providing bread for all the world's hungry. Jesus might have considered the political, religious or economic power blocs of his day but, notes Donald Kraybill,[29] he chose an alternative way.

Jesus could have been the political liberating Messiah, a new Caesar overthrowing the world's powers (Matthew 4:8; Luke 4:6). But as Kraybill points out, Jesus was a revolutionary, who opted for words and acts of love, rather than the Zealot's dagger. Jesus could have begun his ministry with a miracle—jumping off a pinnacle of the Temple and being caught by angels, but the signs that Jesus did perform were never enough and the religious leaders asked for more signs (Matthew 12:38-45; 16:1-

4). Jesus demonstrated his messiahship to his followers, many of whom were repentant sinners, tax-collectors and prostitutes, whom he met in the Galilean countryside.

Jesus could have miraculously fed the poor, the oppressed and the dispossessed masses and so won the hearts of the people. But while this would have been to satisfy their immediate needs, it would not have addressed the idolatry and injustice of the system that led to their condition. When he did feed the masses with bread they tried to make him their popular leader (John 6:14-15) who would always provide them with food (John 6:26, 30-34; Matthew 16:5-6). Instead Jesus offers himself as living bread (John 6:35-58)—a new way and a new foundation for living, through which material bread would be distributed in a new way. We must recognize that the provision of aid to the Third World, or a benefits system in UK, does not in itself address the injustices and inequalities in the system.

For us the question is whether faith controls money, or money controls faith. It is not a simple relationship, but the economic factors in our lives such as what we earn, the income of our friends and neighbours, the value of our house, and our occupation are factors that influence our perspective on life and our theological understanding. We can be tempted to preserve the present economic order and see it as too complex to change, or as making the best of a bad job. This often causes us to skip over much of the biblical teaching on wealth, or leads us to misread scripture, by putting a spiritual gloss on practical instruction. Jesus makes it clear that he expects forgiven and converted people to live in a different way. The Jubilee Manifesto (Luke 4:18-19) is a new way of living for disciples. Jesus does not say that material things are evil but he does speak out against the accepted economic norms which allow inequality and injustice in society.

The late John Smith, MP, together with a number of other Labour politicians and members of the Christian Socialist Movement sought to set a moral agenda for government, in a book entitled *Reclaiming the Ground*.[30] They point out that 'Christianity is a tough religion' and that Christian worship cannot be separated from political and economic justice, but one is left with the feeling that for them the Labour Party is the solution, despite their constant denials of such a biased conclusion. A broader picture of the development of Christian Socialism, and the culture within which it evolved, is presented by Alan Wilkinson.[31] In examining the influence and changes that industrialization, war, General Strike, and the depression of 1920s and 30s brought, Wilkinson explores the lives and views of the main advocates. The author highlights those of great Christian and social conscience, but his account stands as a warning for a middle class church seeking to address the problems of the poor. In the course of discussing William Morris, for example, Wilkinson tells us that 'a former kitchen-maid recalled how she slaved below stairs late at night and early in the morning to serve Morris and his friends upstairs who were discussing socialism'.[32]

Later, when discussing William Temple, the author records the fact that Temple set up the Life and Liberty group within the church during World War 1. He then recalls that Oswin Creighton, son of a former Bishop of London, was one of those perceptive World War 1 chaplains who agonized over the gulf between the church and the trenches. In 1918, shortly before he was killed, Creighton described how he had spent the afternoon and evening in drenching rain, helping to load up ambulances with the wounded and the dying. 'Then I got a memorandum from Life and Liberty asking what the men are thinking about the self-government of the Church' (a proposal with which Temple was engaged).[33] There were of course exceptions; there were the slum priests and those who dedicated their lives to working among the disadvantaged of society, but much of the social and Christian concern was distanced from those for whom care was expressed.

The church as an organism, whatever the political allegiance of its members, has to stand on the outside of political parties, so that it can critique their manifestos and reflect theologically upon their policies. Kenneth Leech[34] emphasizes the dangers of an increasingly individualistic society, where the privatization of the New Right in politics is matched by fundamentalism and private spirituality in the church. He seeks to provide a theological understanding and undergirding for the church's political stance drawn out of his experience of pastoral and social ministry in the East End of London. He maintains that there is a need to rescue spirituality from its captivity to individualism and the culture of false inward piety. In a similar way (as we noted in chapter 3) Pattison encourages those involved in mental health chaplaincy to beware the danger of a 'therapeutic captivity,' whereby the focus of their work is on counselling patients while largely ignoring the social and political issues of the mental health system.[35]

A real concern for the poor, the disadvantaged and the despairing must be a part of our Christian spirituality. We look for a true liberation that is total and comprehensive of all life, and not only human life. Leech directs white Christians in the UK to listen to the Ras Tafari movement, which is the street liberation among young blacks, and then challenges us with a quote from the black theologian James Cone: 'If white Christians are to learn from the black experience, they will need to see that their historic relationship to their black brothers and sisters has been one of oppressor to victim. Spiritual renewal can only come by ending this relationship.'[36]

The Stephen Lawrence Enquiry of 1998 set out to establish the facts surrounding the failure of the Metropolitan Police Force to arrest and effect the prosecution of five white men suspected of the racially motivated murder of a black teenager, Stephen Lawrence. Its conclusions, identifying institutional racism within the police force, must stand as a continuing challenge to complacency by the church as it examines its own institutions. Engaging with social and political issues is never going to be an easy option for the church. In modern politics we find a separation into spiritual and political arenas, a 'two kingdom theology' that allowed Hitler to gain power largely unopposed by the church. We need to recognize the inherent dangers of nationalism, racism and materialism in our own society. If we advocate a Christian socialism then it must be tested against the realities of homelessness, racial oppression, and the collapse of communities. The incarnation must remain our guiding theological and pastoral principle. Leech speaks of personal powerlessness and impotence in the face of the desolation and despair that he encountered in Soho, and judges that much Christian concern for the poor has been condescending, that is, 'compassionate rather than just'. He quotes R.H. Tawney's comment that 'what thoughtful rich people call the problem of poverty, thoughtful poor people call the problem of riches'.[37]

The Gospel we believe, and the Christ we serve, will not allow us to abandon the poor and oppressed within our own communities. While peo-

ple may feel an increasing alienation from government we must not leave
them to feel abandoned by God. When we affirm that humanity is created
in the image of God, we recognize that every person, regardless of religion, ethnicity, gender or social status, has an intrinsic dignity, and should
therefore be valued and accepted. Any form of exploitation, oppression or
discrimination is a denial of that God-given dignity.

I offer the following two examples of ways in which the church can
engage with the issues of politics and power. The first is ECONI
(Evangelical Contribution On Northern Ireland), which grew up as an *ad
hoc* group in 1987 in response to extreme Protestantism.[38] From a reading
of scripture they felt the challenge to work for peace and healing of their
divided community. The first response was to produce a booklet of Bible
studies in 1988 entitled, *For God and His Glory Alone*, which explored
the biblical basis of citizenship, justice, peace, reconciliation and hope.
The title was carefully chosen as a contrast with the rallying cry of the
extreme Protestants, 'For God and Ulster.' These initial moves received a
warm response and in the years since 1988 the Group has developed
study materials, produced a quarterly newsletter, *Lion and Lamb*, and
established an annual ECONI Sunday. It has also published responses to
the Downing Street Declaration of 1993, the IRA and Loyalist cease-fires
of 1994, and the Good Friday Agreement of 1998.

The demand for help from the churches led to the writing of 'action
packs', based on the themes of *For God and His Glory Alone*, and containing Bible study resources, discussion material, worksheets, drama,
material for youth groups and an action list. ECONI believes that it is
essential that they enable the church to move from reflection to action.
The leadership of the group have sought to model this through a public
engagement with politicians and the media. In their 1995 publication *A
Future with Hope*, they conclude that the Bible produces a framework of
theological and moral imperatives, which are to be discussed in a world
of hurt, conflict, fear and hope. They maintain that the realities of this
world dull our expectations as we move toward peace and reconciliation.
But as Christians we must hold on to the lively biblical concept of
shalom, a wholeness of spiritual and social well-being for all people.

They leaders of ECONI have called all people in Northern Ireland to
grasp the opportunity of removing the 'offence' of Christians divided

from each other. They believe that the commitment to serve the community in the struggle for peace, justice and reconciliation, can no longer be an optional extra for Christian people. Their pattern for engagement, in what is a political minefield, began with the experience of people reflecting on their situation. It has developed through an integration of biblical understanding with the activities of the various political parties, and has resulted in action to seek reconciliation and foster peace in the country.

My second example of engagement with politics and power focuses upon the needs, perceptions and gifts of women, which have been largely ignored by both society and pastoral care. Women produce 45% of the world's food, do 66-75% of the world's work, and yet receive only 10% of the world's income and own less than 1% of the world's property. Producing and supporting the human race is not considered to be 'real work' by a male-dominated society. Women are expected to be passive and conforming and as a result have a generally low self-esteem. This is a traditional working class understanding, but also a Protestant attitude; in the church there are sexist liturgies and moralities that encourage a domestic view. Women are also the members of society who are more often single parents, low wage earners, have the burden of children, and care of the elderly. An understanding of the pastoral issues involved is helpfully developed in a collection of essays edited by Elaine Graham and Margaret Halsey, entitled *Life Cycles: Women and Pastoral Care*.[39] There is a need to understand that the patterns of life, both physical and emotional, of women are different from those of men. Helplessness and hopelessness for women are recognized as causes of an increased frequency of mental illness and depression.

So the example I have taken is a strong women's group that uses the Bridge Centre in Belfast.[40] It has grown out of the needs experienced by the women of East Belfast, where desertion, domestic violence, unemployment or sub-employment and debt are common. The group runs workshops for women's health, supports a parents and toddlers group, and generally seeks to increase an appreciation of the dignity of women. Sexuality is approached through sexual humour, although this is seen as a moral anathema by the Protestant church. The group recognizes the need of liberation from sexual issues and stresses the importance for Christians to speak about enjoying sex. The development of the group and the growth in self-worth and self-understanding by the women has been a long process. In 1988 women were coming to the centre for help, often fearful of seeking advice, let alone approaching the authorities by phone or in writing. It may take as long as four or five years before they are able to make a phone call. They find forms threatening and worry about how the council will react to them, fearing they will face condescension. Their growth in confidence is marked by small advances, such as bringing an official form on which they have filled in their name and address. Getting people in an area such as East Belfast to work together is also very difficult as there is a strong ethos of individualism; for example, it took more than four years to set up a residents' association to represent the community to the council. When the church sets out to work with people in the community it needs to be prepared for a long-term commitment.

The parents (entirely women) and toddlers group is a good example of this long unfolding process. Women initially came to this group because there were facilities for the children. While they were at the centre they would often seek advice, on an individual basis, for such issues as domestic violence, multiple debt, tranquilliser addiction or sexual abuse. Over time they chatted to other members of the group and discovered that they had similar needs. Out of this shared experience they asked for discussion and advice in a group separate from the children. The Bridge Centre arranged for the children to be looked after by trained crèche workers, while the women's discussion group was in progress.

Local incidents of sexual abuse and domestic violence within the community brought issues to light for the parents and toddlers group, and as a result the Lower Ravenhill Women's Project was set up. The women have been empowered to organize the group for themselves. They have the ideas for what they want to do and what they want to learn about. As time has gone on they have become accustomed to contacting speakers, meeting them, introducing them at meetings, and entertaining them at meals in restaurants. These are all things they would never have felt able to do in the past. They have arranged meetings with other women's groups and they have made a concerted effort to make contacts across the Northern Ireland political divide.

Here we have an example of women finding confidence, power, value and self-worth. This has been enabled through the community worker placing herself in the background and encouraging the women to take control of their own group. It is now snowballing with the organization of courses for individuals and for the group as a whole. Some are getting involved in training to help others, and a number have enrolled on a business studies course. The important part is getting started, bringing women together to share their experiences and needs. From that point it is important to have a leader who is an enabler, who will encourage the women to take control of their own lives, to help them to reflect on their situation and become informed, so that they are able to respond. In East Belfast this began with a parents and toddlers play group, established by the Bridge Project as an expression of Christian engagement with the community. This is both an example and a challenge for all churches.

The challenge is for the church to be a prophetic community, proclaiming and living the Word of God. We are called to embody the purposes of God in the world of human affairs and to be the incarnate love of Christ, through the power of the Holy Spirit. In this way the church presents the world with an alternative vision: one of transformation and hope. In living out the values of the Kingdom of God, the church will find itself in a place of misunderstanding and dispute, as it challenges the values of a world where human life is often diminished and oppressed. Congregations will listen to the Word of God in the scriptures, in their own prayer and fellowship life, and in the situations of the community and world in which they are placed. Hearing the Word in this way, we are summoned to call the world back to God, while ourselves being a sign of God's promise and purpose.

Exercise 4.3

Consider, under the following headings, either (1) an international political issue such as Third World Debt or reduction of environmental pollution; or (2) a national political issue such as government spending on education and health.

　a. Facts and statistics.

　b. The location of power and control.

　c. The human issues.

　d. Biblical principles.

　e. What has been, and can be, done.

Notes

[1] http://news.bbc.co.uk/1/hi/england/merseyside/4736955.stm; accessed 03.08.05.

[2] S.C.Guthrie, *Christian Doctrine*, revised edition (Kentucky: Westminster/John Knox, 1994), pp. 258-9.

[3] John W. de Gruchy, *Reconciliation: Restoring Justice* (London: SCM, 2002), p. 51.

[4] de Gruchy, *Reconciliation:Restoring Justice*, p. 154.

[5] de Gruchy, *Reconciliation: Restoring Justice*, p. 72.

[6] Paul S. Fiddes, *Past Event and Present Salvation. The Christian Doctrine of Atonement* (London: Darton, Longman and Todd, 1989), p. 175.

[7] Craig Blomberg, 'Implications of Globilization for Biblical Understanding' in A.F. Evans, R.A. Evans, D.A. Roozen (eds), *The Globilization of Theological Education* (New York: Orbis, 1993), pp. 213-28.

[8] Craig Blomberg, 'Implications of Globilization', p. 217.

[9] Laurie Green, *Let's do Theology—a Pastoral Cycle Resource Book* (London: Mowbray, 1990), p. 121.

[10] Ian Fraser, *Reinventing Theology as the People's Work* (Glasgow: Wild Goose, 1988), p. 62.

[11] Andy Bruce, 'Exploring the Far Country' in Steve Finamore (ed), *On Earth as in Heaven: a Theology of Social Action for Baptist Churches* (Didcot: Baptist Union, 1996), p. 22.

[12] David Atkinson, *Pastoral Ethics. A Guide to the Key Issues of Daily Living* (Oxford: Lynx, 1994), p. 234.

[13] John Weaver, *Water into Wine. Marriage as God Intended* (Didcot: Baptist Union, 1996).

[14] National Statistics. http://www.statistics.gov.uk/statbase/Product.asp?vlnk=13412&More=n; accessed 19.09.05.

[15] This is based on a diagram which integrates scientific methods, and which I offered in John Weaver, *In the Beginning God* (Oxford: Regent's Park College/Macon: Smyth & Helwys, 1994) p.16. This in turn was a modification of two models of the structures of scientific and religious thinking proposed by Ian G. Barbour in *Religion in an Age of Science* (London: SCM Press, 1990), pp. 32-6.

[16] Howard Snyder, *Earth Currents. The Struggle for the World's Soul* (Nashville: Abingdon Press, 1995), p. 242.

[17] For worked examples of these films see John Weaver and Larry Kreitzer , 'Part Three: Resources' in Anthony J Clarke and Paul S Fiddes (eds) *Flickering Images. Theology and Film in Dialogue* (Oxford: Regent's Park College/Macon: Smyth & Helwys, 2005).

18 Rated PG-12A on appeal for violence, disturbing images and brief strong language. Runtime: 121 min. Screen play written by Keir Pearson and Terry George. Cast: Paul Rusesabagina—Don Cheadle; Tatiana Rusesabagina—Sophie Okonedo; Colonel Oliver—Nick Nolte; General Bizimungu—Fana Mokoena. Nominated for three Oscars in 2005: best actor; best actress; and best original screen play. Won awards at Toronto International Film Festival; best feature at AFI Festival 2004; and awarded one of the top films by the National Board of Review.

19 See my chapter on *Schindler's List* in Clarke and Fiddes, *Flickering Images,* pp. 175-92.

20 A generally accepted version of some words in Burke's 'Thoughts on the Cause of the Present Discontents': 'When bad men combine, the good must associate; else they will fall ....'

21 National Statistics, *Social Trends 31, 2001 Edition* (London: The Stationary Office, 2001).

22 Ann Bradshaw, *Lighting the Lamp: the Spiritual Dimension of Nursing Care* (Harrow: Scutari Press, 1994).

23 For further discussion see David Atkinson, 'A Christian theology of Work' in *Pastoral Ethics. A Guide to the Key Issues of Daily Living* (Oxford: Lynx, 1994), chapter 10, and Jürgen Moltmann, *On Human Dignity* (London: SCM, 1984).

24 See, for example, Larry C. Spears and Michele Lawrence, *Focus on Leadership. Servant-Leadership for the Twenty-First Century* (New York: John Wiley & Sons, 2002).

25 David Clark, *A Survey of Christians at Work and its Implications for the Churches* (Birmingham: Westhill College, 1993).

26 Cited in Mike West, 'Doing Theology: A Model Examined', in John W. Rogerson (ed.) *Industrial Mission in a Changing World* (Sheffield: Sheffield Academic Press, 1996), p. 45.

27 Stephen Pattison, *Pastoral Care and Liberation Theology* (Cambridge: Cambridge University Press, 1994), pp. 222-3.

28 John Davies, *The Prophetic Tradition in the Contemporary World* (Birmingham: Westhill College, Christians in Public Life, 1993), Position Paper F6.

29 Donald B Kraybill, *The Upside-Down Kingdom* (Scottdale: Herald Press, 1978).

30 John Smith and others (edited by Christopher Bryant) *Reclaiming the Ground: Christianity and Socialism* (London, Hodder & Stoughton, Spire, 1993).

31 Alan Wilkinson, *Christian Socialism: Scott Holland to Tony Blair* (London: SCM, 1998).

32 Wilkinson, *Christian Socialism,* p. 28.

[33] Wilkinson, *Christian Socialism,* p. 113.

[34] Kenneth Leech, *The Eye of the Storm. Spiritual Resources for the Pursuit of Justice* (London: Darton, Longman and Todd, 1992).

[35] Pattison, *Pastoral Care and Liberation Theology,* p. 209.

[36] James H. Cone, *God of the Oppressed* (New York: Seabury Press, 1975), p. 9.

[37] R. H. Tawney, *Poverty as an Industrial Problem* (London: William Morris Press, 1913), quoted in Kenneth Leech, *The Eye of the Storm*, p. 146.

[38] In 2005 ECONI became the Centre for Contemporary Christianity in Ireland: Howard House, 1 Brunswick Street, Belfast BT2 7GE. Website: www.contemporarychristianity.org.

[39] Elaine Graham and Margaret Halsey (eds) *Life Cycles: Women and Pastoral Care* (London: SPCK, 1993).

[40] I am indebted to Christine Acheson, Community Development Worker for the Bridge Community Trust, who shared her insights and reflections on the nature of the Women's Group at the centre. See also the following publications: Christine Acheson, *Churches/Mission Halls and the Lower Ravenhill Community* (Belfast: Bridge Community Trust, 1995); *The Bridge So Far. A History of Bridge Community Trust in Lower Ravenhill 1984-1996* (Belfast: Bridge Community Trust, 1997).

5
Action: Mobilizing the Church

A few days after the murder of Anthony Walker it was reported that, in the nearby Hare and Hounds pub, where Anthony and his friends would often go, people were rallying around the Walker family. The pub manager said, 'His cousins came in for a drink the other night and everyone just went up to them and consoled them.' 'It's good that everyone is coming together. Everyone is dumbfounded by the ferocity and evilness of the attack.'[1]

Anthony's sister, Dominique, said, 'Anthony had so many friends. Everyone who came into contact with him loved him. He blessed so many lives in his unique way. His life was stolen from him. His family and friends are devastated and their lives shattered.' Anthony was a member of a well-loved, church-going family. He was studying law, IT and media at Carmel College in St Helen's and wanted to be a lawyer. He was an avid football and basketball fan, and had trials for the Liverpool and England basketball teams. But he sacrificed a basketball career to spend more time at the Grace Family Church where he was a youth leader, dancer and singer, and played in the band.[2] The support of the local church fellowship was extremely important to the family in the time after this traumatic experience.

In Northern Ireland, in 1987, loyalist paramilitaries were intent on retaliation after the Enniskillen Remembrance Day bomb, but were stopped by the words of Gordon Wilson, whose daughter Marie was killed in the blast. 'I have lost my daughter, and we shall miss her. But I bear no ill will. I bear no grudge,' he told the BBC. 'Dirty sort of talk is not going to bring her back to life.' He said he forgave her killers and added: 'I shall pray for those people tonight and every night.' His words were seen as a fitting memorial to his daughter and to the other ten people who lost their lives, because they encouraged a spirit of reconciliation in the area.[3] He later spoke of going to meet the IRA and of placing his hand in their hand, his humanity reaching out to their humanity.

Out of tragedy, out of our understanding of the Gospel, comes our response in action and the shape of our living.

We can understand the Lord's Supper as a place of reconciliation in action, where in Christ we make a definite move to reach out to each other. The cross of Jesus was the decisive act of God in dealing with the problem of human sin, and for the church of Christ this redemptive activity is focused in the dramatic actions of the Lord's Supper and baptism. As John de Gruchy puts it,

> the sacraments are communal acts of remembering and representing the Gospel narrative through dramatic actions, using material signs and symbols—water, bread and wine, and acts of peacemaking and reparation. The sacraments rightly understood and practised within the worship life of the Church play a central role in shaping Christian community and its witness to God's reconciliation.[4]

The sacraments are a means of grace for healing and transformation, and for creating community. They are actions which lead to many actions of reconciliation, through their shaping of the human actors who share in them.

In her work, *Communion Shapes Character*, Ellie Kreider[5] explores this aspect of the Eucharist. She affirms that communion is Christ's gift to the church, so that through it the great story of incarnation and salvation may be told and retold. She maintains that churches will be renewed when the Lord's Supper, graced by God's presence and Word, orientated to the living Lord and empowered by his Spirit, is fully restored to the place it had in the early centuries of the church. It is in the supper that God, who is Spirit, reaches out to communicate with us through this eucharistic service of bread and wine. We receive forgiveness, joy, healing and reconciliation. Christ, who is our peace, has brought a new humanity into being, breaking down the walls of enmity through his death on the Cross. He has reconciled people to God and to each other (Ephesians 2:11-22), and those who share in the Lord's Supper become people who act out this reconciliation. Kreider warns that 'When gospel and peace are pulled apart, terrible things can happen, as we have seen in countries where Christians have preached a personalised salvation and have not emphasised that the gospel has everything to do with how to live out national or clan identity.'[6]

She stresses that it is important that 'forgiven people are empowered to live as forgiving people, passing on good news of freedom from the compulsions and domination of sin.'[7] Kreider therefore urges us to recognize that *how* we take communion makes a difference, because we act out our communion theology. The way that we act in the Lord's Supper reflects our actions beyond the Supper. Do we truly express our fellowship in Christ or are we merely a group of individuals who have happened to gather for this meal? She believes that 'dead ritual' is easy to spot. A moribund rite is the breaking of bread and pouring of wine in a congregation of people whose lives are in no way broken for the world or poured out in love for their neighbours.[8] It is in confident hope that we receive forgiveness and the daily bread for our life, which are the unmistakable signs of the kingdom coming. We covenant together and become reconciled in the name of Jesus, and then we turn outward to the task of reconciliation that God has given us. In the Lord's Supper this is expressed not only in the actions of breaking and pouring, but in the sharing of 'the peace' with each other.

In the fourth phase of the pastoral cycle we have arrived at response through action. We have honestly explored our experience, analyzed it and sought to integrate the results of our theological reflection with our living in the world as it is. All this calls for action, for the mobilizing of the church. We ask what actions might be possible at all, and which among them would be the most helpful in our particular situation. Above all, we look for actions which match our theological vision of a God who is himself in action, in creation and redemption.

What are we doing here?
A Lent series in the 1980s produced by the then British Council of Churches was entitled 'What on Earth is the Church For?' There is no better question to use as a heading on agendas of church meetings or church councils. We need the constant reminder that we are not so much 'saved from' sin, as 'saved for' the world as salt and light. The church is to be Good News for a world where bad news fills the media. The church is to be light, that is, truth and peace and love, in the midst of the darkness of hatred, violence, and propaganda. The church is to be the salt of hope that preserves and adds flavour in a despairing world, which searches for meaning.

Harvest Festival services give one opportunity to reflect upon the whole of life and work, for it is one time when the church recognizes God's involvement with the whole of creation. They are an opportunity to align our activity with God's. But we will need to be creative as the Bible, hymns and psalms reflect a largely agricultural and pre-technological world, which is remote from most people's lives. A hunt through the more recent hymn books will reveal hymns that speak of our modern world and its industry and commerce, taking us beyond fruit and vegetables. The use of symbols to represent the work and lives of the congregation is another way of involving the whole of life in our worship. All Hallows By The Tower is a church that ministers to the City of London and holds a variety of services and meetings on weekday lunch-times for those who work within 'the Square Mile.' Their Harvest Festival service for the business community, held on a Tuesday lunchtime in early October, begins with the presentation of symbols. The priest says:

> We have come together to worship God, who is present with us in all that we do. In thanksgiving we each offer him our daily lives, and especially in this place, our work. The congregation will remain standing while representatives from the business community bring to the altar symbols of the harvest of our working life. These offerings are presented to God as our thanksgiving for his creative presence in our lives and work.[9]

Amongst the symbols placed on the altar at such a festival service held in the mid-1990s were: sweets and *petit fours* brought by a hotel; a model of the US Space Shuttle Discovery brought by a company that worked for the space industry; a bag of sugar brought by a representative of Tate & Lyle; and canvas money bags brought by a finance company.

All Hallows has a remarkable ministry in the heart of the City of London, which includes in its area the business and financial community, the tourists who visit the Tower of London, and arts centres. Below the present church building there are Roman and Saxon remains, which form part of a guided tour for visitors. Displays in the church recount history from Roman *Londinium* to the Great Fire of 1666, and to the Blitz of 1940. There are documents recalling famous people who were associated with the church, such as Bishop John Fisher (1459-1535) and Archbishop

William Laud (1573-1645) both buried at All Hallows, and William Penn (1644-1718, the founder of Pennsylvania) who was baptized at the church. Yet this church is far from being an historical monument. Through listening to the needs of the business community the church has established discussion groups, lunch-time services, and a healing centre. As a means of listening to the needs of the community the Business Houses Council was established in association with the church. Stress was identified as the one major issue affecting those who worked in the city. In response a stress counselling centre was established in 1990 at All Hallows House, which is the tower of the former church of St. Dunstan in the East (the parish amalgamated with All Hallows), the rest of the building having been destroyed during the Second World War. The centre, known as the Wren Clinic, has developed treatment through a range of complementary medicines, all seeking to enhance the well-being of the business community in the City.

All Hallows gives one answer to the question, 'what on earth is the church for'?

Taking risks in leadership

The ministry described above has been the result of both vision and risk. Dreaming dreams alone in the study, having a vision of God's bright future for the church, is one thing; it is very different to share this vision and allow others to take up the challenge. We have to listen to other perspectives on our vision, accept the insights of others, modify our ideas, and then include others in the performance of the tasks involved. This is risky.

It is said, 'if you want a job done well, then do it yourself.' One major problem faced by those in leadership is a sense of perfectionism. It is difficult to allow someone else to do a job that we are doing well, at least in our opinion. The risk of letting someone else do it is that they may make a mess and others will complain to us; or worse still, they may do a better job than we could and others will praise their ministry.

Building a church so that it may become Christ for the world is a key task for leaders, and leaders might be advised to begin by reflecting upon how they arrived in a place of leadership. My earliest memories of taking part in church activities revolve around the Sunday School Anniversaries: having to stand up before a full church to sing, or recite a piece of scripture or a poem. I recall the smile on my mother's face, the worried look of my father, and my Sunday School teacher encouraging me to speak out and look up. Through the Christian Endeavour movement we were encouraged to take part in leading services: giving Bible readings and offering public prayer, solos, choir pieces, and short addresses. We were invited to take the whole Sunday service at some of the South Wales valley chapels. Looking back, I can see only too well that leaders, ministers and churches took risks in encouraging us in ministry. Later on, as a student on a ministerial training course, church placements and preaching engagements allowed me to test out my gifts, and 'experiment' with new insights and understanding. I shall forever be indebted to a small Baptist chapel in Berkshire, where I took my first infant dedication service, baptismal service, wedding, and funeral. They encouraged and loved me through my mistakes and, hopefully, I learned from both the people and the mistakes, and developed in ministry. Taking risks involves the willingness to fail and to allow others to fail, and without risk-taking there can be no action.

In counselling, counsellors recognize their own humanity. Pastoral care must come out of the consistency and depth of the caring person's own character. Integrity includes failure, and there needs to be a move away from the emphasis on competence, and a readiness to see both success and failure in terms of growth. Failure may belong to both the person who comes for counselling and to the pastor; failure is a common feature of pastoral ministry. Failure and sin are not the same, although sin may rightly be seen as moral failure.

We must face up to failure in ourselves, our attitudes and actions. The Christian church should be a place where people fail, and are seen to fail, learn from their mistakes, and are forgiven. There is a problem of success-driven congregations in a success-driven society. Maria Boulding gives helpful encouragement:

> If we cannot endure failing and being weak, and being seen to fail and be weak, we are not yet in a position to love and be loved. . . .
>
> Christ has gone down into the deepest places of our failure and claimed them as his own, and now there is no possible failure in our lives or our deaths that cannot be the place of meeting him and of greater openness to his work.[10]

What is true of pastoral counselling is also true for the exercise of leadership, which honestly faces up to its own weaknesses and failures, and is ready to encourage others in leadership and, in love, living with their mistakes and failures.[11]

It is often said that 'marriages may well be made in heaven, but they need to be worked out on earth.' The same is true of each contribution to the life and ministry of the church. We receive our gifts from God; they are events and abilities of the Holy Spirit within Christians (Ephesians 4:11-12; Romans 12:6-8; 1 Corinthians 12:1-11; 1 Peter 4:10-11), but these gifts have to be recognized and given opportunity for expression within the fellowship of the church, and within the society we are called to serve. It is for this reason that Paul is anxious to point to the need for encouragement, acceptance, unity, and humility in the use of these God-given gifts. Effective action needs the gifts of all to be deployed.

Good leadership is vital here; Paul speaks of apostles, prophets, evangelists, pastors and teachers equipping God's people for works of service, and of the whole body growing and being built up in love (Ephesians 4:11-16). How is this equipping, growing and building to be achieved? Leaders will clearly have to open the scriptures with their congregations, but words are not enough. Leaders will need to make opportunities for people to recognize each other's gifts, and also make room for the exercise of those gifts. I have found it useful to take the church fellowship away for a day or weekend, away from the familiar church surroundings to a neutral place where they are free to think new thoughts. Here I might use small groups of six or eight and invite the group to identify the gifts they recognize in each other. In a neutral place thoughts are not confined to what people do in the church at present. New perceptions that are arrived at on such a day may then become the basis for the further development of ministries within the congregation.

We now recognize why Paul emphasises love when speaking about gifts. (Ephesians 4:16; Romans 12:9f; 1 Corinthians 12:31ff) It is only love that will let others take their part; only love will give others preference; and only love will deny self. Leaders, especially, are expected to demonstrate such congregation-building love. They are to be self-emptying, empowering others, and providing the opportunities for others to be creative. It is a leadership, that in love, lets others be the people God created them to be, within the church and world.

Asking dangerous questions

So, what on earth is the church for? Such a question runs the risk of upsetting the comfortable. While surveys reveal that many churches do not tackle issues of work and aspects of daily life within services and Bible study, I suspect that many people do not want such questions raised anyway. For many people in our congregations church provides a respite, an oasis, and a time for spiritual recharging, after a tough week of work and family life. It is not only the former Prime Minister, Margaret Thatcher, who wants the church to concentrate on saving souls, and not stray into politics. Yet, in response, we can agree with Bishop Desmond Tutu that 'When people say that religion and politics don't mix, I wonder what Bible they're reading.'

The starting point of any move toward an understanding of social and community issues will be information and experience. On a world scale the facts are perhaps too enormous for our minds and hearts to handle. For instance, the World Watch Institute noted the following statistics of the state of the world at the turn of the century. One in three children is malnourished; 30,000 children died every day in 2005 as a result of extreme poverty; 1.2 billion people lack safe water to drink (over one fifth of the world's population); three million children die every year from diseases that are preventable (through immunization) and one million women die annually from preventable reproductive health problems. The 1992 Earth Summit at Rio de Janeiro, and the subsequent summits at Kyoto in 1997 and Johannesburg in 2002, highlighted the environmental deterioration which threatens the quality of life, especially for the poorer southern continents, where overpopulation, deforestation and over-farming is leading to flooding and the creation of dust bowls.

We have begun to recognize the interconnectedness that exists within the natural world, and we have heard the questions that science and theology pose for each other. Nowhere do these find clearer expression than in the environmental debate. No discussion of the mission of the church can ignore the care of the planet. We live at a time when there tends to be a self-centred paternalism, or worse, hypocrisy, with rich western nations wanting to prevent the poorer developing nations from doing what they have already done, in using natural resources to further economic development. The just answer will be for the rich nations of the world to share their resources with the poorer nations, so enabling them to develop without further destruction of the environment.

There are important questions to be addressed by the church in the areas of conservation, pollution, ecology, stewardship, and justice. For example, the earth is heating up as the result of burning of fossil fuels, creating a build-up of Carbon Dioxide gas in atmosphere (the Greenhouse effect). Ozone depletion mainly caused by chlorofluoro-carbons (CFCs) used in fridges and air-conditioners is causing the harmful effects of ultra-violet radiation to affect all life on the planet. Sulphur Dioxide, produced in large quantities by power stations and other industries in which coal and oil is burnt, combines with water in the atmosphere to become the main source of acid rain.

The impact of global warming will be seen in sea level changes. In low lying countries a rise of one metre in sea level by 2050 would be devastating: for example, over six million people in Bangladesh live below the one metre contour. Deforestation will lead to both drought and flood, and drier climates will have a great effect on agriculture. The result of all this is that there could be up to three million new environmental refugees each year, which is 150 million by 2050.

Added to the pollution is the rapid exhaustion of non-renewable sources of energy such as oil and gas. Questions that need to be addressed include our use of energy in heating and cooling our homes and places of work; the enormous increase in the use of private cars, and in air travel, mostly for pleasure. Christians have a contribution to make. God created the earth, entrusted it to human beings, and will redeem the whole of creation (Romans 8:18-21). We must learn to think and act ecologically and repent of extravagance, pollution and wanton destruction; we must recognize that human beings find it easier to subdue the earth than they do to subdue themselves. There is a need to be re-awakened to the Gospel ethic, and recognize that human greed is at the root of the environmental crisis. There is a price to pay through fair prices for Third World goods and through higher taxes to allow the support of development in Third World countries.

Christians face the task of articulating the Gospel with relevance, in order to speak prophetically and relevantly to the environmental and social issues of our day, and to rediscover a holistic doctrine of creation. Sadly often the church misses the opportunity and others take on the task, which is particularly the case with the environment. The growth of the Green Movement is the clear example, where Christian involvement has been slow to gather pace. The Jubilee 2000 Charter (published by the Jubilee 2000 Coalition in 1996), for example, has sought to present a Christian response to Third World debt, aiming, in response to Jesus' call to bring Good News to the poor, to liberate the poorest nations from the burden of the backlog of unpayable debt owed by their governments to international financial institutions or to commercial banks. To achieve this liberation, and a return to sustainable development, they suggested the unrepeatable one-off remission of unpayable debts of the poorest countries by the year 2000. This aim was only partially achieved.

In 2005 the Make Poverty History campaign was launched, picking up the themes of cancellation of debt, trade justice, and more and better aid. The Make Poverty History campaign is a member of the Global Campaign Against Poverty. Through the championship of British Chancellor of the Exchequer, Gordon Brown, the G8, at its Gleneagles summit in July 2005, agreed to the cancellation of the debts of a significant number of Third World countries.

The native American Cree people have a saying: 'Only when the last tree has been cut, the last river poisoned, and the last fish caught, only then you will realise that one cannot eat money.'[12]

Awareness must be converted into action. As the Church begins to understand this situation, as it listens to its brothers and sisters throughout the world and contemplates the facts, so it will seek a partnership between 'North' and 'South' in bringing about the transformation of the Kingdom of God announced by Jesus (Luke 4:18-19). We must also recognize that we in the 'North' are the beneficiaries of an economic system that the 'South' experiences as oppressive. To understand this fully we would need to experience it ourselves. Perhaps travelling to the other side of the world is not an option for many people, but we all can walk to other parts of our own community and listen to the people there.

Eric Blakebrough challenges us through his consideration of ministry in London: 'Frankly, the well-off majority of Londoners do not need the poor minority; they do not know them, or care much about them. In this way the poor are isolated, and since they are a minority in most boroughs they have no political power.'[13] These people are voiceless and powerless and see little change in their future lives. When we consider some of the facts and figures for London we find that one-parent families have almost trebled in number in the last 20 years. While racially motivated attacks are common, racial inequality is an even more significant feature. Ethnic minorities are concentrated in low quality housing and are exploited in the job market, finding themselves in low paid work or unemployed. Women, often lone parents, also find their employment prospects bleak and insecure. As benefits are cut, many find themselves with severe problems of debt and frequently turn to 'loan sharks,' which has the effect of deepening their crises.

Blakebrough is right to challenge the church, noting that it has the independence to speak against injustice, and urging that 'it is not good enough simply to condemn; it is required of local churches that they become much more involved in relieving the suffering which exists near to their doors. In this matter, actions speak louder than words.'[14] In this, leaders risk upsetting the comfortable and, in taking a prophetic stance on political issues, risk being misunderstood. The church needs leaders who will enter into the experience of their community, learn from the people, enable the people to understand and analyse their own situation, help them to integrate their experience and understanding with biblical and theological perspectives, and then to plan an active response. It is worth looking back to chapter 1 and noting what we saw of Bob Holman's work with the people of the Easterhouse Estate in Glasgow, and to the insights of Kenneth Leech in London, in chapter 4.[15]

We are identifying a number of important points through our exploration of the world for which Christ died. First there is the question of whether pastoral care is unwittingly on the side of the powerful against the oppressed, especially in our western (or 'northern') context. Second, we must recognize and address issues of conflict, injustice and inequality within our own community, as well as being concerned for those who live 'on the other side of the world'. Third, to regain its prophetic voice the church will need to be socio-politically aware in its pastoral care, looking beyond the concerns of the individual we are seeking to help. There is the need to tackle preventable suffering which has social causes, and the church must deal with the causes as well as the symptoms. Fourth, we will look for a creative theology that moves from experience to reflection and analysis, and through biblical and theological integration to action.

Exercise 5.1

a. Identify key issues: (1) what are the issues facing your church? (2) what are the main concerns within your community or town? (3) what issues should be tackled, as a priority, by the world leaders?

b. Discuss how you can act on each of the issues that have been raised, and identify the Christian principles that are involved.

Helping groups towards action

In the last chapter we saw that the successful establishment of a women's group at the Bridge Centre in Belfast was the result of leaders who patiently, over a number of years, worked with the group, empowering them to discuss, come to decisions, and take action. As we have already said, leaders must value group members, and believe that the group has valuable insights to offer, and that they, as leaders, still have much to learn from others. Members of the group must also listen to, and appreciate, each other. In this respect the leader has the added responsibility of modelling an attitude that values the contribution of others.

Establishing a new group, or enabling an established group to function in new ways that lead to appropriate action, involves a number of steps. When setting up a group for the first time we might identify people who share a common concern, for example, those involved in education: teachers, support staff, and school governors. Such a group would meet with the specific objective of working out their faith within the field of education. At an initial meeting, the group members will get to know each other through telling their own stories and speaking of their experiences in education, such as the stress of teaching in a primary school or with a Year 10 class (15 year olds), or producing a school budget, or representing the concerns of parents. When common themes and concerns are identified the group can begin to produce an agenda for discussion and reflect upon issues for faith within their work situations. Following such a deductive approach, where members individually and collectively recount, reflect upon, and think seriously and creatively about their work situations, courses of action or response can be suggested for individuals, the group or the church. The group should continue to meet in order to evaluate the results and subsequent new experiences brought about by any action taken.

Groups should be small, ideally no more than 8-10 people, in order to allow the development of confidence and trust. There are some obvious benefits in bringing together a group whose work is similar, or even in the same company; but there are also advantages in bringing together a more diverse group so that different perspectives are heard. If a pre-existing study or fellowship group is the location of these reflections, it is likely to be a mixed group. Unless a church has a large congregation, groups are likely to be mixed, rather than specialist.

In any group it is important that there is ample opportunity to tell and listen to each other's stories, but Rachel Jenkins gives some additional suggestions for the ways in which a mixed group might effectively operate.[16] She states that it is unlikely that the group will reach a consensus on every issue. There is therefore a need to respect different experiences and points of view that have been shaped by those experiences. It is important that members of the group understand each other and therefore members should always give explanation of the meaning of the words (jargon or technical terms) they use. In building trust within any group there is an absolute requirement of confidentiality, unless otherwise agreed by the people involved. All these features of a group will take time and will require a commitment to each other by the members of the group.

Jenkins outlines the process as follows:

- Group members arrive with rich experiences, mixture of skills, difficult decisions, a strong sense of commitment to their own values, but also with a struggle of relating faith to their work.
- In the group they build trust, which enables them to begin to see their values in context.
- On the basis of this they are able to analyse their situation and through reflection discover a new understanding of their strengths and weaknesses, and the situation of others.
- All this leads to greater confidence in what they may achieve and enables them to make strategic plans for action.

This may be over-optimistic, but what is important is that connections are made, issues raised and support is found which enables people to be

more effective in living out their Christian discipleship. The attitude of
the group leader, and the kind of environment for discussion that is created, will be of paramount importance in achieving the objectives set out
above. Generating the following values will be important: respect for all
members of the group; listening to and using the experience of all those
present; encouraging participation, discussion, and humour; use of a variety of methods, recognizing that some people respond more easily to
written or verbal information, while others find visual material or role
play more helpful; giving the group responsibility for their own learning;
and providing a safe environment, where mistakes can be made and dis-
agreement is accepted.

It is also important to have specific strategies for the running of any
group. These include having aims and possible outcomes that are discussed by the group at the beginning, and the encouragement of
interaction both in discussions and socially. It is also important to reduce
individual exposure and risk. This can, in part, be aided through encouraging members of the group to work together. It is important to work
creatively so as to involve all members of the group. This can be achieved
through such methods as: the use of a variety of examples that will
engage with different people's experiences; the explanation of an issue in
more than one way; open questions that can involve everyone; and group
work and practical tasks, where people can contribute from their own
experience. Leaders should give non-threatening and non-judgemental
feed-back, and encourage theological reflection to develop out of both
practical experience and biblical knowledge.[17]

A good house group or study group is the envy of all. Sadly, the full
potential for the development of creative debate and enjoyment of social
interaction in group meetings is seldom realised. It is important to build
strong relationships through the exchange of thoughts and feelings. People
will need to be told what is the purpose and underlying philosophy of the
group. If there is an open invitation to join a group, people are able to join
freely, but then the way in which the group is to operate must be defined
and its life-span is made clear. People will want to know the nature of
commitment they are making and whether the objectives are realistic. As
we have emphasised already, the attitude of the leader/enabler in valuing
the experience of others, is vital. Leaders need to reflect honestly on their

feelings about this method and about the people who will make up the group, and prepare their material carefully. Leaders will find it helpful to think creatively; this will involve writing down their ideas and thoughts, perhaps using a connected thought diagram, structuring their material, and formulating questions that will help discussion to develop. I have also found that eating together is a helpful group-building activity.

In the conduct of a meeting, communication is important. This involves careful listening, picking up the non-verbal messages through body language and voice tone; it requires understanding, empathising, and then reflecting back to people what the leader has heard them say. Discussion, where people bring their own experiences, can become unfocused, and the leader will need to help people to make connections between their specific experience and the general points under discussion.

The brainstorming approach can aid this process. The following is an example of an initial meeting of five churches who wanted to plan a joint evangelistic mission to their community. Several questions were asked, and responses given.

Why do young people and some partners of congregation members not come to services?
• Peer pressure.
• They want to do their own thing.
• They feel that the church tells them that they shouldn't do what they want to do.
• The church is irrelevant.
• Going would be an admission of weakness.
• They don't like singing.

When do people attend who wouldn't normally come to church?
• Weddings.
• Funerals.
• Special occasions.
• Baptisms, infant thanksgivings.
• Brigade services and services where their children are involved.
• Remembrance Sunday.
• Christmas.

What is it about these occasions that attract people?
• They are traditional — with familiar songs and stories.
• They are family occasions, a time for being with friends.
• They are comforting.
• In a larger congregation people can be anonymous.
• Events are less churchy, and people can be more at ease.
• Sermons are shorter.
• Food is provided.

What are the concerns and questions of the people in your community?
• Why do bad things happen to good people?
• Unemployment.
• Relationships.
• Crime; fear of a breakdown of society.
• Injustices.
• Truth and tolerance.
• What can I get out of God?

As a result of the brainstorming the churches began to think of the sort of services that might be planned to attract people, and the ways in which the questions raised might be tackled in services or other meetings. Beyond a planned mission the churches might then continue to think about alternative ways of being church and engaging in worship.

As an encouragement to good practice, there has to be an evaluation of how the group functioned: a feedback of what was negative or positive, helpful or unhelpful. The group, themselves, might consider how such an evaluation should be conducted. This might be facilitated by asking each member of the group to write down one or two things that helped or hindered their participation in the discussion. Each person reads out what he or she has written, and the group decides, on the basis of this information, how they will proceed in future.

Finally, it is important that the activity of the group is not merely that of discussion, As Paulo Friere has said: Reflection without action is mere verbalism; action without reflection is activism. The group should have an on-going life of action and reflection. This may be aided in the following way. Group members bring their current experiences to the group.

They are encouraged to keep a diary of experiences and any responses that they have made, or action taken, in response to the group discussion. This may help people to have other thoughts about their lives and experience. There is a regular challenge to come to conclusions, take decisions, and make changes. At subsequent meetings there is an opportunity to look at the experiences of seeking to make changes or to take action, which leads to further reflection, discussion, and decision for action.

Helping the church to combine action with reflection
During the early history of the Church, in an attempt to protect the Church's doctrines, people's experiences of life and the world were largely ignored as possible dangerous influences. The Church councils and theological institutions became the guardians of orthodoxy and the places for reflection. The Church, however, needs not only to guard the faith tradition, with its interpretations, but also to enable open reflection and conversation by all its people. Theology is a conversation, which takes place both within the church tradition and within the practice of Christians who seek to live as disciples of Jesus Christ. In our discussions study of the Bible and the traditions of the Church will be sources of theological reflection about the nature of God, the way God interacts with the world (particularly through Jesus Christ), and for our life as Christians in the world.

Paul Ballard and John Pritchard observe that the key question is: 'What is the relation between the specific theological activity of describing the nature and content of the Christian faith, and what Christians actually do in their lives?'[18] We need to help people to tell the Story and their own story as part of their natural living out of the faith. This is the essence of evangelism. Iris Cully maintains that the church has largely ignored this aspect of education. She states that:

> Secondary education is supposed to challenge adolescents to think and explore ideas. By the age of eleven or twelve they are beginning to ask questions about God and to question stories they have been told from the Bible. Frequently they do not raise these questions in church settings. Either they do not want to shock their pastor and teachers, whom they respect, or they expect to be rebuked for questioning sacred texts.

Teachers need the gifts of conviction and openness. Commitment makes it possible for a person to explore options and to realise that a growing faith is one that can be enriched and deepened by new insights. Adults as well as young people need to be engaged in the task of verbalising their faith. This calls for discussion methods that probe beneath the surface when raising questions that have more than one answer. Sometimes people need to be unsettled in their thinking before they can become settled on a firmer foundation.[19]

Young people who have left the church speak of just 'going through the motions', and so feeling hypocritical. They find that as they are growing up they change, while the church remains unchanged. The worship services feel mechanical and formal, especially when compared with much of their leisure activity. They complain that the church is hierarchical and status-conscious. They say that the church feels like 'another planet' and fails to connect with the rest of life. They tend to disagree with the church's stance on key moral issues, believing the church to be narrow, old-fashioned and stuck in its views. They also observe, correctly, that most of their friends do not attend church.[20] While some of these comments may simply be excuses, almost all young people will say that their concerns and interests are not addressed in church. Some of the issues and questions that dominate the thinking of young people are: personal relationships, sex, marriage, homosexuality, racism, law and order, the Third World, work, environment, and unemployment. Most important of all, young people want security, to feel valued, and to be given responsibility.

When we consider the total environment in which adults live, we recognize that living in a family brings conflict as well as satisfaction. There are the tensions that arise between the various generations within families, health and financial problems or concerns, as well as the joys of parenthood and family celebrations. At work there will be tensions such as job security, harassment, deadlines, or lack of resources, as well as the satisfaction of achievement and promotion.

There is a need to explore all these experiences and situations in ways that are useful to our growth as disciples of Christ. Theological reflection is the crucial core in our involvement in the mission of God; reflection is necessary for effective action. Ballard and Pritchard describe theological reflection as 'holding together the practice of ministry with the resources of theology and allowing the interaction to guide what we do'.[21] We each bring our experience of life, our knowledge of the Bible, our thinking about the faith, and our knowledge and experience from other disciplines; and out of these critical discussions comes reflection on the nature of God, his activity in, and desire for, the world. As we have emphasised already, we learn by doing, and as we become involved in the story of the Bible it is important to live as it teaches. So reflection and action belong together.

People will bring their own patterns of studying the Bible, which may be very traditional. This may prove a good place to begin, by exploring with people why they may wish to rest in the security of the familiar and not face the more difficult questions that the Bible presents, for example, when interpreted or contextualised. Making a direct connection between a situation and a biblical text or doctrine may seem to have the advantage of being rooted in scripture, but it may ignore God's continuing revelation and God's use of other disciplines of learning.

Consider the example of Genesis 1:1-2:3, where we read the Bible's account of the creation of the world we inhabit. How do we interpret this account, as those who live in the twenty-first century, with our scientific understanding of the universe?[22] One answer is to begin with the context in which Genesis 1 was written. Through a consistent process of teaching in the church, we might tell the following story and enable people to read Old Testament scripture with it in mind.

The people of Israel had been in exile in Babylon for a number of years, and their situation was depressing in every way. They were aliens in a foreign land, with a different culture, different religion, and different climate and environment from their own. On top of this they were prisoners with an existence that was not far from slavery. The understanding of their captors was that the gods of Babylon were victorious over the God of Israel, and they were often tempted into believing this version of the truth. They were living in mud-brick houses alongside the irrigation channel, called the River Chebar, in an inhospitable climate and land. They had been granted permission by their overlords to establish their homes, and they had sought to bring a degree of order and meaning to their existence, but the local inhabitants made fun of their plight and derided their religion. Spiritually they were depressed. Their temple in Jerusalem, the place where they had believed that God dwelt in a special way was over a thousand kilometres away, and worse still, it was in ruins. Their view was that they were far away from God, and that their very condition demonstrated his impotence.

In the face of this their prophets, Ezekiel and Isaiah, declared that God was not confined to the land of Israel and the temple in Jerusalem, but was with them in Babylon, and that he was ready to forgive them and bring about a new exodus.

It is in this context too that the writer of Genesis 1 began to reflect upon the faith of Israel. The religious leaders of the people in exile reflected upon the traditions of their faith, the writings that the religious community had preserved and brought with them into exile, and upon the history of God's dealings with his people. They thought about the story of God's relationship with them over the years, from the Patriarchs to Egypt, from the Exodus to David, and from Solomon's Temple to the exile. To this they added their experience of the world, and the religious views held by their Babylonian captors. The writers took all these experiences, and under the inspiration of the Holy Spirit a newly edited version of the scriptures took shape. The very first belief that they wanted to express was that the covenant God of Israel was the God of all creation. Out of their experience they opened their major work with what we now know as Genesis 1.

Here is their declaration: *In the beginning, Yahweh—the God of Israel.* Through Genesis 1-11 creation is linked with the history of Israel as God's chosen people, beginning with Abraham. We see that they clearly understood that the God of the covenant, the sustainer and redeemer of Israel, is the creator of the universe.

Their faith is strengthened. The stories from the past reminded those in exile in Babylon of what God had done in the nation's history, and that even in times of suffering and rebellion he had not deserted them. He was the God that they had experienced as the God of the covenant, he was the God who had been with them throughout their history—in Egypt, through the Sea of Reeds, through the wilderness, into the promised land and the establishment of the Davidic Kingdom. He was the God who went ahead as pillar of cloud and pillar of fire; he was the God of the prophets. The God of their salvation history was the God of creation, and was the God of new beginnings. It is to this hope that the prophets of the exile looked (Isaiah 43:16-19).

Isaiah speaks of God guiding the course of all history; the creator God of Israel's covenant is the God of the universe and the nations. When Cyrus became emperor, events took on more global proportions, beyond little nations and their deities. Israel's faith would need to be of universal proportions if it were to make sense of the events of history. It is into this situation that God's prophet Isaiah speaks (44:28-45:4) and looks towards a new exodus (43:14-21). Cyrus is God's instrument in history. God is creator and lord of history (40:21-28; 44:24-28); he is doing a new thing (43:19); he is proclaiming a new covenant, like that with Noah (54:9), like that with David (55:3b-5), and redemption through a new exodus (43:14-21). There is in the work of these religious leaders in exile a polemic against the foreign nations and their gods (41:1-5,21-29; 43:8-15; 44:6-20; 45:20-25), and an assertion of the ever present connection between God's word and events. It is God who foresees the fall of Babylon (46:1-2), and this demonstrates his superiority over Marduk, the god of Babylon.

Now, the opening chapters of Genesis express their faith in these truths. Genesis 1 transcends all the myths of the ancient world, especially those of Israel's captors. Its view of God comes through the writers' faith in, and meditation upon, the covenant. It presents the love, faithfulness and sovereignty of God over the course of the nation's history. It expresses their living awareness and reliance on nature and God's faithful will, even in times of darkness and despair. In the same way, as Christians we affirm our trust in the incarnation and resurrection of Christ. God's relationship to creation is experienced and understood as a personal covenant of gracious love. Genesis 1 is not exhortation or parable or prophecy or song or a list of the contents of the storecupboard of creation—it is an explicit theological affirmation that everything, the whole universe, is dependent upon God.

The overall picture is of God creating a world ruled by space and time that provides living space for human beings. In the first three works of creation God separated and named the light (3-5), the firmament (6-8) and the sea-land (9-10). God carefully defines the space in which life can develop and in which human beings can live and thrive. The land produces vegetation—the earth is the mother of life. God through his creative word creates heavenly bodies, animals in the seas, in the air and on the land. Last of all, come human beings. All creation is fertile; it has a purpose; and is all part of God's story. Everything has a purpose and this purpose reaches its goal with human beings, created in God's image; and with human beings creation moves forward into history. The final goal of creation is seen in the seventh day, the worship of the creator—worship of God is the ultimate purpose of creation. This passage is not a scientific account; it is a proclamation of faith, which is a confession that creation is God's gracious gift.

The starting point of the world, in which we live, is outside of human beings and human control. The universe is created, the plants spring up, and animals live their own lives. The fact that the first page of the Bible speaks of heaven, earth, sun, moon, stars, plants, trees, birds, fish and land animals is a sign that God is concerned with the whole of creation, not only human beings. Yet we are created in the image of God—in relationship with God, with capacities and abilities, sexuality and mutuality, creativity and fruitfulness. We become truly human through relationships of love. This love, in relationship to God, is expressed in the worship of the seventh day (which has not yet come to an end).

The second story of creation, in Genesis 2 gives us the view from earth. Here we find God living on the earth, the fatherly God who is with us. And when we reach Genesis 3 the narrative describes something happening between God and human beings, and the man and the woman become the subject of the story. It is important that we see these chapters (and indeed the Bible) as a whole. We discover God the creator, we discover his desire for us, and we discover that we are only truly human beings in community, in relationship with each other. The closeness of God's relationship with us is seen in the forming and shaping of the first human being from the earth, as the artist or potter shapes and creates. The craftsman has a sense of pride, a sense of fulfilment, care, love, and negatively frustration and anger. And it is the breath of God that brings Adam to life. Human beings share God's creativity and have the responsibility of caring for creation.

In distinct contrast with the myths of the ancient Near East, the writer of Genesis states that God created the whole universe out of nothing—a rejection of the idea that matter existed before the gods, and was essentially evil. The sea monsters and the astral bodies are created by God, they are not rival deities. Human beings are not servants of the gods—they are God's representatives on earth. Four features of their faith are emphasised. First, God is without peer or competitor. Second, God is more than creator: he is the law-giver and the orderer of the world—light and dark, land and sea, night and day. Third, the whole world reflects its creator, being the perfection of God's will. Fourth, the true nature of human beings is to be in the image of God, in relationship with God and each other, and able to subdue the earth with responsibility.

Having helped people to recognize the community of faith that preserved and was first addressed by the scriptures, we might use other approaches of theological reflection, which allow us to hear the biblical passages in our own context. We can brainstorm a situation, making connections through lateral as well as linear thinking. Or we might use case studies, which help us to get into the habit of asking theological questions about situations. I have offered examples of this approach for Bible study and preaching in chapters 3 and 4.

We might ask people how their experiences fit with the biblical story. This can produce a lively Bible study, in which everyone takes part, but care should be exercised lest the meaning is distorted. There will always be a need of good hermeneutics. The value of this approach may come through the difficult questions that arise out of experience, which do not fit with comfortable superficial answers.

The narrative approach, in which we tell our own story, exploring our recent life, or significant events for the church in past years, or current world events, can be a useful approach to theological reflection. For example, following the death of Mother Teresa of Calcutta, we might have asked what significance could be attached to the giving of a state funeral for a Roman Catholic nun in a Hindu country. There might be reflections upon the impact of the witness of a servant ministry. Stories are important for all of us. Stories help us to understand the meaning of life and to make sense of human behaviour. Imagination is important in listening to stories and allows us to enter into the experience of others. Stories are told to give reason for action and to build up community identity. Where these stories support conflict, as in Northern Ireland and in Israel/Palestine, we need to encourage the different groups to listen to each other's stories. Peggy Heeks makes the following helpful observations.

> Two things especially give richness to our personal stories. First, they intersect with other stories, especially those of family and our faith and literary heritages. At a very deep level, individual stories gain meaning by a sense of connection with God's story, with God's creative purposes. The second point is that our stories are inhabited by other people. As in a novel, each of these has a role and a purpose. Each has a message, which we can discover if we welcome them into our story and share theirs.[23]

Our own stories are important to us, as they change and develop through our life experiences. Our self-identity is tied in with our story, and through sharing our stories we grow to understand each other, and ourselves, at deeper levels.

Another form of reflection can be developed through the church's prayer ministry for its locality. Members of the group may be encouraged to walk around their town or area, watching, listening, making notes, picking up significant objects left lying around, and maybe taking photographs. In the group they bring together all their observations, together with local newspaper cuttings, and discuss the topics for prayer. In such a discussion theological reflection will arise over issues such as: how and where God may be present; how and where the church may get involved; and how and why God may be expected to act.

Asking questions that generate discussion and give rise to new insights is probably the most important aspect of theological reflection. Peter Price presents a useful list of questions related to an action-reflection model:

Experience: What is happening? What are the needs? What are the churches doing? What are other agencies doing?
Analysis: Why is this situation as it is? Who makes the decisions? Who benefits? Who loses?
Reflection: Where is Jesus present? What Gospel values are present? Where are Gospel values missing? How does the Bible reflection help?

Action: How can we respond? How can the church respond? How can people respond?
Celebration: What has been achieved? What is there to celebrate? What is our experience now? What next?[24]

As I suggested earlier, the key questions that we will hold at the front of our minds for our discussions or with our learning groups are:

• What does this teach us about God?
• How does this help us to understand how God works in the world and through human lives?
• What might this suggest about God's desire for us, for our community and for our world?

Through response to these questions we will equip the church to become the agent of God's mission in the world. For, having worked through the reflection, it is important to complete the learning cycle by making a response. Ballard and Pritchard observe that Jesus combined profound reflection with committed action. In our mission we must move on from reflection to action. Ballard and Pritchard outline six types of change that may take place:

• Cognitive change—new things are learned about God, about ourselves, about the mission of the church.
• Affective change—in emotions and attitudes, for example, male understanding of the pain experienced by women in a male dominated church/society.
• Behavioural change—new skills are learned and put into practice.
• Interpersonal change—learning how to relate and care for others.
• Social and political change—looking to make radical transformation in society.
• Spiritual change—a unifying change in belief and practice.[25]

All reflective study should lead to action. When we ask, 'What does this biblical passage say to us?', the answer should make a difference in our lives and the lives of others.

Exercise 5.2

a. Recount a story that has special meaning for you, or your family, or your community

b. If we recognize that our lives go through various stages, accompanied by differing emotions at different times: (1) what story can you tell today? (2) what story would you have told ten years ago? and (3) what story would you like to be able to tell in five years time?

c. How do these various stories help you to understand your faith in God?

d. What action needs to be taken in the light of your reflection on the stories?

Relating spirituality to action

The purpose of relating our faith to our life is to encounter God with us, sharing our experiences, and through this to be drawn into a closer relationship with God and into deeper engagement with God's mission. We learn to accept for ourselves that as Creator, as incarnate humanity in Christ, and as ever-present Holy Spirit, God knows more about our job, concerns, life, and relationships than we do. Our spirituality involves the whole of our life; our life-stories often carry our deepest beliefs and values. Ballard and Pritchard are right to conclude that 'it is not surprising, therefore, that any spirituality which seeks to be in touch with the deepest realities by which we and others live will be drawn to narrative, metaphor and poetry. Stories are evocative and open-ended; they engage the listener; they make him ask and answer questions.'[26] Jesus knew this, as demonstrated in the ways he engaged people with stories.

Our experience of God's presence and activity in our own lives, in the church and in society will affect and instruct our worship and our personal prayer life. Prayer which involves listening, discernment, obedience and wholeness is crucial to our lives in Christ. We depend on the guidance and strengthening of the Spirit, using the gifts that the Spirit's presence in our lives brings. But it is a mark of true spirituality to recognize the complexity and insoluble nature of world situations and seek to live as Christ where we are. Faithfulness is the mark of such discipleship. I remember an interview with Mother Teresa of Calcutta, when the interviewer suggested that her sacrificial work among the poor and destitute of Calcutta had not resulted in great success. Her reply was simple and devastating: 'God didn't call me to be successful, but faithful.'

I suggest that we can identify three aspects of this world-affirming spirituality.

• *Our spirituality is based in God.* This basis for all spirituality is helpfully stressed in the exploration made by Paul Fiddes into the grounding of pastoral practice in the being of God as Trinity.[27] For Fiddes our participation in the life of God affects the way we do theology; we are not observers of God, but are involved in the energy and patterns of the divine life. When we ask *how* we live and move and have our being in God (Acts 17:28), Fiddes suggests that the image of dance helps us to move away from rational doctrines to a participation in the triune movements of God. Such participation leaves us freedom to respond in different ways and to different degrees, and is the outworking of the creative purpose of a God who in love allows us to be. However, God always seeks to encourage us in his desire for our life. Fiddes is surely right to affirm that the whole world is a place to encounter God. It is in the universe that we see God's creativity continuously at work. We have a sacramental universe that displays God's grace, love and faithfulness, and which in this sense can be described as expressing the body of the trinitarian God, just as Christ expresses what it is to be truly human. The following is a useful summation of Fiddes' argument:

> We should envisage sacraments drawing us deeper into the heart of the interweaving flow of relationships in God. The key is participation, so that God is always open to make room for the world, while remaining an event of relationship in God's own self. God has a body, in so far as finite bodies are in God, and so movements of love and justice in God are expressed through bodies.[28]

This suggestion echoes what I have said earlier about our participation in Christ, and his death and resurrection life for the world, through the Lord's Supper.[29] The same point can be made with respect to believer's baptism, where the candidate dies with Christ, is buried, and is raised to a new life of discipleship in the power of the Spirit (see Romans 6:1-11). Through such participation the church and its individual members become both a sign and a sacrament of the Gospel, that is, Christ's body for the world. While the image of God's participation in the world is important for us to hold, we should not lose sight of God's transcendence as creator, sustainer, and the one through whom the universe will reach its final consummation. Fiddes expresses the demands of discipleship through an understanding of what it means to participate in God:

> We should feel through their [our neighbours'] reaction the real pain of facing the particular. This is the kind of cost to be carried by those who are willing to be 'living sacraments.' The sacramental life is one that is open to the presence of God, and can open a door for others into the eternal movements of love and justice that are there ahead of us, and before us, and embracing us. This openness can be felt like the invitation to a dance, but sometimes like the raw edges of a wound.[30]

• *Spirituality involves the whole of life.* A significant aspect of our life is likely to be our work, both paid and unpaid, and this must also be seen as part of our Christian discipleship. Janet Hagberg helps us to see this in the conclusion to her study of faith and work:

> By applying our work skills, be they creativity, discipline, critical thinking or nurturing, to our faith we contribute more consciously to the deepening of our faith. . . . One sure way to grow spiritually is to ask God to deepen the way in which we think about our faith and work connection. Deepening our faith is what the critical journey (of reflective faith) is all about. But we must be careful what we ask for. We might get it.[31]

It is also important therefore that our work, and indeed every experience of daily living, is included within the worship of the faith community. So much of our worship is directed inward. With an emphasis on stewardship, visitation and evangelism demonstrated in the content of sermons, testimonies and prayers it is not surprising that when we ask people how they serve God their answers will revolve around the church.

'Ask them how they serve God in their places of work,' says William Diehl,[32] 'and they may be surprised by the question.' David Clark goes further when he suggests that:

> the problem is not the lack of Christians deeply involved in public life. It is that they are so often left by the church, as an institution, to undertake this task unrecognized and unsupported. Their struggles and their questions, their discoveries and their insights remain theirs and theirs alone—few affirm, listen to or learn about their work for the Kingdom in the world beyond the parish.[33]

He continues to state that the support and inspiration of the church deals mainly with the personal and the familiar, but that 'the public domain, where the stranger and the unfamiliar are regularly encountered, has become hostile territory. The church gathered is recognized, acknowledged and resourced; the church dispersed is unacknowledged, forgotten and adrift'. Mark Greene, in his book *Thank God It's Monday*, bemoans this situation in terms of the mission of the church. He recognizes the fact that most church members are unprepared for evangelism in the workplace, where their main 'warm contacts' are to be found.[34] But I want to emphasise that we should not think only in terms of evangelistic opportunities. We need a theology of work which affirms the nature of Christian mission and ministry in every sphere of life.

Our spirituality develops through our life's journey, through our conversion, our experiences of the nearness of God, our encounters with doubt, and through the pain and cost of discipleship. As we open our mind and heart to the Holy Spirit's direction we begin to see ourselves as God sees us. We come to terms with our own personality, prejudices and failures, while knowing that we are loved and accepted in Christ. It is then that we begin to recognize the experience and faith of others. Growth in spirituality means understanding the importance of community, as we recognize each other's need for support and encouragement in sustaining the transforming vision of the Kingdom of God. Such an understanding of community reaches beyond our own local church or denomination, and we recognize that we are part of one universal church, charged with taking one Gospel to the whole world.

• *Spirituality issues in holistic mission.* A spirituality like this leads to activity. It is orientated towards a mission that cannot be divided into the sacred and the secular, or evangelistic and social action. It is a whole mission of the whole church. Sarah White and Romy Tiongco found that a search for wholeness is in fact a theme that emerged through their study of development in the Third World. They stress that:

> This means overcoming the dualisms and dichotomies between rich and poor, material and spiritual, North and South, private and public, individual and collective, personal and structural, religion and politics, men and women, humans and other creatures, and text and context. The way to achieve this [wholeness] is not by denying tensions and conflicts that exist, but to struggle toward reconciliation.[35]

For such reconciliation to take place we must all participate in the process and recognize the holistic nature of the Gospel. Reconciliation is a costly journey for both the ones who may be able to offer forgiveness and for the ones who need to be forgiven. It will be realised through genuine relationships and solidarity one with another. These are relationships where we listen to and value the views of those with whom we do not necessarily agree. They are relationships where we will seek forgiveness for our own prejudices.

An important part of this process will be the recognition of the spiritual experiences and needs of those outside the church. In one national opinion poll 76% of those asked stated that they had had what they would describe as a 'spiritual experience' in the previous five years. Laurie Green reflects on the singing of 'I'm forever blowing bubbles' at a funeral of a life-long West Ham supporter. He observes that 'it will not be easy to analyse the religious experience of inner-city people. It is fragmentary, fragile and broken. It is born of suffering, hidden and evasive. It's very difficult to describe—but it is overwhelming in the experience'.[36] He believes that people have a sense of place, a sense of the history of their community. They also have a sense of God, although the history of institutional oppression makes them reluctant to hear God through the usual church channels.

Statistics reveal that less than 2% of inner city people attend church. Yet they have a sense of sin, as they realise that they are trapped by the sinfulness of those who hold power. Some people in urban priority areas can feel that they are being punished for some sin of their own and this leads to apathy, whereas in point of fact they are powerless to do anything about it, because the power, and indeed the sin, is lodged elsewhere.

Such situations lead Ballard and Pritchard to call for a spirituality which is biblical and radical; it sees the Bible as a radical, challenging and often subversive document, used by God to unsettle his people even as he assures them of his steadfast love. They suggest that

> to read the Sermon on the Mount in a tower block in Gateshead is to have a different set of questions asked of the reader, and will produce a different set of emotional responses to the text. The crucial questions of our time, whether they be about urban deprivation, Third World debt, ozone depletion or ethnic warfare, are unlikely to be addressed sharply enough by the conventional biblical exegesis offered to suburban churches in the Home Counties. The deeper, unsettling consequences of a riskier hermeneutic, however, can engage these issues in a way which revitalises the Church's confidence in its biblical heritage.[37]

They maintain that a spirituality that is socially and politically earthed will see the division between sacred and secular breaking down. 'It will not be concerned with defending its boundaries, keeping its life from dirt and danger on the roads. Indeed it will seek 'contaminating contact' with the world for which Christ died, for there the struggle for life rather than death is keenest, and there the liberating story of Jesus will be heard most clearly.'[38]

Such spirituality engages with suffering and celebrates resurrection; we enter life's hard places, unafraid to face the difficult and painful issues. We have seen already this in the experience of Bob Holman in Glasgow.[39] Ballard and Pritchard are right to observe that it is likely that

> those who are committed to the transformation of lives and of society through the dynamic of loving service, will be sustained by a lived experience of resurrection which has come about through hard work and not a little suffering. Those who are most involved in life's hard places

often have an inner core of celebration which they have discovered through their Good Friday experiences and without which they would simply not have survived.[40]

We conclude that this spirituality is what Fiddes has described as 'participating in God,' which he explores through the themes of community, power, intercessory prayer, suffering, forgiveness, death and spiritual gifts. Above all, I think, participating in God is a sharing in his mission in the world. The needs of a broken world lead us toward a spirituality which has depth and integrity. We celebrate this through broken bread and poured out wine, where we enter into God's story of salvation, forgiveness and new life in Christ.

Connecting worship to activity in the world

We need worship in depth, which takes us beyond ourselves and into an encounter with God. Life and work can leave us bruised and battered. Studs Terkel prefaced his best-seller, *Working*, with the statement that:

> This book, being about work, is, by its very nature, about violence—to the spirit as well as to the body. It is about ulcers as well as accidents, about shouting matches as well as fistfight, about nervous breakdowns as well as kicking the dog around. It is, above all (or beneath all), about daily humiliations. To survive the day is triumph enough for all the walking wounded among the great many of us.[41]

Sadly, the same is often true for many carers and home-makers. Worship must be constructed to make the connections, to recognize God's universal presence and sovereignty in all of life, and to provide teaching that lays a theological foundation for work and leisure, joy and pain, celebration and suffering. Good liturgy will be grounded in what we share in common, recognizing that all that we do and are is part of God's creation. Liturgy needs to become the people's work, their expression of their lives. Yet as David Westcott laments, some work is considered to be more Christian than others. Westcott challenges us to look at the prayers of intercession in our churches, and to consider that people often only speak of 'witnessing' at work, when asked about their jobs.

> There is no sense in which the whole of work belongs to what God has called us to do in the world. People often do not see that computer technology, hairdressing, brewing, rolling steel has anything to do with God's purposes in the world. We express our creativity in work, and in our worship of God we can offer the product of our work and in so doing recognize the presence of God in all that we do.[42]

Likewise we must encourage people to offer their fear, anger, frustrations and anxieties to God, for it is only as we give these to God that God can deal with them and encounter us in them. Then, we begin to find God in the most unlikely places.

It was in the Enlightenment that a division was made between reason and belief, the public and the private worlds. This led to a dualism that separated the natural from the supernatual, and resulted, as Westcott rightly observes, in eighteenth-century businessmen who could worship in church on Sunday and engage in slave trading for the remainder of the week. Ministers of religion could preach the Kingdom of Heaven from the pulpit and ignore the hell experienced by the members of their congregation who worked in the local factories. This can still happen today.

It is the incarnation of God in the human flesh of Jesus that rescues us and our work from the dominion of darkness. It does this by making all of life, including our work, an arena in which not only to serve, but also to meet God. It gives work the possibility of being sacramental. All we do, all the things we make or produce, can be seen in the light of God's command to act as stewards of the earth. As we bring our lives before God we recognize that this will involve a rich mixture of word and sacrament, symbol and art form, music and dance, songs of praise and silent reflection. We bring all this into focus at the Lord's Supper where the whole of life is offered as a sacrifice to Christ with whom we have died and been raised to live the resurrection life. We might make a prayer of self-offering at the commencement of the Lord's Supper such as the following, used in the chapel of Regent's Park College in Oxford:

Father of all, we bring these signs of your creation,
the harvest of grain and vine;
we bring these signs of human labour,
the money which we earn and spend;
we bring the hours of the past week, and
the work of the days to come;
now in your mercy receive this our sacrifice of praise and thanksgiving,
and help us to value all things by the measure
of your gift of love in Jesus Christ our Lord.[43]

In a culture that emphasizes individuals and their personal growth it is especially important to stress this corporate dimension in linking life, work and worship. We should not lose the centrality of the Lord's Supper for worship. Yet Ruth Etchells is right to caution us against seeing this as the only focus of our Christian life, when she says, 'But God does not cease to be at work in his saving story when we leave the holy table and its churchly context. So the eucharistic community, the believers gathered regularly round his table, are commissaries in re-enacting that drama of salvation in their secular lives: i.e. they are to carry that eucharistic reality with them and live it in the world.'[44]

Our praise is not only with our lips, but also with our lives. We meet around the table as the gathered church to be strengthened in our ministry as the scattered church in the world of our daily living. One Good Friday morning in Rushden, Northamptonshire, the members of the local Council of Churches were holding their usual open air presentation of the Passion, in the middle of the High Street. At the end of a dramatic presentation of the Crucifixion, each of the clergy took a loaf of freshly baked crusty bread and walked out into the crowd. We each broke off pieces of the loaf and gave it to those who had gathered to watch the drama. We shared the broken body of Christ with the people of the town. In the symbol of pieces of bread from the one loaf, we shared the Gospel, the life of Christ, with our community. To be the people of God, sharing bread and wine, and receiving forgiveness, and resurrection power for living, helps us to understand that God's grace is active in the world, even in the most adverse and dispiriting situations.

We recognize with Luke (Luke 8:22-56) that Jesus is Lord over nature, the demonic, sickness, and death, and, as we observed earlier in Luke 5:1-11, he is seen to be Lord of our work. He is Lord at all times, in all places, in all circumstances; and we offer our life as part of the story that we celebrate at the Lord's Supper. But, as Etchells observes, re-enacting the saving story in our secular living also involves sacrifice. We are called to confront the chaos in society, at the heart of humanity—in family, community and politics. Here our believing moves into the public arena.

Francis Dewar,[45] as we noted in chapter 1, helpfully identifies two invitations from God. The first is an invitation to a relationship with God, to the discovery and offering of our true selves into God's hands. The second is an invitation to *do*, to give ourselves wholeheartedly to what we do. It is God who calls us to offer our very self in initiatives that require us to step out on unmarked paths. This will mean responding to God's promptings, changing direction, and taking risky steps of faith. Such steps are followed, not preceded, by God's confirmation, and in the future they are followed by further steps. This must be accompanied by an openness to the world's pain, which entails listening to people and to situations with an open mind.

Part of hearing the pain of others includes hearing and owning our own pain. In all of our desire to hear and do the will of God, we recognize the need for guidance. Dewar is convinced that the will of God will coincide with our deepest longings. But for this to be accurate and not wishful thinking, we will need to be in touch with our deeper self and discern God's personal call on our lives. It is, as St. Augustine is reputed to have said, a matter of: 'Love God and do what you like.'

In our regular weekly services one way in which the connection between our worship and work might be made is through intercessory prayer. Prayers for the community and the lives of the people who make up the community would be normal for most churches, but this could be extended through a focus on a particular area of work. For example a teacher or factory worker, a nurse or manager could share something of their work and the particular issues and concerns that they faced each day. The congregation could then enter into prayer with their sister or brother in Christ for their work, for those who work with them, and for the impact that that place of work has within the community. All of this becomes a part of the pastoral care that the church gives to each other, and which enables the whole congregation to grow in understanding and effectiveness in Christian discipleship.

Ben Patterson reminds us that in the Bible there is a unity between worship and work; both are forms of service to God. 'The former is the liturgy of the sanctuary; the latter is the liturgy of the world.'[46] Worship has the ability to transform our work, as we ourselves are transformed through giving ourselves wholly to God (cf. Romans 12:1-2, and Mark 8:34). Patterson reflects the feeling of many ministers when he notes that nothing is more irritating than talk of the 'real world.' When someone tells the pastor that 'it was such a good service it's a pity we have to return to the real world on Monday', he comments that 'the assumption is that what happened in worship was a pleasant and therapeutic diversion. But the real thing is out there in the rough-and-tumble of the world.'[47] It is rather that, in the light of the reality of worship of the living God, we return to the world of lies, and live the truth; we return to the world of dispute and division, and live peace and reconciliation; we return to the world of hatred and envy, and live love.

Another annoying accusation laid at the door of the minister is that they, themselves, do not live in the 'real world.' While leading a retreat for a group of church leaders, a Junior School headmaster challenged my comments about the church's mission, suggesting that I did not understand how real people lived, because I didn't have 'a proper job.' I did not feel that it was right to challenge this statement in public, but I later reflected on my activity in ministry over the previous few months. I had spent three nights at the local hospital with a couple whose new-born baby was dying. I had been supporting an elderly woman who was at her wits end caring for her husband who had had a severe stroke, which had left him paralysed, unable to speak, and extremely irritable and aggressive. I had been working with local secondary school teachers, where as the result of the merger of two schools, all the staff had to reapply for their own jobs, with no guarantee of re-employment. I was also supporting an alcoholic and a woman who was being abused by her husband. In addition there was the 'normal' round of visiting the sick, the bereaved, and those seeking marriage. I concluded that I, like most clergy, may have been more in touch with the harsh realities of life than that headteacher.

Andrew Walker says that liturgy is vital—it is part of an oral culture and leads us into the life of faith, the wonder of the story. He states that

> Liturgy is both mystagogy [teaching of mystical doctrine] and mission.
> It nurtures soul and body and draws us 'further up and further in'
> towards the story. At first we hear the word, accept it, and see that it is
> true. Then we taste it, and know that it is good. Liturgy is participatory
> religion drawing us in, taking us deeper, holding us up. It also calls out
> to a lost world to come and see for itself.[48]

The local Christian community is a *witness* to the truth of the Gospel. It is also the *hermeneutic*—that is, a people who are living the story are *interpreting* it for others. When celebrated in faith, the story is God's chosen way to bring light and healing and encouragement to us. For when we believe the gospel story, the Bible says, we are, in some mystical way, 'in Christ:' his death becomes our death to sin, his resurrection becomes our resurrection to new life and his promised return becomes our hope. In short, his story becomes our story.

The most vital aspect of all that we have been considering is that the story which is 'acted out' in the liturgy of Sunday worship should transform the stories we live out in our living and in our work Monday through Saturday. The worship of Sunday provides the context, the support and encouragement for our daily lives; it is the place where our story is part of the Story, and is given significance. Through worship we are equipped to be a sign and a sacrament of the Kingdom of God. This Story is a story to live and to die for.

Exercise 5.3

a. Suggest ways in which your celebration of the Lord's Supper could be shaped to be an encounter with the Christ who died for the world.

b. Consider some creative ways in which your church's intercessory prayers might fully engage with local, national and world events.

Notes

[1] http://news.bbc.co.uk/1/hi/england/merseyside/4739569.stm; accessed 03.08.05.

[2] http://www.blink.org.uk/pdescription.asp?key=8331&grp=55&cat=199; accessed 03.08.05.

[3] http://www.iraatrocities.fsnet.co.uk/enniskillen.htm; accessed 03.08.05.

[4] John W. de Gruchy, *Reconciliation: Restoring Justice* (London: SCM, 2002), p. 96.

[5] Ellie Kreider, *Communion shapes Character* (Scottdale: Herald Press, 1997), reprinted in UK as *Given For You: A Fresh Look at Communion* (Leicester: IVP, 1998).

[6] Kreider, *Communion shapes Character*, p. 109.

[7] Kreider, *Communion shapes Character*, p. 120.

[8] Kreider, *Communion shapes Character*, p. 153.

[9] Service sheet for the 'Harvest Thanksgiving for the Business Parish,' All Hallows By The Tower, London, Tuesday 4th October, 1994.

[10] Maria Boulding, *Gateway to Hope* (London: Collins/Fount, 1985), pp. 12, 74, quoted in Stephen Pattison, *Critique of Pastoral Care* (London: SPCK, 1993), p. 168.

[11] Further helpful discussion is to be found in: Paul Beasley-Murray, *Power for God's Sake. Power and Abuse in the Local Church* (Carlisle: Paternoster, 1998); Paul Goodliff, *Care in a Confused Climate. Pastoral Care and Postmodern Culture* (London, Darton, Longman and Todd, 1998); David Lyall, *Integrity of Pastoral Care* (London: SPCK, 2001); William Willimon, *Pastor. The Theology and practice of Ordained Ministry* (Nashville: Abingdon, 2002).

[12] Cited by Margot Kassmann, 'Covenant, Praise and Justice in Creation' in David Hallman (ed.), *Ecotheology: Voices from South and North* (Geneva: WCC/New York: Orbis, 1995), p. 49.

[13] Eric Blakebrough, 'London's Unwanted Citizens' in Eric Blakebrough (ed.), *Church for the City* (London; Darton, Longman and Todd, 1995), p. 49.

[14] Eric Blakebrough, 'London's Unwanted Citizens', p. 56.

[15] See Bob Holman, *Faith in the Poor* (Oxford, Lion, 1998) and Kenneth Leech, *The Eye of the Storm. Spiritual Resources for the Pursuit of Justice* (London: Darton, Longman and Todd, 1992); Leech, *Through our Long Exile* (London: Darton, Longman and Todd, 2001).

[16] Rachel Jenkins, *Christians in Public Life* (Birmingham: Westhill College, 1992), Position Paper G4.

[17] For a careful examination of the educational aspect of learning with adult groups see: John Daines, Carolyn Daines and Brian Graham, *Adult Learning, Adult Teaching* (Nottingham: University of Nottingham, Continuing Education Press, 1993).

[18] Paul Ballard and John Pritchard, *Practical Theology in Action: Christian thinking in the service of Church and Society* (London: SPCK, 1996), p. 43.

[19] Iris V. Cully, *The Bible in Christian Education* (Minneapolis: Fortress, 1995), p. 67.

[20] For further discussion of these points see Philip Richter and Leslie Francis, *Gone but not Forgotten. Church Leaving and Returning* (London, Darton, Longman and Todd, 1998); Alan Jamieson, *A Churchless Faith. Faith Journeys Beyond the Churches* (London: SPCK, 2002); Gordon Lynch, *Understanding Theology and Popular Culture* (Oxford: Blackwell, 2005); Steve Chalke, *The Complete Youth Manual Vol 1* (Eastbourne: Kingsway, 1987); Pete Ward, *Youth Culture and the Gospel* (London: Marshall Pickering, 1992); Ward, *Worship and Youth Culture* (London: Marshall Pickering, 1993); Ward, *Liquid Church* (Carlisle: Paternoster, 2002).

[21] Ballard and Pritchard, *Practical Theology in Action*, p. 118.

[22] The following is based on pasages in John Weaver, *In the Beginning God* (Oxford, Regent's Park College/Macon: Smyth & Helwys, 1994), chapter 6; and Weaver, *Earthshaping, Earthkeeping. A Doctrine of Creation* (London: SPCK, 1999), chapters 1-3.

[23] Peggy Heeks, 'Stories for a Journey', *The Friend*, 21 May, 1999, p. 8.

[24] Peter Price, *Seeds of the Word: Bible reflections for small communities* (London: Darton, Longman and Todd, 1996), p. 26.

[25] Ballard and Pritchard, *Practical Theology in Action*, pp. 140-2.

[26] Ballard and Pritchard, *Practical Theology in Action*, p. 161.

[27] Paul Fiddes, *Participating in God: A Pastoral Doctrine of the Trinity* (London: Darton, Longman and Todd, 2000).

[28] Fiddes, *Participating in God*, p. 300.

[29] See the discussion in chapter 1 of the stories that are told at Passover and the Lord's Supper.

[30] Fiddes, *Participating in God*, p. 302.

[31] Janet Hagberg, 'The Faith-Work Journey: Developing and Deepening the Connection between Faith and Work' in Robert Banks (ed.) *Faith Goes to Work. Reflections from the Marketplace* (New York: The Alban Institute, 1993), pp. 182-3.

[32] William Diehl, 'Bringing the Workplace into the Worship Place' in Banks (ed.), *Faith Goes to Work*, p. 148.

[33] David Clark, *Christians in Public Life* (Birmingham: Westhill College, 1992), Position Paper B3.

[34] Mark Greene, *Thank God It's Monday. Ministry in the Workplace* (London: scripture Union, 1994), pp. 10-14.

[35] Sarah White and Romy Tiongco, *Doing Theology and Development: Meeting the Challenge of Poverty* (Edinburgh: Saint Andrews Press, 1997), p. 214.

[36] Laurie Green, 'Blowing bubbles: Poplar' in Peter Sedgwick (ed.), *God in the City: Essays and Reflections from the Archbishop of Canterbury's Urban Theology Group* (London: Mowbray, 1995), p.72.

[37] Ballard and Pritchard, *Practical Theology in Action*, p. 154.

[38] Ballard and Pritchard, *Practical Theology in Action*, p. 156.

[39] See above, chapter 1, section 5.

[40] Ballard and Pritchard, *Practical Theology in Action*, p. 164.

[41] Studs Terkel, *Working* (New York: Pantheon Books, 1972), p.xi, quoted in Ben Patterson, *Work and Worship: Serving God in everything you do* (Leicester: Inter-Varsity Press, 1994), p. 30.

[42] David Westcott, *Work Well: Live Well. Rediscovering a Biblical view of Work* (London: Marshall Pickering, 1996) p. 57.

[43] *Regent's Park College Prayers and Orders for Worship* (Oxford, Regent's Park College, 1994) p.81. Prayer by Paul S. Fiddes.

[44] Ruth Etchells, *Set My People Free* (London: Harper-Collins/Fount, 1995), p. 101.

[45] Francis Dewar, *Called or Collared? An Alternative Approach to Vocation* (London: SPCK, 2000).

[46] Patterson, *Work and Worship,* p. 87.

[47] Patterson, *Work and Worship*, p. 95.

[48] Andrew Walker, *Telling the Story* (London: SPCK, 1996), pp.198-9.

6
New Experiences: Growth in Community

As Huyton tried to come to terms with the brutal axe murder of black student Anthony Walker in July 2005, the sense of sorrow and shame was palpable. There was sorrow at the senseless slaying of a promising and popular young man, and shame that this racially-motivated killing had taken place in their own backyard. Huyton (population 40,000) is predominantly white, with a mix of comfortable semi-detached and Victorian houses as well as local authority estates.

Kevin Mello, a black man from nearby Kirkby, said he now feared for the safety of his own children. 'This could have easily been my sons standing at a bus stop being targeted because of their colour,' he said. Some people were sceptical that the murder was racially motivated. 'Anthony was in the wrong place at the wrong time, this could easily have happened to a white lad,' said one woman, who did not want to be named for fear of being targeted. 'I think there must have been some kind of history between him and his attackers. It's a small minority of individuals who are evil.' Another woman said: 'I went to Asda yesterday and for the first time I realised that I was being served by a Chinese man and an Asian man. I'd never noticed before—you just don't think about it. You see the person, not the colour.'[1]

In Huyton, the community found itself in a new situation in the aftermath of this tragic event. Some were changed by it and others, it seems, were not.

There is a clear need for forgiveness and reconciliation in our world, within our church fellowships and in our personal relationships. In the wake of terrible events, there is a need for community to be renewed and healed, for new beginnings to be possible. Christian reconciliation is founded on God's pattern—'The Word became flesh.' It is not an abstract philosophy, a doctrine, or some utopian thought, it is grounded in historical reality. As John de Gruchy puts it, 'Reconciliation is an event, a praxis, a process and celebration, before it becomes a doctrine or a theory.'[2] The infant church embodied reconciliation (Acts 2:42-47; c.f. Ephesians 2:11-16), which is not to say that the early church did not have its rifts and divisions, as we see in Paul's first letter to the Corinthian church. He encouraged them to rediscover the meaning of healing divisions through the Lord's Supper, when celebrated aright (1 Corinthians 11).

Reconciliation cuts through all the divisions that society creates, and for the infant church this included the Jewish-Gentile split. The church is to be an example of a reconciling community (2 Corinthians 5:11-20). Reconciliation is eschatological and is part of a future hope in which all will be one in Christ. It involves letting go of the past and embracing God's future. The Christian faith sets up signposts of reconciliation and the Church is God's agent of reconciliation in the world.

When we fail to strive for forgiveness and reconciliation we run the risk of marring our life on earth and our eternal destiny. We recognise the damage and bitterness when people find it impossible to forgive, for whatever reason. William Blake's poem 'A Poison Tree' expresses the truth about unforgiveness:

> I was angry with my friend:
> I told my wrath, my wrath did end.
> I was angry with my foe:
> I told it not, my wrath did grow.[3]

The bitterness of an unforgiving heart can destroy someone so that their personality becomes distorted and unattractive. But as de Gruchy concludes, 'covenanting to restore justice, covenanting together as a people reconciled to God and one another, covenanting to restore relations with the 'other', requires then a commitment to live and work in anticipation of what God promises.'[4]

Our Baptist ancestors spoke of 'walking together and watching over each other in love.' We covenant together as fellowships of God's people, we seek to be reconciled with each other in Christ, and we offer each other the sign of the Peace. These are the marks of a church which celebrates the Lord's Supper at the heart of its worship. The church offers itself as a sign to the world that communities can be renewed even in the face of evil and hatred. A new beginning is always possible.

The last phase of the pastoral cycle is actually not the end, but the beginning of a new cycle of experience, analysis, integration and action. The result of the action we take in response to reflection is new experience, affected and shaped by what has gone before. We find ourselves in a new situation, with new insights in a world that has changed in some way. Christian discipleship is to follow this never-ending path, open in trust to God's future. But this is not the lonely journey of an individual; there are companions on the way as a new community is created which offers hope to the broken communities of the world.

Life-changing events

There are events that change our lives and lead to new ways of looking at the world. When we reflect on these experiences and respond to them, we find that we change and grow in understanding and maturity. The following story from an article in the *Guardian* newspaper for May, 1999, illustrates this vividly.

The phone rang in the office of Professor Charles Villa-Vicencio, head of research at the Truth and Reconciliation Commission in South Africa. The man at the other end of the line was an officer in military intelligence who had been particularly hostile when interviewed by the commission some weeks before. The man was suave, sophisticated and utterly ruthless. 'I'd like to meet,' he said. The officer arrived at the meeting place, tall, athletic, apparently confident. A lawyer by training, he had planned and directed operations of unspeakable terror against black activists, but had never pulled a trigger himself. 'I want to tell you a story,' the man began. It was not what the Commissioner was expecting.

A few days earlier, after the publication of the activities of the secret death squads the man's 23 year-old daughter had come to him and said: 'Daddy, sit down, I want to talk to you. All my life you have taken me to church, sent me to Sunday School and raised me to be honest. And all my life I was told never to ask where you had been when you were not at home. Now I want you to tell me the truth. I want to know what you have been doing for the past twenty years.' The Truth Commissioner looked at the murderer. 'I did not know what to say to her,' the man blurted out. 'I could not start even to think how to tell her or even where it had all begun.' He began to cry, as bewildered passers-by looked on. 'It was,' he eventually said, 'the truth moment of my existence.' It was then that Charles Villa-Vicencio realised that perhaps a change in South Africa was possible.

Such events also take place in our own lives. Three events took place in one short week in March 1995, which changed the way in which I have viewed my life and ministry ever since. On 24th March I worshipped in the chapel of the Cancer Hospital in San Salvador, on the fifteenth anniversary of the murder of Archbishop Oscar Romero, killed because of the stand he took for justice on behalf of the poor. He was shot down as he celebrated the Mass for patients, their families and medical staff. A couple of days earlier I had stood in the Rose Garden in the grounds of the University of Central America in San Salvador. A plaque in the garden carried the names Ignacio Ellacuria, Amando Lopez, Joaquin Lopez, Ignacio Martin-Baro, Segundo Montes and Juan Ramon Moreno, and the date 16 de Noviembre de 1989. On that date in this garden six Jesuit priests and their housekeeper and her daughter were tortured and murdered by a secret death squad, also because of their stand for truth and justice. As I contemplated the lives and death of these priests, in the garden, and in the service at the chapel, I had to come to terms with my own commitment as a servant of Christ. I discovered that my earthly life was very precious to me and I wondered whether I had the strength to take such a costly stand for God's truth in the world.

A few days later, together with two missionaries, on the day before I was due to return to the UK, I was robbed at knifepoint. The local Salvadoran Baptists were surprised that we had lived to tell the tale. Back in Oxford the reality of that incident dawned and life has taken on new meaning. I now live in the light of these three experiences.

A changing society brings new experiences
Modern western society is dominated by individualism, which is one characteristic of post-modernism. So much of life appears to be controlled by the maxim 'what is best for me,' for *my* pleasure, my development, my fulfilment, my success. The late John Smith MP, leader of the British Labour Party, was right to coin the phrase 'the Me generation' in describ-

ing the UK society of the 1990s. Many people construct a faith of their own that suits them: trust in the market place economy is actually a manifestation of belief, and the so-called 'New Age' religion exemplifies the eclectic nature of many people's attitude to faith.

Our society—whether in the UK or the USA—is no longer monochrome in culture, nationality, ethnicity or belief. There is a wide variety of cultures and sub-cultures, each of which will have a different worldview. One obvious change is the rich variety of food that is now available in shops and restaurants, but, more importantly, each group of people will also bring different perspectives to the view of society and its needs or problems. Each will have different questions and different answers. This means that those of us who seek to understand our neighbours will have to listen very carefully in order to understand the stories, beliefs and concerns of others.

Employment and leisure now figure highly on our agendas in an increasingly automated society. We recognise that the political ideal of full employment is no longer a realistic objective. Part-time work and job-sharing are common; this is especially true for female members of the workforce. There will therefore be a greater number of people with increasing amounts of leisure time, which they will wish to find creative ways of using. The upward spiral of information technology is having an effect on employment in a number of different ways. The rapid increase in the requirement of new skills is leaving many people behind, especially among older workers, with the result that many in the 40 plus age bracket are being made redundant. Another feature of the IT revolution is the greater scope for people to work from home, their only requirements being a computer and a telephone line. While there may be some positive results of these changes, many people are left with a low sense of self-worth—'on the scrap-heap at 38'—and a high degree of isolation and stress, where there are no co-workers with whom to discuss problems or decisions. Another, more recent, aspect of employment in the UK is that a falling birth rate and fears about adequate pension provision are resulting in the need for people to work well beyond the current retirement age of 65 years.

For much of society, the media dominates leisure time, especially in the form of cable or satellite television, DVDs, and computer games.

Recent figures reveal that in the UK on average men watch 24.1 hours and women 26.9 hours of television per week. The figures range from children under 15 years watching between 17.9 hours (girls) and 18.6 hours (boys) per week, to those over 65 years of age watching 36.5 hours per week.[5] There is increasing evidence of the influence, both constructive and destructive, of the media in shaping people's ideas, values, emotions, and activities, to say nothing of how we spend our money. Violent and pornographic videos have been cited as contributing factors in a number of violent crimes.[6] On the positive side, documentaries dealing with ecological studies have heightened the nation's awareness of environmental issues, conservation of energy, and the protection of the countryside with its plant and animal species.

Many people find that in a fast-changing world they need space to think and talk with others about how they feel. The church is one place that can provide that space where groups can help people to discuss the issues, reflect upon their experiences, and consider what they want out of life and what they want for the world and future generations. Older people are especially concerned about change, but, as we have already noted, young people would value a safe place where they can express anger, find security and value, and make relationships. The Christian church offers the perspective of the Creator God who desires all people to experience the fullness of life as he planned it. It is God's plan and purpose for creation revealed in Christ that is the focus of the Christian hope. I believe that the church can make a valuable contribution to our present society by providing opportunities for building relationships and community. This can be achieved, at least in part, by creating a place where all people, inside and outside the church, can reflect upon their experience of life, their hopes and fears, and ask questions about the place of God in their life and in the world. As the outcome of this process, they can find themselves in a new situation, where the process of reflection and integration can continue, enriching life without end.

A changing society and new ways of being church

The late John Wimber, who was leader of the Vineyard Fellowship, California, spoke at one of his first public meetings in UK in the early 1980s about his conversion to Christ. He said that he came from an unchurched background and first heard about Jesus through friends at university. Intrigued by the lifestyle of some Christians he went along to a Bible study in a fellow student's room. Here, he says he was so attracted to Jesus Christ and to his Gospel that he surrendered his life to Christ at that meeting. After the meeting, one of the student leaders suggested that Wimber might like to attend a church service. This he readily agreed to do on the following Sunday. When the service was over, Wimber asked his friend, 'Is that all there is?' His friend replied that the service was over and that they were free to go home. 'But isn't there anything else?' enquired Wimber. His friend was a little concerned and said that sometimes there was coffee after the service and on rarer occasions a bring-and-share lunch, but that on this occasion no such thing was programmed. But Wimber continued to insist that there should be something more, to which his friend was bemused and asked what Wimber meant. Wimber then said, 'We've sung about it; we've prayed about it; we've read about it; we've listened to the preacher speak about it; we've even given to it; but when are we going to do it?' 'Do what?' asked his friend. 'The Jesus stuff! When are we going to do the Jesus stuff?'

In similar vein, Donald Kraybill presents us with a picture of the church as an upside-down community ('These men have turned the world upside down': Acts 17:6). Citizens of the 'Upside-Down Kingdom' do not do their own thing, rather they follow God's will together. 'Jesus' kingdom words on riches, power, love and compassion assume that his people share a corporate life together.'[7] We are faced with a membership that has increasing commitments outside the church, but Jesus calls for a prior commitment to the body. Kraybill encourages us to see that 'creating a new style of corporate life is more critical than having all the right answers to the question of political and economic involvement. In a real sense the creation of *bona fide* Christian community is a political act since it represents a distinct social reality.'[8]

As a people in the world but not of the world Jesus forewarned us that we would be despised (John 15:18). We need to resist the temptation merely to accommodate and assimilate the values of our culture; we function within a cultural context but our life is not determined by it. Again Kraybill provides a helpful comment: 'The community is also necessary to discern the real issues in modern life. An individual can easily be overwhelmed by the media blitz. . . . The individual cannot always detect the depravity behind much of the rhetoric in modern life. The Holy Spirit in the community of faith helps God's people truly discern the times in which they live.'[9]

We can identify a western church which is in trouble, and realise that discovering new ways of being church is the crucial task that faces us today. Our so-called 'post-everything' generation has more questions than answers, and the church is no different. Church-planting experiments and Alpha courses have been partially successful, and have provided a catalyst for fresh thinking about church life. Yet, despite growth in some congregations, the church is in decline. Even growing congregations are increasingly distant from contemporary culture, and the church is also failing to connect with their own committed members, as Michael Fanstone's research discovered.[10] His survey of 500 people who had returned to church, as we noted in chapter 2, identified issues of irrelevance of services for everyday life, lack of personal care, support or help offered by the church, and failing leadership.

We need models of church where the boundaries between insiders and outsider are blurred. We need to make a move away from the model of the 'gathered church' toward a 'gathering church', where belonging precedes believing. The Kingdom agenda is more important than church programmes and strategies. This will mean taking care that we do not confine ourselves to 'middle class' values and the agendas of professional people. Christian communities will be involved in offering legal and social services to the needy; they will take social action to modify unjust social structures; they will cooperate with political and industrial organisations (so long as they are faithful to the Kingdom agenda); and they will offer dissent in the face of racism, militarism, oppression and injustice. This must all flow out of a vital experience of worship and prayer within the community of faith. In following such an agenda we must take care not to be paternalistic or patronising in our dealings with people. As we have already said, we must work with people and so empower them to take control of their own lives. We are talking about 'doing the Jesus stuff.'

Alan Kreider poses some pointed and challenging questions, which we shall have to address as we seek new ways of being church in the twenty first century:

> How about your congregations? In the way that they function and worship, are they becoming communities of peace and freedom which are evidences of the truth of the Gospel? And your catechism: as you prepare people for baptism, are you equipping them to live freely in the face of the addictions and compulsions of your time? Are you teaching them new narratives and new folkways, so that they are being reformed into people who are distinctively Christian? Finally, in your worship, what do your rites (for you all have them) say about your churches' beliefs and priorities? Are your rites strong and living, enabling you to address the issues that really trouble your communities? Do you evaluate your worship primarily by how it makes you feel, or by the extent to which it shapes your character—as communities of faith and as individual Christians—so you look like Jesus Christ?[11]

As we noted in chapter 2, the authors of *The Prodigal Project* present a picture of post-modern society, which has largely rejected the church, and a post-modern church-goer who is mostly unhappy with the routine of church life. They ask whether such discontent may be the voice of God's Spirit prompting the church to seek new ways of being the body of Christ for the world. Important aspects of the new models of church that they describe are honest and vulnerable relationships, community, and worship that provides a space for worship rather than a managed programme. One fundamental question that they pose bears repeating: Even if we change the format so that the church takes place in, for example, a café style, has anything significant changed in the way we are being the church for the world?[12] This must remain an important question for the church as it searches for relevant models that are true to Christ, in a new age.

I want to hold on to a vision of being church that includes honesty, openness, integrity, and real love. Church is the place where I can be me, 'warts and all;' it is a place where there are people who will accept me as I am. This means that each of us will be ready to disagree in love, listen to stories of failure and weakness, as well as those of triumph and faith, and accept our sisters and brothers in Christ. Church is a community of love that lives for others, shares the journey with others, weeps with those who weep and rejoices with those who laugh, prays with each other, and offers real support and practical care. The local church is, as I suggested in chapter 1, *the children of the Father, who meet in the presence of the Holy Spirit, and seek the mind of Christ.* For our relationships are bound together in the relationship of the Trinity, a relationship of eternal love, participating in God, as we observed in Chapter 5.

The modern hymn, *Servant Song*, by Richard Gillard[13] expresses much of what a new way of being church might include. Here are just two verses which catch the tone:

> Brother, sister, let me serve you,
> let me be as Christ to you;
> pray that I may have the grace to
> let you be my servant too.
>
> I will hold the Christ-light for you
> in the night-time of your fear;
> I will hold my hand out to you,
> speak the peace you long to hear.

When the hymn is sung it should be sung together, looking from one to another, as we sing: we are saying, 'this is what *you* mean to me, this is what *I* will seek, with God's help, to be to you'. This leads us on to discuss the nature of our communities, their leadership, and their worship.

Creating community in new circumstances

At the beginning of a conference to discuss ways of being a learning community we began with a brainstorming session, giving answers to the question: 'What has changed in your lifetime in the way people relate to each other?' The following were some of the answers:

• from a few telephones to text messaging and the Internet;
• from extended family to nuclear family or no family;

- from team games to individualism, represented by video and computer games;
- from real games with real people to fantasy games and virtual reality;
- from little travel to frequent global travel;
- from family meals to many different individual meals from the microwave;
- in tragic situations, a move from concern to litigation;
- of public leadership, from trust to mistrust and suspicion;
- of services, from the personal to the impersonal telephone recorded options;
- of society, from the local community to fragmented individualism.

In my childhood there were many opportunities to learn and build relationships. We made music, we played board and card games as a family, we prepared meals and did the washing up together. At church there were the same or similar activities. All of these places were times to talk, to tell stories and share jokes, and to listen to the memories of older members of the family or the church. In a society where we have so many opportunities to use the latest information technology, we may have deliberately to create a space where conversation, sharing memories, and learning and playing together can take place. In a fast moving society where so much information is available almost instantaneously we need to recognise that community and relationships take a great deal of time to create. But this will be time well spent.

Let me offer a parable. There are two ways of reaching the top of Snowdon. One way is to get on the Snowdon Mountain Railway at Llanberis (you will probably have to queue) or you can walk from Pen-y-Pass at the top of the Llanberis Pass. Many people want to see the view from the top of the mountain, or just tick the summit of Snowdon off their list of places to visit. For them the railway is the quickest and simplest way. For those who walk it will take a lot longer, but they will see so much more. They will walk along the shore of Llyn Llydaw, and look at the variety of grasses and wild flowers. They will enjoy the fragrances, the wind, sun, or even rain on their faces, the spring of the turf, and the roughness of the rocks. There will be the colours and shapes of the rhyolite lavas of a volcano extinct for over 400 million years, and the ripples

on the surface of the water of the lake. As they get to the foot of the central peak, they will walk past Glaslyn, a circular lake, deep blue in colour
and with a sheer rock wall at its back. Then comes the final steep climb to
the summit. Those who reach the top by this route will be tired, sweaty,
and grubby, but they will have many stories to tell. They will also have
enjoyed many shared stories on the journey.

Community involves commitment, and the important expression of
covenanting together. The Puritan understanding of 'walking together,
and watching over each other' in Christ, is a good model to follow. We are
companions on the journey of faith. The word 'companion' comes from
two Latin words: *cum* and *panus*, meaning, 'with bread'. At the Lord's
table we covenant together and share bread. To take the bread without
understanding the nature of our relationship of covenantal love, is, says
Paul, tantamount to failing to discern the body (1 Corinthians 11:29). The
community that gathers around the Supper table is not divided, nor does it
make distinctions; all are sinners in need of grace; none of us have anything of which to boast. So at the table there is no male or female, slave or
free, Jew or Gentile, black or white, intellectual or uneducated, possessing
one spiritual gift as opposed to another (cf. Galatians 3:28; Ephesians
2:11-22; 1 Corinthians 12:12-31).

We are created beings, given a share in who God is and what God
does; and we exist in relationship to all that God creates and loves
because we are created in the image of God. We are fallen, but there is
reconciliation and restoration through a new covenant. As Susanne
Johnson rightly observes: 'Our Story is about fall, bondage, slavery,
oppression, exile, alienation, and estrangement, the symbols of disrupted
community and disrupted relationships. . . . But our Story is also about
exodus, promised land, covenant, advent, resurrection, and new life,
about community forfeited and redeemed. It is about death and rebirth.'[14]

Christian spiritual formation is messy, with failures and progress,
doubts and certainties, mountain-top experiences of God's presence and
the dark valleys of despair. Yet, in the Christian community, we grow
together, in the truth of the Christian Story which is about redemption,
sanctification, and hope. Through the Lord's Supper we celebrate the
covenant, with Christ as creator, redeemer and sustainer, and with each
other as fellow pilgrims. In this act of sharing bread and wine we will tes-

tify to the quality of our relationships and express ministries of servant love.

This community will, however, only be able to serve a changing society if it relates itself both to the world of work and to those on the margins of society. To have a view of work that focuses on paid employment is far too narrow; it devalues or fails to value much of people's activity in their daily lives. A strong theology of work will see all people as being involved in God's creativity, moving us away from the dualism of sacred and secular and helping us to value all of our abilities, experiences and activities. Such a view encourages us to listen to each other and learn from experiences that are shared.

David Ford is right to remind us that 'issues of dignity are very near the surface where there are poverty and severe problems with housing, unemployment, crime, violence, family break-up, healthcare, education and lack of amenities.'[15] In the church there is a place for practical help, but also we celebrate our dignity in Christ; we each have value rooted in God (Ephesians 1) and in his love (Ephesians 3:14-21). Community is essential to all this. In situations of deprivation and brokenness the church and other communities may offer hopeful beginnings of transformation, creating community against all the odds. Ford concludes that, 'this is community with a crucified man at its heart, a gathering around one who was poor, rejected, persecuted and executed. It not only affirms community in general, but indicates that there is a special promise from God attached to the creation of community around the weak, marginalised and those not valued by society.'[16]

Exercise 6.1

a. What are the events that have shaped or re-shaped your life?

b. How has the world changed since you were a teenager, and what implications do these changes have for the mission of the church?

Shared stories

When a church in Northamptonshire, where I was the pastor, celebrated its fiftieth anniversary we decided that we would publish a book of anecdotes that expressed something of the church's life and history. The church had been built at the same time as the council housing estate which it served, and telling the church's story involved the story of the estate and its families. The church minute books recall the removal of all iron railings from the estate and church in 1940 to be melted down for armaments. There was a long running battle with the authorities for their return or for compensation; it was rumoured that the railings were still on a scrap heap in Wellingborough in 1946. A terse note reported that £6 was eventually received, but that the new railings cost £100. The same minute recalls that the use of the A.R.P. (Air Raid Protection) hut on the estate was sanctioned for the storage of Sister Freda's bicycle—further compensation, no doubt. The resulting booklet was given to every household on the estate and was accompanied by an exhibition in the church hall. Many people came to share their memories, and this became an opportunity for the church to make connections with the lives of those it sought to serve.

Shared stories become our shared experiences of learning. We are challenged and encouraged by the stories of others and their stories inform us. Stories of people in other cultures become a lens through which we can gain new insights into our own culture. For me the stories of communities in Central America, stories of the life and death of Archbishop Oscar Romero, and the witness of the murdered Jesuit priests in San Salvador, have forced me to reassess my understanding of the mission of Christ in the world. It is from the experience of the base ecclesial communities in Central and Southern America that many churches throughout the world have seen the possibility of new ways of learning. They have set a pattern that has been copied in many places: commitment to the community around, an analysis of the social situation, a re-reading of the biblical stories from the perspective of stories of people today, and a relating of all this to pastoral practice and to action for change in society.

We have already discovered that stories have an important place in our learning processes. Stories were an important part of Jewish life and we have found Jesus to be a master-storyteller. The Old Testament presents us with an example of the way in which the story of the exodus from Egypt was continually reflected upon as the people of God sought to make sense of their experiences through settlement, monarchy, exile and return. Today, in Third World communities, we find that the exodus story continues to be a motif for the poor and oppressed, and for marginalised minorities.

One story that Jesus told that is frequently referred to in our society, demonstrates the forgiveness, acceptance and restoration that is at the heart of the Gospel. It is the story of the Prodigal Son (Luke 15:11-32). It is a well-known story about a foolish young man who thinks only about himself. Having persuaded his father to give him his inheritance he goes off to live a life of self-centred pleasure. But when the money runs out, the rebellious youth finds that his life is no longer any fun. He recognises his mistake; realises that life would be better at home, even as a servant; he returns, admits his foolishness, and asks for forgiveness. This is a story that resonates, because we have been this young man.

The story has also been seen as a picture of a father's love, entitled by Helmut Thielicke[17] as 'the Waiting Father.' Here we find a picture of God: the patient, loving father, who having given his son the chance to choose how he will live, now accepts the consequence of giving him that freedom. In spite of the choices that the son makes, the father lovingly awaits a change, and is ready to accept him back, forgive him, and treat him with extreme generosity. We empathise with this story because many of us have sought to be this parent, or have received such parental love.

But this story can take us a lot deeper in reflecting upon our lives. It is certainly about coming to our senses and finding new life 'at home' with God our Father. But the story is told to a group of Pharisees, religious people, who were complaining about tax collectors and outcasts and sinners eating with Jesus (Luke 15:1-2). So, we ask, who represents the Pharisees in Jesus' story? The lost son represents the tax collectors and sinners who come to Jesus, and the father's accepting love represents Jesus. So who represents the religious people? They are the elder brother, the third character in the story, who is lost while still remaining at home. He is sure of his own goodness, and indignant at his father's accepting and forgiving love. He thinks the worst of his brother, going beyond the evidence of his frivolous living to refer to prostitutes; he is judgmental and unforgiving. This can be a real danger for religious people; we can be tempted to decide who is unforgivable.

A very angry woman phoned my wife one Sunday morning before the service began. 'Does Frank go to your church?'

'Yes.'

'Well, do you know that he is divorced, and now he's living with Sally? Don't you think that someone like that should be excluded from worship at your church?'

Sheila said, 'Do you think that you have to be good to come to worship God?'

'Yes.'

So Sheila spoke to her about the fact that all of us are not particularly good and that the Bible speaks of God's love and acceptance.

The elder brother is so sure of his own character. He has never put a foot out of line, has always done what he has been told. But we might wonder about the attitude with which he has done all these things. He refuses to go to the party. He tells his father just how hard-working he has been. But this appears to have been a grudging duty; it has not done out of love. It is like another story that Jesus told, about a tax collector and a Pharisee in the Temple, bringing their prayers to God, where it was the tax collector who went away right with God (Luke 18:9-14). There are wrong and right attitudes to have about ourselves before God. And how do we view God? The elder brother is very angry with his father. He does not understand his father's attitude towards his younger brother. He is jealous of his father's response to his brother's return—a party, when his grudging duty has never been rewarded! He cannot understand his father's compassion; he has no love for his brother; he only knows that religious rules have been broken.

Hearing the story, we recognise that we were once the younger son of the story, but we have come to our senses; we have found the Father's forgiving love, and now have a new relationship with the creator of the world. But we also hear a warning about the danger of being lost at home: the danger of self-righteousness, of being sure of our own goodness, which sees us lost once more, even if we are at home in the church. We love as Christ has loved us, and this is demonstrated by our daily behaviour with others, both inside and outside the circle of the church.

In the same way as the Jewish people of the Old Testament retold and participated in the Passover story, so Christians retell and participate in the story of the crucifixion and resurrection of Jesus through the Lord's Supper. Our story becomes part of the Story, and in this one human story, we find hope. In this we learn to value individual experience; we encourage the community of faith to reflect upon one another's stories; we help people to own their insights; and we excite each other with the relevance of the faith. Alan Kreider comments that 'We act as we do because we have been shaped by stories and experiences which shape our inner identity and reflexes . . . the story of the Bible . . . the story of the church . . . the story of our communities themselves; and our personal stories'.[18]

But is the church in a position to express such a community model? Following George Ritzer, John Drane suggests that the church demonstrates a 'McDonaldization' process. It imititates the production line of McDonalds and other providers in our consumer culture through four features: efficiency—a pre-packaged church; calculability—quantity not quality; predictability—including both programmes and beliefs; and control—a 'like us' uniformity. Drane rightly argues that people's lives are messy, that God is not predictable, and that the church is in danger of being consumed by a social reality that is at least partly of its own making. The danger he sees in this is that the faith will be dismissed along with the culture in which it feels most at home.[19]

We may believe that we are seeking to reach all parts of society, but we are probably relating only to traditional Christians and the upwardly mobile professional families. The poor, the pleasure seekers, the spiritual searchers, and secular society are largely untouched. Much of current church programmes, such as Willow Creek and Alpha, are successful, but mostly with the traditional churchgoers and professional people. Can we see just a touch of the older brother in Jesus' story here?

In a world of movement and drama, can we create community in settings where we spend most of our time looking at the back of other people's heads? We need to engage with people's stories. The Bible is story, not philosophical or religious ideas, and we are discovering story as a means of connecting with society. Enlightenment reason through critical scholarship may have led us to think that stories are peripheral and that intellectual abstraction is the real thing, but this view does not fit with the ways in which human beings think and relate. In our modern world it is possible to connect and to make sense of things through stories, shared experiences and relationships. Worship should create a context in which people can be themselves, where people who are friends can help each other towards personal maturity, without having to apologise for their uncertain, tentative, and provisional understanding of God.

Sharing stories and learning together is an important way for building community. In El Salvador I came across the following incident, which provides a useful lesson for church congregations everywhere. Just before their church anniversary in 1994, El Cordero de Dios (Lamb of God) Baptist Church in San Salvador decided that they would produce a new mural to hang at the front of the church, behind the communion table. They met together one evening and looked at a series of slides, which showed scenes of the church's life during the previous couple of years. Then each member drew pictures to represent something of that pilgrimage. After a little while they came back together and placed all the pictures on the floor and discussed them. They chose images that the group felt best represented their life as a church. These images were then brought together into a montage by a member in the church, who was gifted in drawing. The resulting picture was sketched on a large plastic sheet (about 2x4 metres) and painted by the whole group. It was almost dawn when the mural was completed. The result is a striking banner of images that the whole church can appreciate and recognise as its own story.

Exercise 6.2
a. If your fellowship wanted to produce a mural to express its life over the last 5 years, what images would you want to include?

b. If you were asked to choose a Bible story to explain the heart of God's message for the world, which one would you select? Why did you choose it?

Communities and leadership in learning
I once asked one of the church-based students at Regent's Park College, Richard Burfoot, how his ministerial training had shaped him. The following are some of his comments:

> My training has developed my ability to think on my feet about a wide
> range of pastoral, ethical and life situations; it has greatly broadened my

understanding of people (not just Christians), and the love that God has for all of humanity; and I am learning not to form judgements hastily. I can now see God at work in places and situations which beforehand I would never have considered or noticed; it has given me the ability to stand back from life and reflect on the wider picture of what is going on around me, something which I am sure many people miss; and along-side my greater love for people has come a greater belief both in them as individuals and in their potential. My understanding and practice of leadership has developed beyond my time as a manager in business. I am now able to let people do what they do best. (Still a long way to go!) But sadly, not all has been positive. I have become very cynical about much that goes on in church life, such as: our individualistic faith and ghetto mentality; the abuse of ministers and their families; and our orgasmic, but shallow worship—a reflection perhaps of our shallow spirituality.[20]

In some ways the expression of Christianity in UK has become locked into books and words and this is often reflected in the ways in which ministers and leaders are trained. Whilst ministerial formation does indeed require academic input, those involved need to be aware of issues of communication with people, particularly where books are not the main source of information. We need to be aware of the cultures and 'world-views' of those to whom we minister.

When we speak of a 'pre-modern' society it is more accurate to think of a Christian story underlying people's exploration of the world, rather than a single worldview. In the same way, it is also dangerous to suggest that the majority of people in our society today will hold a scientific, rational worldview, as this largely belongs to an intellectual elite. We need an open mind that recognises a variety of world-views. If we are to com-municate the life-changing message of the Gospel we must be prepared to meet with and listen to people where they are. One positive aspect to col-lege training is that students are able to ask and reflect upon theological questions and air views about God and his activity in the world, in a 'safe' environment. We need to create such safe places where this can be done by all the members of a church congregation—places to ask questions, express doubts and disbelief, anger and bemusement, in our quest to understand God.

When we concentrate on the more academic aspects of the Bible and theology we are more likely to produce leaders and congregations who miss the cultural mark. There is a need to equip leaders who enable people to reflect on the place of God in their everyday experiences of life, and not upon those issues that only focus on church structures or which are rooted and remain in the first century. We look to build communities of faith that function as redemptive communities in and for the world. This is the place where Christians learn their discipleship and learn to relate their faith to their life and work. Doing theology is the ability to engage in a living dialogue between contemporary issues in faith and the witness of scripture and church tradition. To do this we will need leaders who are open to the experience of their congregation and who know that they are also learners. Richard Burfoot comments that in college students are often encouraged to 'read' theology, whereas in the churches we must enable people to 'do' theology—a practice whereby faith and life meet on the same road and find a workable interpretation and framework within which to live.

As one who seeks to train ministers for churches, I believe that it is vital to encourage leaders who listen to others, and value others for the experiences, gifts and abilities that God has given to them. The gift of Christ through the Spirit is the appointment of those who will equip all God's people for the work of Christian service, in order to build up the body of Christ (Ephesians 4:11-12). It is important to prepare ministers who are: enablers, encouragers, trainers, open to people, and open to their community, as well as being communicators and preachers of the Gospel.

A new way of learning requires a new way of teaching. The leader will value the experience of all people and enable them to discover what they already know about life and faith—to discover the places where God is already revealing himself to them in their everyday lives. The leader will be a resource person for the congregation, but all will learn from each other's stories and insights. The action-reflection approach which I have been commending and practising throughout this book, frees us to discover our true human worth. Adults have a wide experience and have learnt a great deal from life. Until the gap between the teacher and learner is closed, the dialogue is impoverished and the learning is therefore impaired. Leaders certainly need to have a good background understanding and knowledge of scripture and of church tradition, so as to be able to give appropriate input and guidance. But they must recognise that the insights of others have value, and that God does bring important insights through other people, even those with no formal training.

The church in the UK and the USA has already rediscovered the involvement of all its members and has begun to emphasise (at least in its words) the priesthood of all believers and the ministry of the whole body of Christ empowered by the Holy Spirit. This pattern of discipleship can be developed through learning in community. This will involve listening to each other's stories; valuing each other's experiences; integrating our biblical and theological understanding with experience; and responding through action, which itself is then evaluated. In this way we discover that our stories and the story of our local church is a part of the great Story.

Such learning does not stop this side of eternity, as we continue on our journey of faith. The refrain of George Rawson's hymn[21] reminds us that: 'The Lord has yet more light and truth to break forth from his word.' We live in the light of this truth, and respond to it in our lives. As we have seen (figure 1.2), an action-reflection model of learning is a spiral: our response to bringing our experience of life into the light of the Gospel leads us to new experiences, which in turn will be reflected upon.

Community life and worship

Feeling like a fish out of water, or perhaps an Eskimo at a cricket match, might be a fair description of the feeling of some who drop into worship from the world of work or leisure. We need to address such alienation between the worlds of church and daily living. Indeed, there is a clear need to relate our worship to the rest of our lives and to bring our whole life into our worship. Underlying this is the principle that the whole of life for a Christian disciple is worship. Our worship should then, at least in part, be committed to an empowering of Christians for their life outside of the church community. For this to take place we will need to develop ritual and liturgy, symbols and words that express the lives of the whole congregation. Such worship will involve all and be led by all. Our liturgy should free the whole congregation to express itself to God, to hear and support each other. Congregational worship is a place of renewal for the people of God; to hear the word of God and to feel the touch of God in the voices and from the hands of their fellow Christian pilgrims.

Worship is a vital part of our pastoral care. There will always be a place for individual counselling, but the therapeutic community of faith, where we are able to find and develop our true personhood, created by God for relationship, is a fundamental part of being the people of God. The development of the church community is important for understanding God and making sense of life, and it is where we strengthen our hope in Christ.

Pastoral care is exercised by the whole church; it is concerned with the needs of the whole person—body, mind and spirit; and it is directed towards individuals and community. It is important for the church as a community to socialise, play and eat together, as well as worshipping and studying together. Weddings, funerals, infant thanksgivings and baptisms, should be the focus of fellowship life. It is important for church members to be present at these occasions, whether the participants are congregational members or not. These occasions are opportunities for the church fellowship to express their pastoral concern through their commitment to pray with and support the people and families involved.[22]

The church does need to create time and opportunity to break down the division between faith and work, between worship on Sundays and the rest of life. Worship must be constructed to make the connections, to recognise God's universal presence and sovereignty in all of life, and to provide teaching that lays a theological foundation for work and leisure. Good liturgy will always be grounded in what we share in common. It will be important for preaching and teaching to address the issues that are facing members of the congregation and the community in which they live. Worship will also be enhanced if it is earthed in the experiences and pressures faced by the people. Work, and family responsibilities and concerns, should figure all the time in the prayer life and testimony of the church.

The impetus for going out and getting on with our Christian discipleship, for being the mobilised people of God, will come from our gathering together in worship. We might begin with an emphasis on the centrality of the Lord's Supper. Here we celebrate the new covenant in Christ through the sharing of bread and wine. We are one body who share one promise of forgiveness and new life; one experience of the empowering of the Holy Spirit to live the Jesus-life in this world; and one hope of an eternal relationship with God, over which death cannot place a full stop. It is appropriate for this celebration to be the time when we celebrate and lament, laugh and cry, with and over world, community and family issues. We will create space for the sharing of family news and community events. We will give space to reflect upon national and international events: the horror of war, the tragedy of an earthquake or flood, the tensions between people groups, or a time of local or national celebration.

Communion with Christ is more than warm feelings; we must 'discern the body' — to perceive the meaning of our actions, and catch the implications of our behaviour. There is a need for the church to recover a true sense of community and hospitality through sharing meals, which are transformed through acted memory by Christ's own presence and love.[23] Ellie Kreider[24] challenges the church to imagine early Christian communities gathered around tables for their *agape* meals, probably on evenings after work. Hosted by householders, these meals were occasions for social fellowship and economic support, as well as spontaneous worship. The focus was on thanksgiving, much as it was in the Jewish festival tradition — praising God for creation and his continuing intervention on behalf of his people. After the resurrection of Jesus such a Passover celebration continued. The Christian communal meal served as a strong focus for the identity of the church. It was an arena in which the church had to tackle questions of the inclusion of women, slaves, and non-Jews. This communal meal kept alive the memory of Jesus, and was the place where teaching, economic sharing, and discipleship were worked out.

Kreider reflects with sorrow on the medieval period when she believes that there was a change in emphasis; an elaborate penitential system shifted the focus from a continuously reconciling community to an emphasis on the status of individuals before God, where priests and people alike asked the dreaded question, 'Am I worthy?' Church assemblies lost the atmosphere of a joyful redeemed community celebrating their living hope in communion with the risen and returning Lord Jesus. Required to confess and take communion at least once per year, medieval European Christians were no longer active participants but watchers. The mass was a priestly act, where ordinary people participated by looking on.

With the Reformation came a renewed emphasis on scripture in the rite, accompanied by the removal of some ceremonial actions. In Anabaptist theology and practice the Lord's Supper was creatively distinct. Here the believing community gathered around the table of the Lord, sharing bread and wine, knowing Christ's presence. The Spirit shaped the community's life in conformity to the cross of Christ and to his sacrificial life of love.

Keith Jones describes the Anabaptists as Christ-centred; he challenges the church today to avoid an exclusively Pauline diet, and instead to find the four Gospels as the hermeneutic key. He observes that the Anabaptist 'gathering church' was a dynamic community working together with others, hearing the voice of Jesus in the Bible and then going and living that out in society. The Anabaptist emphasis in church life was community. It was a gathering, not gathered, church; it was not complete, but believers gathering together on their journey of faith. They did not opt to join because they liked the music, or the preacher; they were involved with each other, in the life of the Kingdom. There was an anti-clericalism, but they were not anti-intellectual, a distinction we sometimes fail to make today.[25]

Today, in many parts of the church, our view of the Lord's Supper is individualistic, narrow, and small. We can, with Jones, identify two important distinctives for our life as the church of Christ. First, our discipleship must be understood neither as a vocation for the few nor an esoteric discipline for adepts, but as a life transformed into service by the lordship of Jesus Christ (signified by believers' baptism). Second, our expression of community must be understood not as a privileged access to God or to sacred status, but as sharing together in a storied life of obedient service to Christ and with him (signified by the Lord's Supper).

The challenge for us is to recover the insights of early Christian communities for whom forgiveness, joy, healing and reconciliation were the fruit of a loving relationship with God. The meaning of the cross is clearly seen in our worship, which proclaims the Lord's death. Christ's own self-giving is mirrored in the relationships that we develop within his church. As Ellie Kreider suggests, the church should be encouraged to explore thanksgiving, feasting, sharing, reconciling, forgiving, healing, covenant, discipline, serving, and justice. Such exploration will shape our character and the character of the church.

In re-telling the story of God's creating, redeeming and liberating love, we find that the Spirit is able to minister to our individual and community needs. Coming together in unity at the Lord's table, we renew our identity as people of God. Our vision of God's will and reign lifts us above the daily grind. In confident hope we receive forgiveness and the daily bread for our life — unmistakable signs of the Kingdom coming. We reconcile our differences in the name of Jesus, and we pledge to share generously what we have. Then we turn outward to the task God has given us.

Exercise 6.3

a. Design a communion service, which you feel expresses both the Gospel of Christ and the meaning of Christian community.

b. What images and symbols (in addition to the bread and the wine) would enhance your celebration of the Lord's Supper and inspire the church's mission within the community that it seeks to serve?

Epilogue

The church of Jesus Christ will hear the call to worship, and be ready to take a prophetic stance in its society. The prophets of God do not side with government nor with church; they represent God on behalf of those who are disadvantaged or are suffering. They will stand on the outside of political parties, critique their manifestos and reflect theologically upon their policies. They will listen to the people within the community they seek to serve, analyse the situation, hear the word of God, and act.

Alan Roxburgh observes that pastors in the later twentieth century became characterised as teachers, counsellors, and professionals, but that these descriptors have ceased to be meaningful at the beginning of the twenty-first century. However, because the paradigm is so entrenched, 'practically the only model presented to each new generation of potential leaders is pastor as professional and teacher; the caretaker and chaplain of dwindling, ageing congregations.'[26] Young creative leaders with the passion and skills desperately needed in the churches, see this model and turn elsewhere for vocational fulfilment.

In a time of declining congregations Roxburgh notes that there is a need for leaders who listen to the voices from the edge. 'This is where the *apostle*, the *poet*, and the *prophet* are found. These are the metaphors for congregational leadership today.'[27] These are different leaders, who are encountered by, and in turn encounter, our culture with the Gospel. The apostle holds out the Gospel story in stark contrast to the cultural context, leading churches into a missionary encounter and equipping disciples. The poet is an articulator of experience, who images and symbolises the unarticulated experiences of the community, identifying and expressing the soul of the people within their culture. The prophet addresses the Word of God directly into the experience of the people of God, and offers a vision of God's purposes for them in the transformation of culture.

Engaging with social and political issues is never going to be an easy option for the church and it will lead to misunderstanding and abuse. Our role is to listen, to reflect and to help society to find transformation in Christ. The church needs leaders and members who will enter into the experience of their community, learn from the people, analyse the situation, bring a biblical and theological perspective, and plan an active response.

We must remove any thought of dualism and allow our faith to become fully engaged with our daily experiences and our work. In this way we will become the revolutionary church of Christ. As Verna Dozier and James Adams challenge us to see, 'When the Christian church chose to worship Jesus *instead* of following him, it tamed much of what was threateningly radical in this disturbing person'.[28] Our call is to be this Christ in the world through the Holy Spirit. So to be, we shall never stop reflecting upon our life and work, in the light of our faith in God.

Notes

[1] http:news.bbc.co.uk/1/hi/england/merseyside/4739569.stm; accessed 03.08.05.

[2] John de Gruchy, *Reconciliation. Restoring Justice* (London: SCM, 2002), p. 75.

[3] William Blake, 'A Poison Tree' from *Songs of Experience* (Etched 1789-1794).

[4] de Gruchy, *Reconciliation,* p. 213.

[5] National Statistics, *Social Trends 31, 2001 Edition* (London: The Stationary Office, 2001).

[6] Regular viewing of *Rambo* videos was said to have influenced Michael Ryan, who carried out a series of random killings, one summer's day in Hungerford, in 1987, before killing himself. Violent videos, such as *Child's Play*, were said to have been a contributing factor that led two boys aged 10 and 11 to abduct and brutally murder a toddler, James Bulger, in Liverpool in 1993.

[7] Donald B. Kraybill, *The Upside-Down Kingdom* (Scottdale: Herald Press, 1978), p. 303.

[8] Kraybill, *The Upside-Down Kingdom,* p. 304.

[9] Kraybill, *The Upside-Down Kingdom,* p. 306.

[10] See Michael Fanstone, *The Sheep that Got Away. Why Do People Leave the Church?* (Tunbridge Wells: MARC, 1993).

[11] Alan Kreider, 'Worship and Evangelism in Pre-Christendom'. The Laing Lecture 1994, *Vox Evangelica* 24 (1994), p. 30.

[12] Cathy Kirkpatrick, Mark Pierson, Mike Riddell, *The Prodigal Project* (London: SPCK, 2000), p. 45.

[13] Verses 1 and 3 from 'Servant Song', written by Richard Gillard, with music by Richard Gillard and Betty Pulkingham; copyright 1977 scripture in Song, administered in Europe by Thankyou Music. Quoted by kind permission.

[14] Susanne Johnson, 'Education in the Image of God' in Jack L. Seymour and Donald E. Miller (eds), *Theological Approaches to Christian Education* (Nashville: Abingdon, 1990), p. 132.

[15] David Ford, 'Transformation' in Peter Sedgwick (ed.), *God in the City: Essays and Reflections from the Archbishop of Canterbury's Urban Theology Group* (London: Mowbray, 1995), p. 201.

[16] Ford, 'Transformation', p. 206.

[17] Helmut Thielicke, *The Waiting Father. Sermons on the Parables of Jesus* (London: James Clarke, 1960).

[18] Alan Kreider, *Lessons from Intentional Communities: Mennonite Perspectives.* Unpublished paper presented at the Baptist Union Consultation on Living and Learning in Community, 1995, p. 4.

[19] George Ritzer, *The McDonaldization of Society* (Thousand Oaks: Pine Forge Press, 1993, 1996), cited in John Drane, *The McDonaldization of the Church* (London, Darton, Longman and Todd, 2000), pp. 28-32.

[20] Richard Burfoot was a student at Regent's Park College in Oxford from 1995 to 1998. He was a church-based student at Chalford Baptist Chapel, near Stroud, of which he has since become the full-time minister. These comments appeared in Richard Burfoot and John Weaver, 'Forming Church Leaders in Today's World—some questions for discussion', *Mainstream Journal*, 61 (January, 1998), pp. 28-33.

[21] George Rawson (1807-1889) hymn: 'We limit not the truth of God'. The refrain quotes the much-celebrated words from John Robinson's parting speech to those leaving his Leyden congregation to sail to America on the *Mayflower* in 1620.

[22] For a full exploration of this point see William Willimon, *Worship as Pastoral Care* (Nashville: Abingdon, 1979).

[23] This theme is helpfully developed by Eleanor Kreider, *Communion Shapes Character* (Scottdale: Herald Press, 1997); also published in the UK under the title *Given For You: A Fresh Look at Communion* (Leicester, Apollos/Inter-Varsity Press, 1998).

[24] See note above.

[25] Keith G. Jones, *A Believing Church. Learning from some Contemporary Anabaptist and Baptist Perspectives* (Didcot: Baptist Publications, 1998).

[26] Alan Roxburgh, 'Pastoral Role in the Missionary Congregation' in G. Hunsberger and C. Van Gelder (eds) *Church Between Gospel and Culture* (Grand Rapids: Eerdmans, 1996), p. 321.

[27] Roxburgh, 'Pastoral Role in the Missionary Congregation', pp. 325-6.

[28] Verna J. Dozier and James R. Adams, *Sisters and Brothers: Reclaiming a Biblical Idea of Community* (Boston: Cowley Publications, 1993), p.11. My italics.

Index